IMAGES
of America

Appanoose County

I0806222

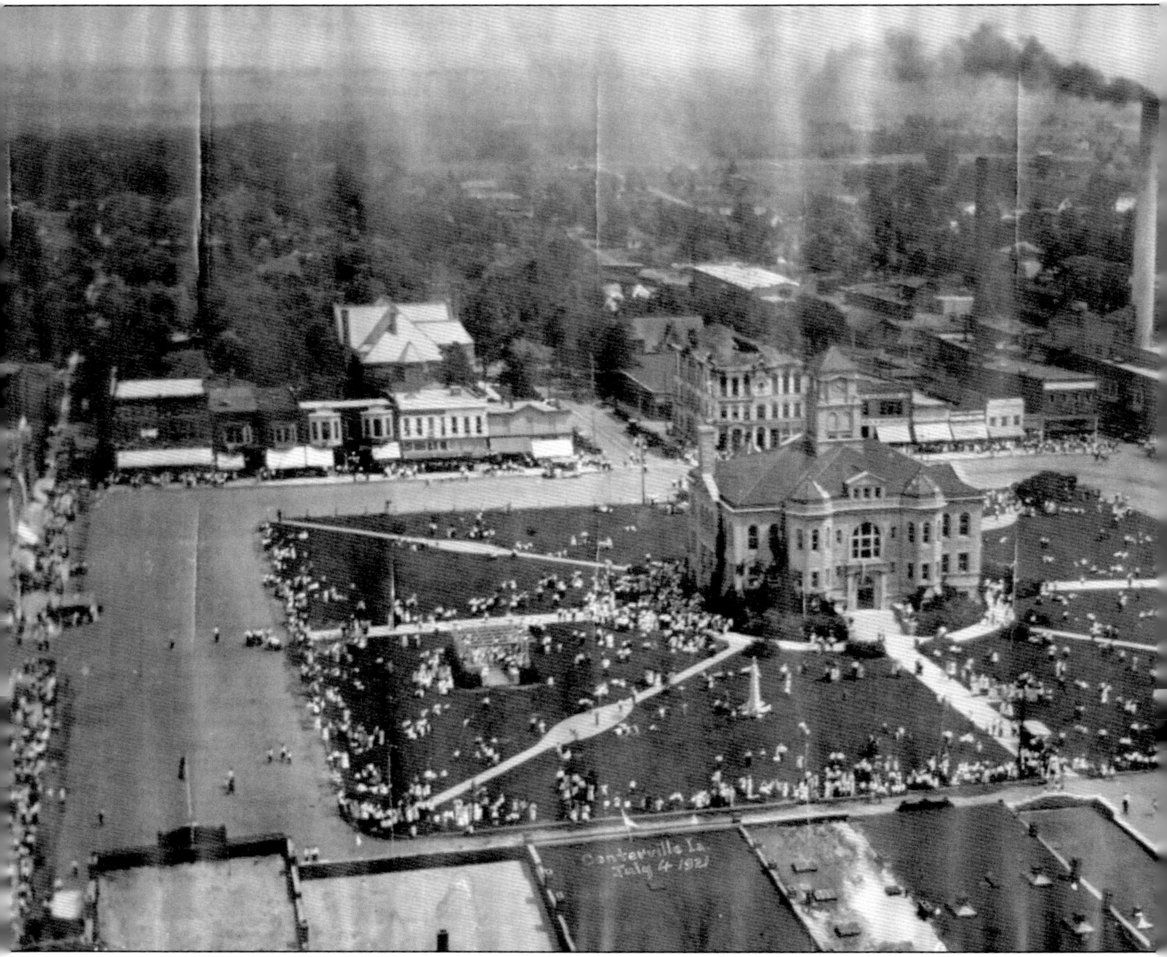

It was reported that 15,000 people came to the Square to celebrate Independence Day in 1921, despite heavy rain. The fireworks show, held at 4:30 in the afternoon, consisted of "day bombs," a type of firework that sailed high, then exploded with ribbon streamers and tiny toys that children hunted for on the ground. (Courtesy of the Appanoose County Historical Society.)

On the Cover: On August 26, 1922, the US Bureau of Mines and Centerville leaders hosted the Iowa State First Aid Tournament on the courthouse lawn. Teams from Appanoose County mines and some from as far away as Des Moines competed in the successful completion of tourniquets, splints, and general care of the wounded. Prizes were awarded, from cash to collar buttons. This was the only such meet in the country in 1922. (Courtesy of the Appanoose County Historical Society.)

IMAGES
of America

APPANOOSE COUNTY

Appanoose County Historical Society

ARCADIA
PUBLISHING

ISBN 978-0-7385-9899-4

Published by Arcadia Publishing
Charleston, South Carolina

Printed in the United States of America

Library of Congress Control Number: 2012952165

For all general information, please contact Arcadia Publishing:
Telephone 843-853-2070
Fax 843-853-0044
E-mail sales@arcadiapublishing.com
For customer service and orders:
Toll-Free 1-888-313-2665

Visit us on the Internet at www.arcadiapublishing.com

To the residents of Appanoose County who came before us, thank you for leaving us with a rich heritage from many cultures—people who were strong and worked hard and were proud of their accomplishments. To the youth of Appanoose County, may you be as proud of your heritage as your ancestors were.

Contents

Acknowledgments		6
Introduction		7
1.	The World's Largest?	9
2.	Beyond the Square	35
3.	The Levee, Walsh, and South Centerville	49
4.	Give Us Guidance	61
5.	At Your Service	77
6.	Black Diamonds	89
7.	Trolley Tracks	99
8.	Coming Together	111
9.	Favorite Pastimes	119
10.	When the Going Gets Tough . . .	125

ACKNOWLEDGMENTS

On behalf of the Appanoose County Historical Society, I would like to thank those people and businesses that supported the Newspaper Digitization Project, without which the captions in this book would be lackluster and nondescript. The newspapers from the Centerville area are gold mines of information that are just waiting to once again be read and digested, as they were in the old days. This database is available to all and can be found by going to the Appanoose County Historical and Coal Mining Museum website, www.appanoosehistory.com, and following the link to the digitized newspaper database. Or, one can go directly to http://centerville.advantage-preservation.com/search/site.

Additionally, I would like to thank Gary Craver, Dana Moritz, Patty Timmens, and Tyler Morgan for their help with research, writing, proofreading, and fact-checking. I could not have done it without them. And huge thanks go out to Enfys McMurry, who has brought Appanoose County's history back into the limelight with her comprehensive book, *Centerville: A Mid-American Saga*.

—Lisa Eddy, Curator
Appanoose County Historical & Coal Mining Museum

Unless otherwise noted, all images in this book are courtesy of the Appanoose County Historical Society.

INTRODUCTION

Appanoose County is like no other county in America. Its character is multifaceted, from its populace, which is a true melting pot, to its oversized historic business district, which has been in place since the platting of the town in 1846.

To *read* the story of Centerville and Appanoose County is an eye-opening experience. Author Enfys McMurry has recently written the most important, comprehensive history of Appanoose County that has ever been attempted, *Centerville: A Mid-American Saga* (published by The History Press). In those 750 pages, readers will discover details about Appanoose County's beginnings that are astounding.

To *hear* the story of Centerville during one of McMurry's live presentations is incredible. She takes it to the next level, breathing life into the extraordinary stories of Appanoose County's unique, multicultural background with her passion and excitement.

The book you're holding now will help you *see* Appanoose County's history. For some, it will help them wrap their minds around the format of the county itself, as well as the town of Centerville and its various business districts and neighborhoods. Though not a comprehensive history, it will enhance the mental images while consuming McMurry's book. We would like to think of it as a companion book in some ways. For others, this book will merely be a great way to reminisce about the good old days in Centerville and Appanoose County.

One of the most precious collections stored at the Appanoose County Historical & Coal Mining Museum is the archive of photographs. We can explain our artifacts and their functions, but photographs make the connection, bringing the artifacts to life and giving them meaning. The collection within this book is just a small fraction of the photographs that are in our vast archive. Some subjects are not covered in this book, for the simple reason that there are still so many photographs out there that have not been donated to the museum. We extend our apologies if the picture you were anxious to see is not within these pages—it simply means that we do not have that photograph in our collection, or the constraints of space between the covers could not accommodate all of the images we would like to have included.

We are always looking for more photographs taken within Appanoose County that explain an event, a building, or a location. If you have one, we would love to see it, scan it, and show it to our visitors. The Appanoose County Historical & Coal Mining Museum is a great place to grab onto your heritage, learn about the amazing people who shaped the county, and take pride and ownership of this community.

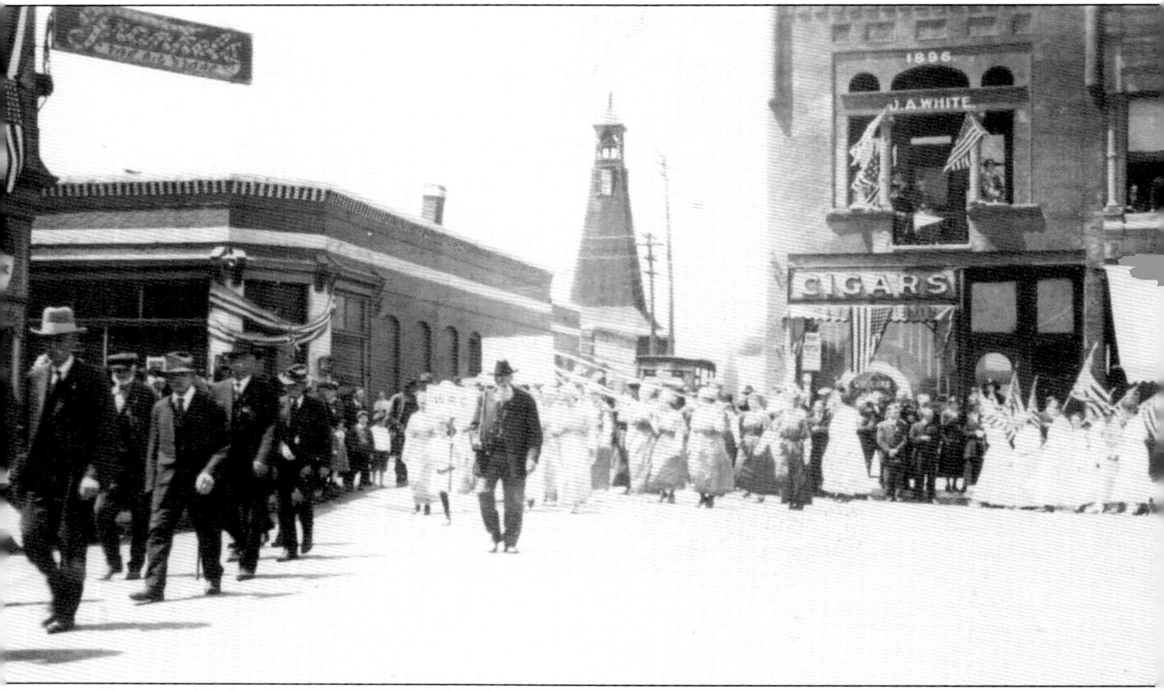

Centerville has hosted thousands of celebrations over the years. This parade on May 17, 1919, celebrated the return of Company D from World War I. This section of the parade features veterans from previous wars, including the Civil War and Spanish-American War. Behind them is the Women's Relief Corps. This photograph shows the southwest corner of the Square and West Jackson Street, with a great view of the hose tower at the Centerville Fire Station. The fire station and Centerville City Hall were located on West Jackson until 1959. On the right is the J.A. White building, known for the wooden Indian in the window during its time as a pool hall and cigar store.

One

THE WORLD'S LARGEST?

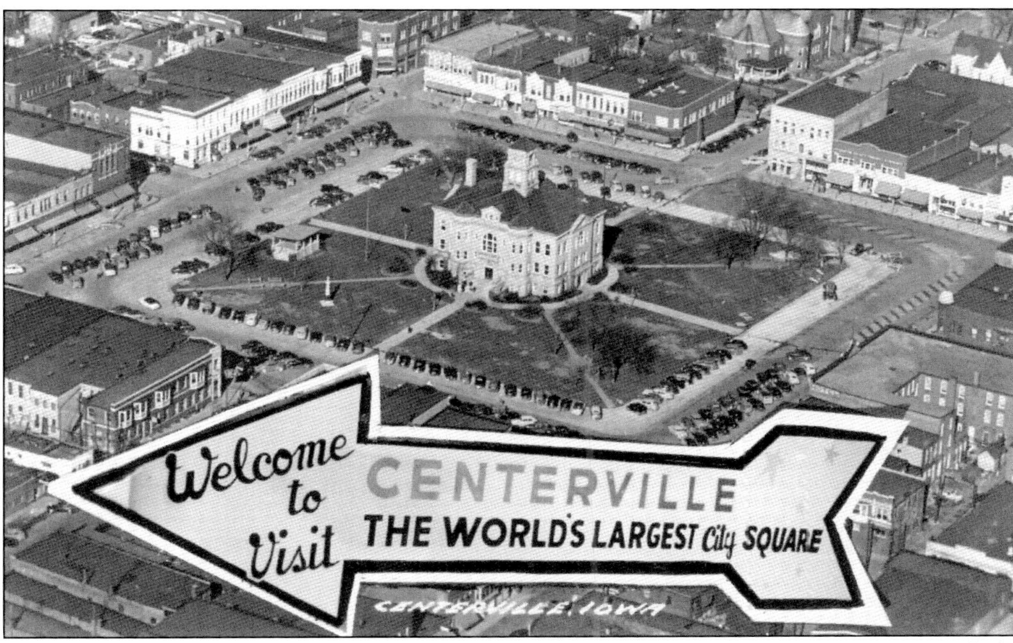

The idea that Centerville, Iowa, has the largest square in the world is a misconception. It might be more accurate to say "the largest square in Iowa" or "one of the largest city squares in the world." The phrase was coined by the Association of Commerce in the 1940s. The arrow-shaped sign transposed onto this aerial photograph hung over the intersection of Maple and Main Streets for many years, pulling visitors into the Square.

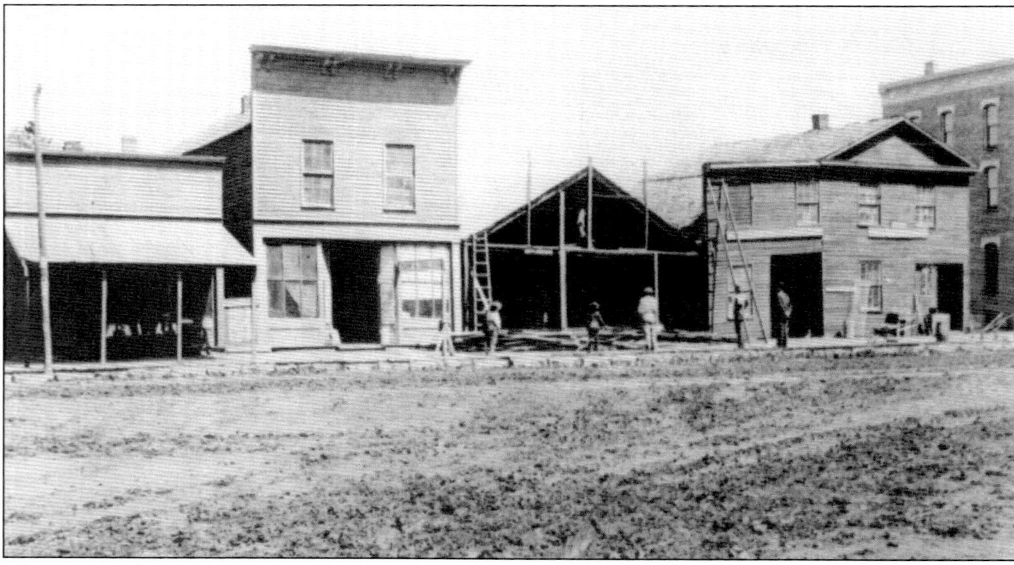

The original town of Centerville, including the Square, was platted by Jonathon Stratton in January 1847. Wooden buildings began cropping up around the perimeter of the Square, which stretched for a total of eight city blocks, two blocks per side. Here is the east side of the Square, north of State Street, around 1895. To the right is the Continental Hotel, the original of which had burned in 1893 and was replaced with the structure seen here.

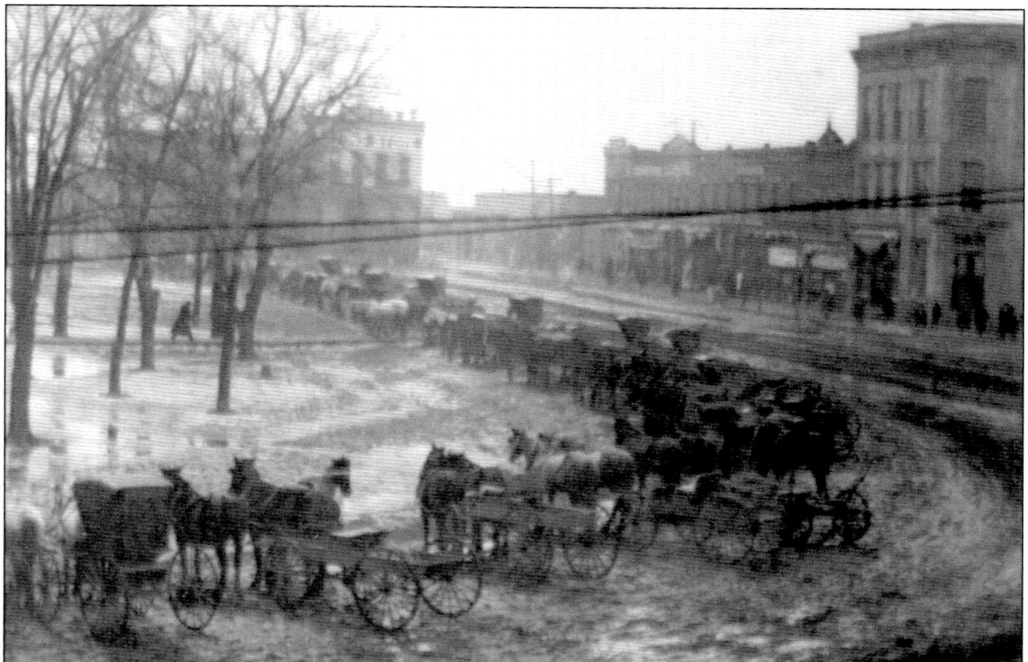

By 1900, most of the buildings on the Square were brick, but the streets were still dirt. Shown here on a rainy day around the turn of the century is the southwest corner of the Square. Even on nastier days, the Square was busy. Hitching posts around the courtyard provided plenty of parking for the horses. The Square was paved with brick in 1904.

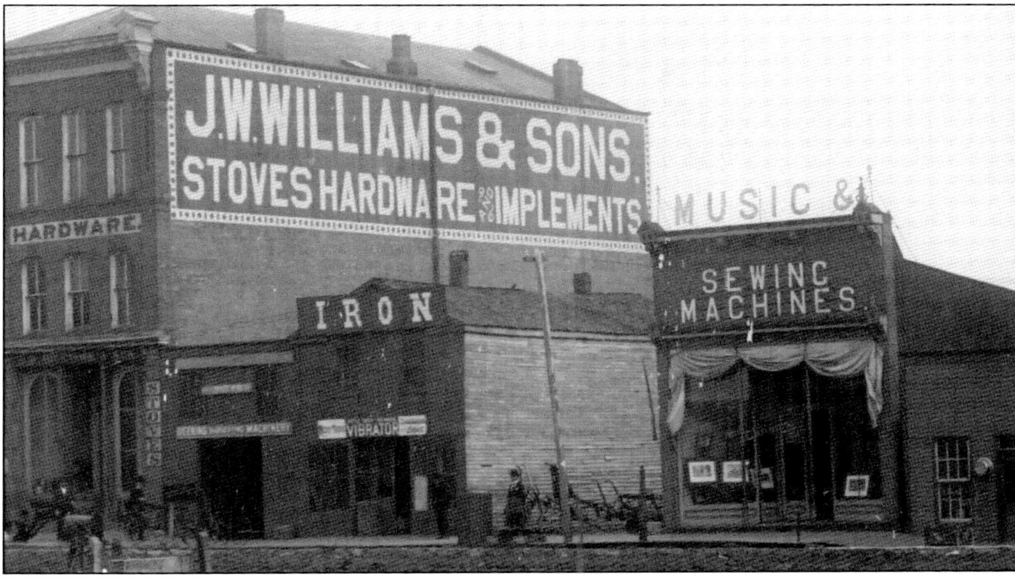

This is the Square's north side, east of Main Street. J.W. Williams operated a hardware business on the Square beginning in 1855. He sold the hardware business to Little & Vickery in 1898. It was purchased by H.E. Luther in 1904, and sold to the Davison Brothers in 1907. A huge fire in December 1911 destroyed the building, still owned by J.W. Williams, and the inventory of Davison Brothers Hardware.

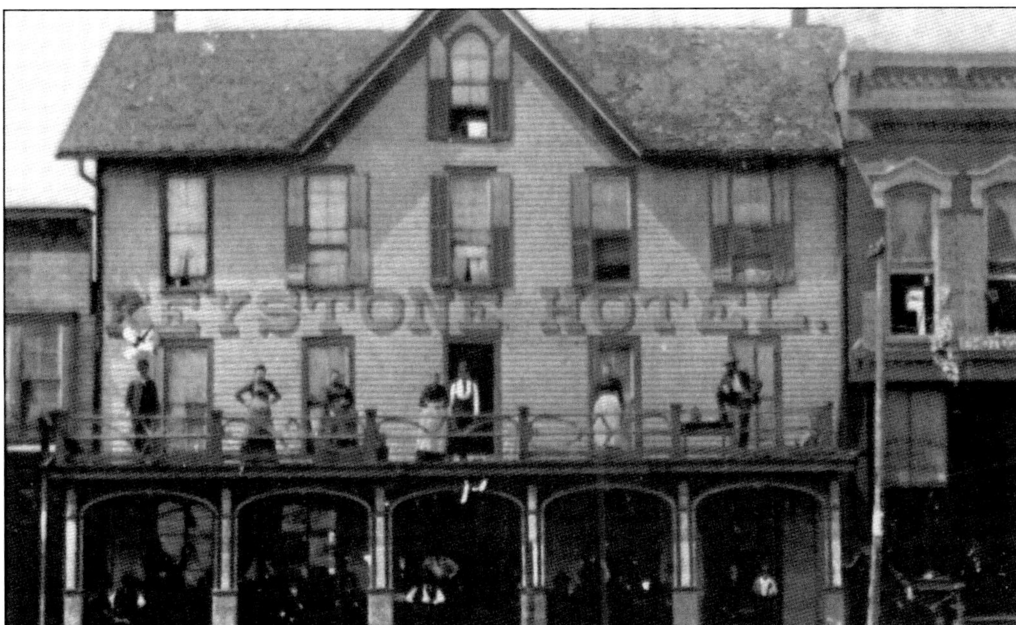

The Keystone Hotel was on the north side of the Square, west of Main Street. Built in 1855, it was considered an Appanoose County landmark. On Valentine's Day, 1888, an African American man and a Caucasian woman from Macon, Missouri, were married in Centerville, then boarded a streetcar in front of the Keystone Hotel, surrounded by a crowd of curious onlookers. The Keystone Hotel burned down in September 1894.

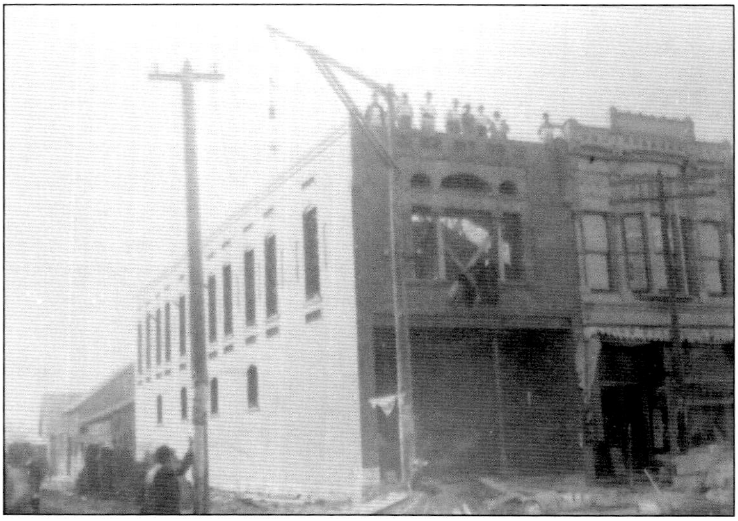

The J.A. White building on the Square's southwest corner was constructed in 1898, after a fire consumed Vollmer's Restaurant at that location. White offered the lot to the city to widen Jackson Street, but the city declined. Instead, White built a pool hall that would be well known throughout most of the 20th century, with its signature wooden Indian in the window.

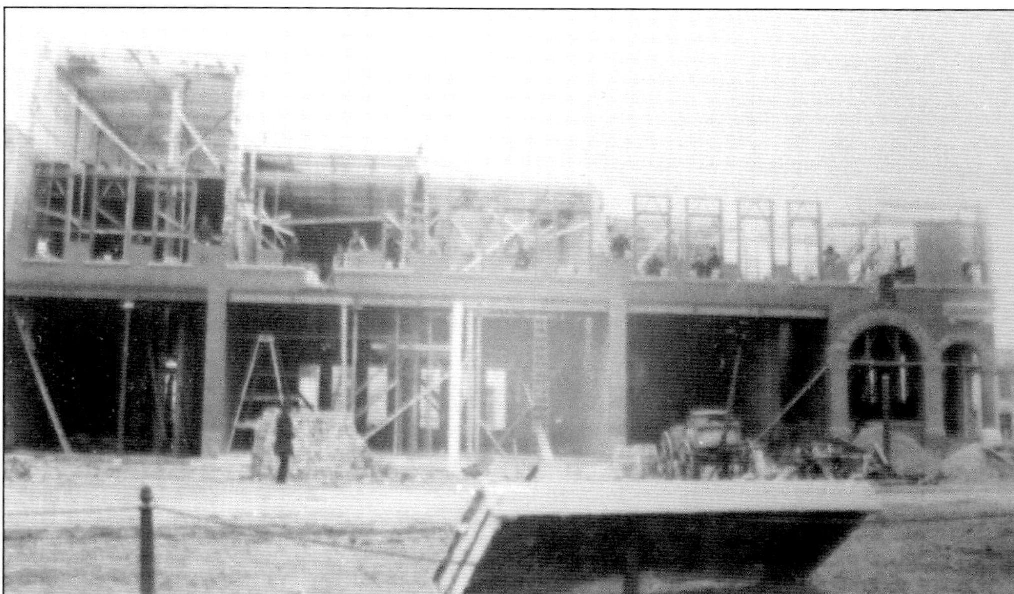

The Bradley-Hamilton-White block of buildings was erected on the east side of the Square in 1895. The corner of the structure was built by William Bradley for a bank. The next 20 feet of the structure was built by David Hamilton as a hardware and implement business. The next 40 feet was built as wholesale rooms with a top-notch freight elevator. J.A. White built the three-story structure north of the Hamilton building.

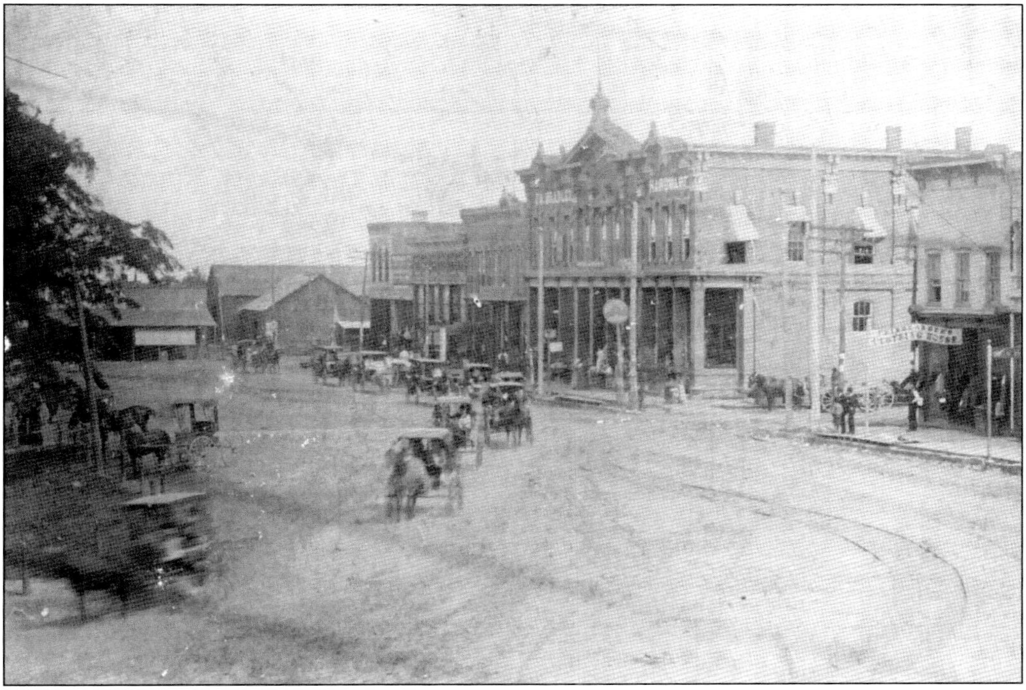

The large, ornate building on the south side of the Square was labeled with many interesting names before the 1920s. It was actually three storefronts, all with different occupants. Over the course of many years, the peak was labeled "Merritt Bros," "D.C. Bradley," and "The Surprise."

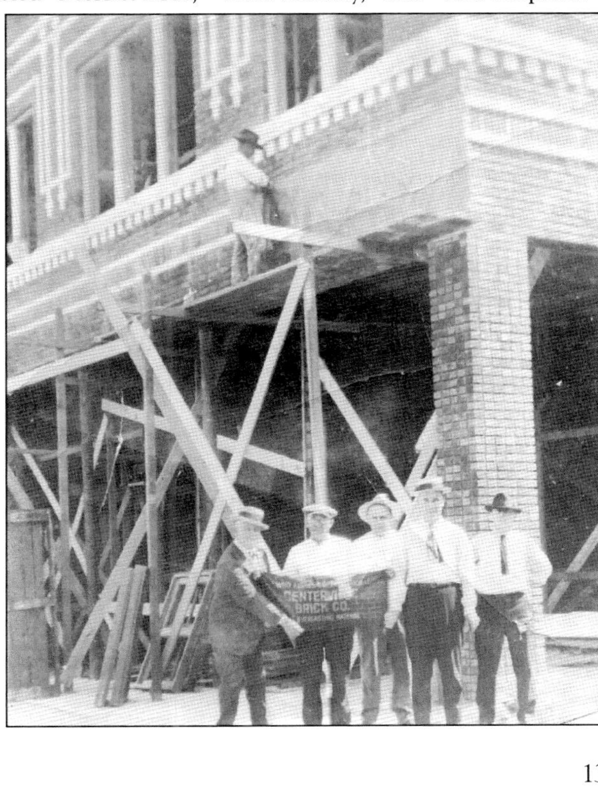

The Dinning Building, on the southeast corner of the Square, was built by David Dinning in 1922. For years, this area was known as "Hatzenbeeler's Corner," after the merchant Jacob Hatzenbeeler, who owned the property and operated a meat shop on the site. The first occupant of the new building was the J.C. Penney Company, one of the first "chain stores" to inhabit the Square.

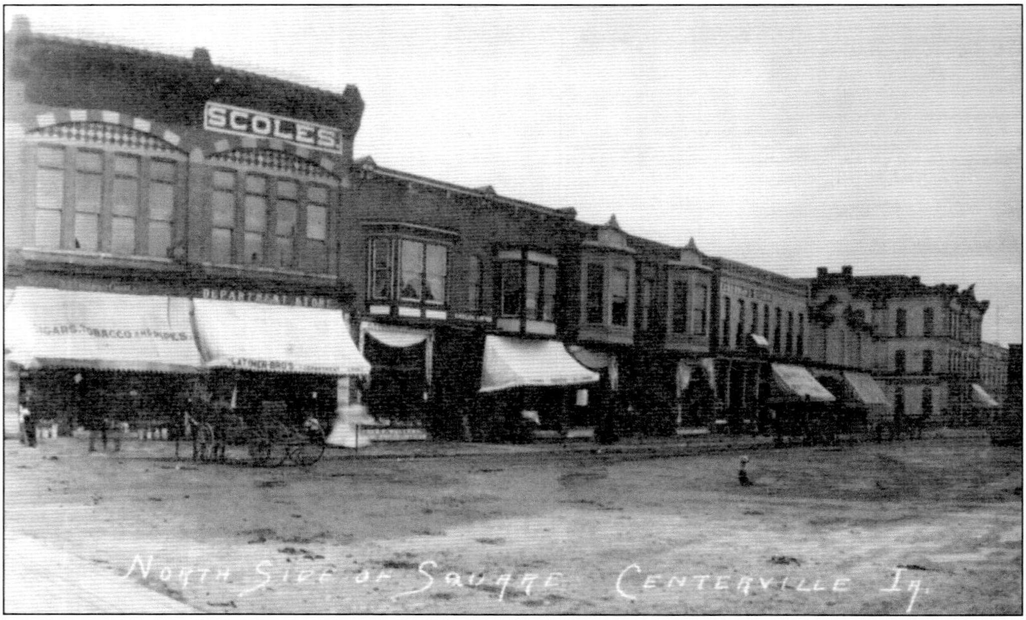

The north side of the Square, west of Main Street, included the venue that was known as Russell Hall. It occupied the second floor in the building on the far left, and was the scene of many dances, classes, parties, and other social events. In 1885, Joseph Herriford became the first African American to graduate from Centerville High School. The graduation ceremonies were held in Russell Hall.

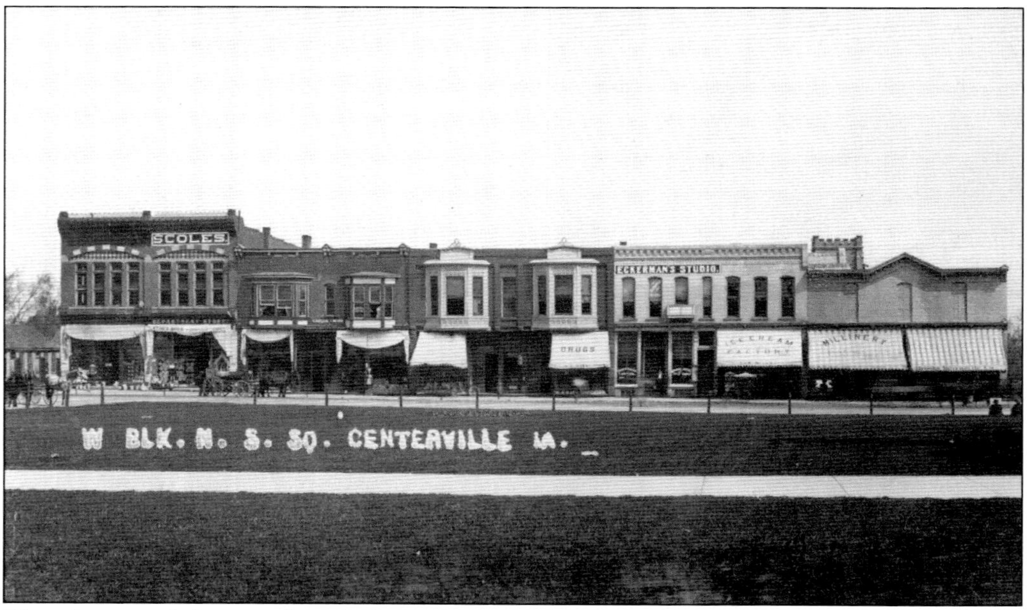

This photograph features Santi Milani's Ice Cream Parlor. Over time, the younger Milanis took up law practice here and partnered with the likes of Vermillion, Fee, and Tannehill. The building marked "Ice Cream Factory" is home to the current Milani law practice. The inside is still decorated with the ornate plaster moldings hand-created by the Milani ancestors.

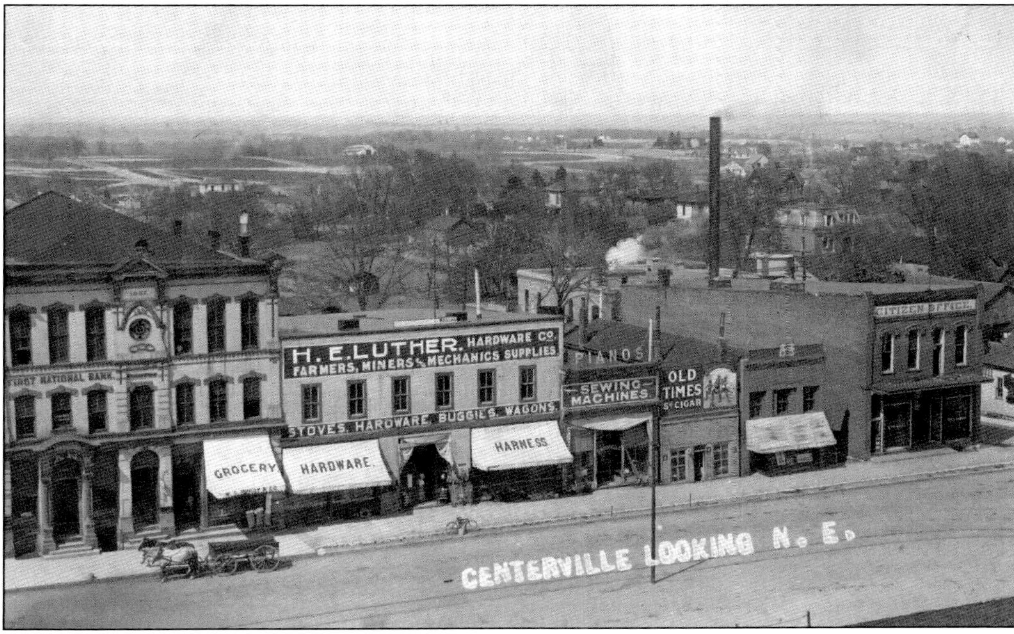

The north side of the Square, east of Main Street, featured the Citizen building on the east end. The offices of the *Centerville Citizen* newspaper only occupied the basement and front of the second story. The main floor housed the Centerville Post Office until 1903. In 1908, the New Majestic Theater opened in the vacated post office space, prior to becoming the Orpheum and the Ritz.

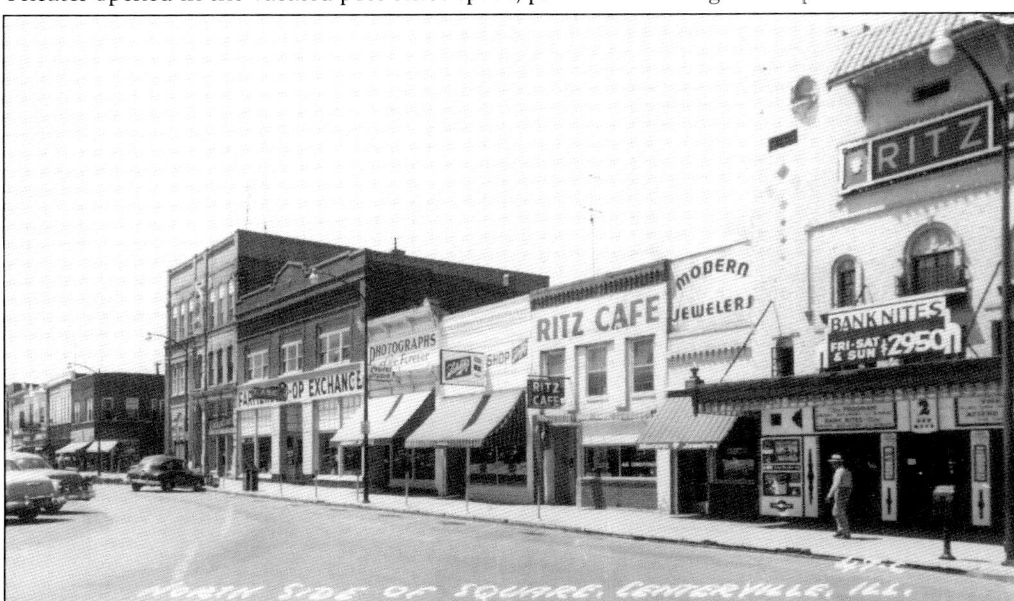

The *Centerville Citizen* was bought by the *Iowegian* in 1916, and the building became home to several other businesses, most notably the Orpheum Theater, which later became the Ritz Theater. The next space west of the Ritz is the tiniest building on the Square. It has housed several businesses, including the Stewart Shoe Store, the Ritz Barber & Beauty Shop, and Modern Jewelers, among others.

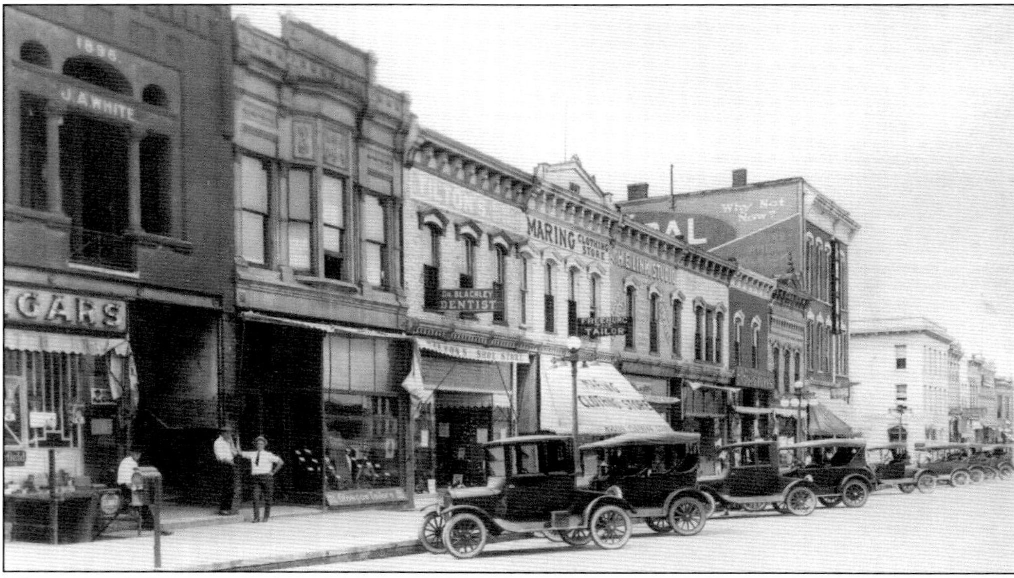

This c. 1915 photograph shows the west side of the Square, south of State Street. During the early 1900s, every space in a building was used by businesses. In the upstairs level of the buildings were photographers, tailors, doctors, and lawyers. The main level was most often occupied by retail businesses. The basement levels were often barbershops.

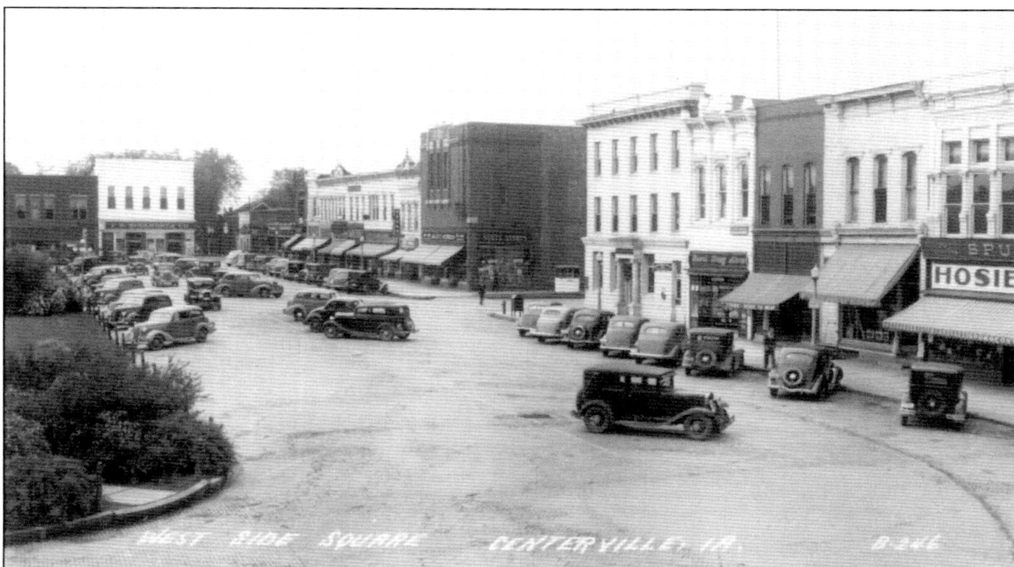

This photograph shows more of the west side of the Square, a few years after the image above. One of the buildings had burned down and was replaced by another stately structure that housed Scotts Stores on the main level and a grandly appointed Masonic Lodge upstairs. Just around the corner was Jack's Popcorn Stand, operated by Jack Jones, who also played in the pit orchestras that provided music for silent movies in Centerville.

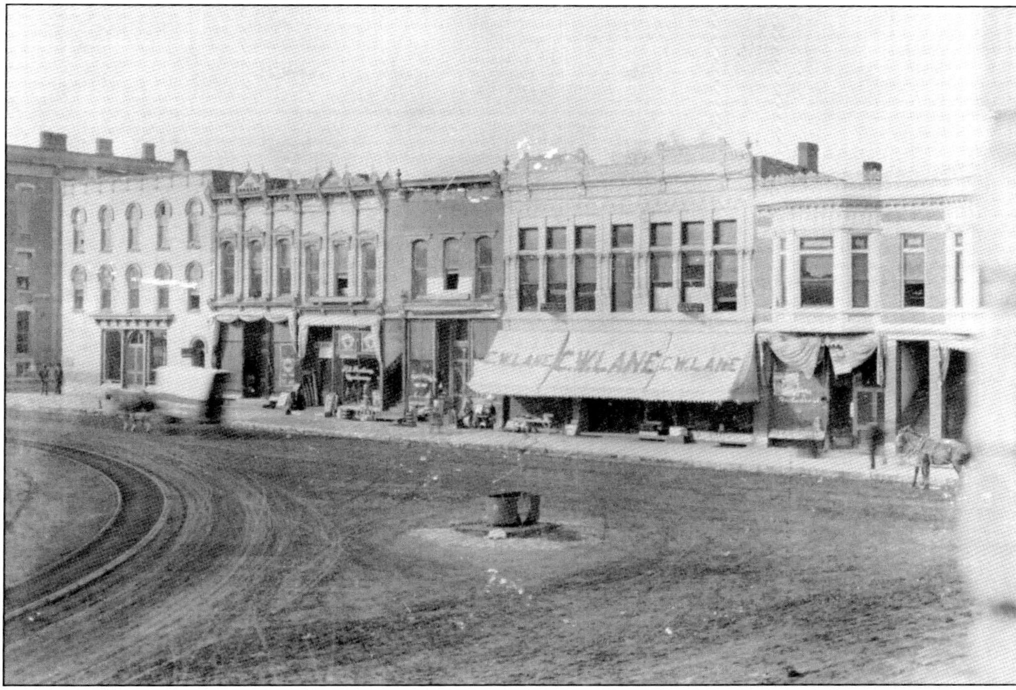

The west side of the Square, north of State Street, has an interesting history. Gov. Francis Drake was part owner of a dry-goods store known as Drake & Lane. That same building later was the first HyVee self-service supermarket, where customers served themselves using shopping carts. Men were hesitant to use them because they looked like baby buggies, so free candy bars were placed in the carts to entice them.

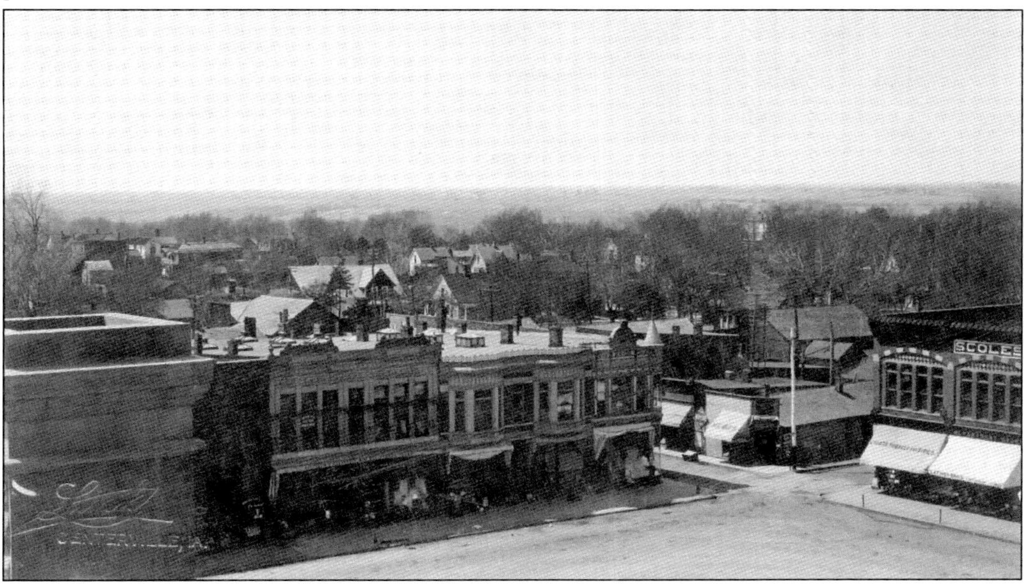

This view of the west side of the Square shows the Salinger & Goldstein store and wooden structures on the corner of the Square. Both photographs on this page were taken before 1904, confirmed by the presence of dirt streets and wooden-plank sidewalks.

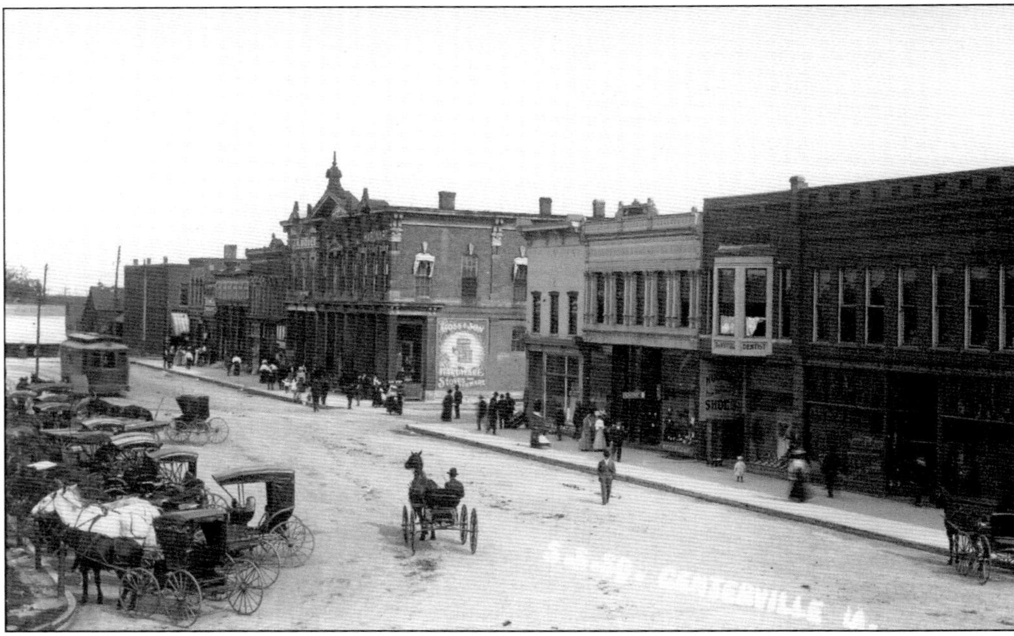

The Square hosted bustling business every day. From this one place, residents could satisfy all of their needs: food, clothing, banking, hardware, doctors, lawyers, dentists, and barbers. Even the post office was on the Square until 1903. People came to town in their buggies, or rode the streetcar to the Square to do their business.

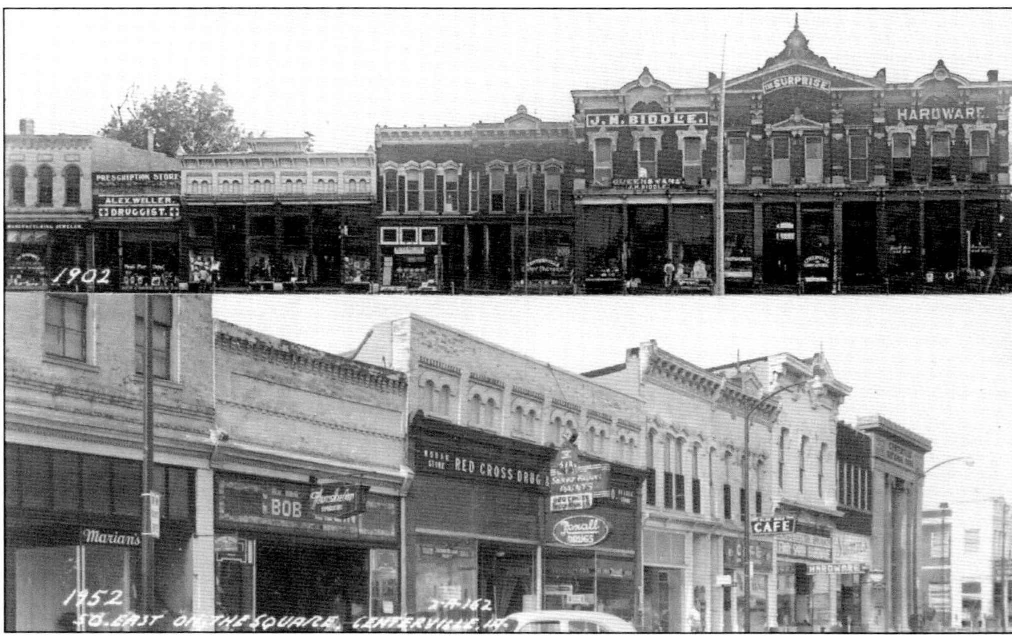

These photographs of the south side of the Square, east of Main Street, illustrate the changes in the block between 1902 and 1952. Most of the architecture remained the same, with the exception of the end of the block. Centerville National Bank reconstructed and remodeled the building on the west end in 1924, giving it a very stately, elaborate facade.

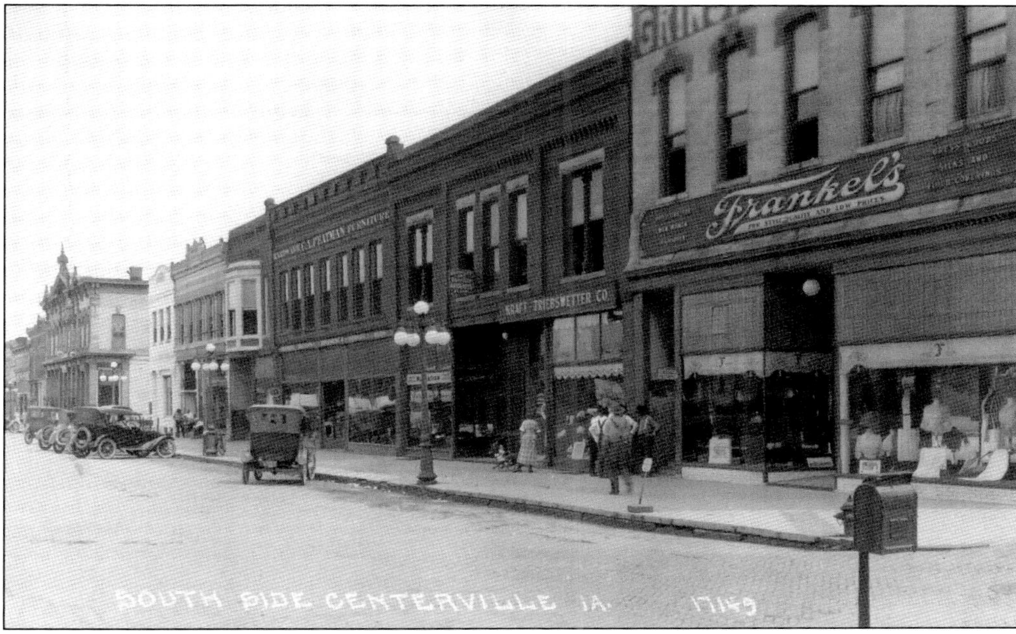

This block on the south side of the Square has housed many clothing stores. At one time, however, a "hole-in-the-wall" was operated there by Quick McCue, one of Appanoose County's earliest liquor establishments. It was a tiny building, about six or seven feet wide, located about 15 feet east of the Frankel Building. The tiny place sold hard cider, cigars, tobacco, and candy.

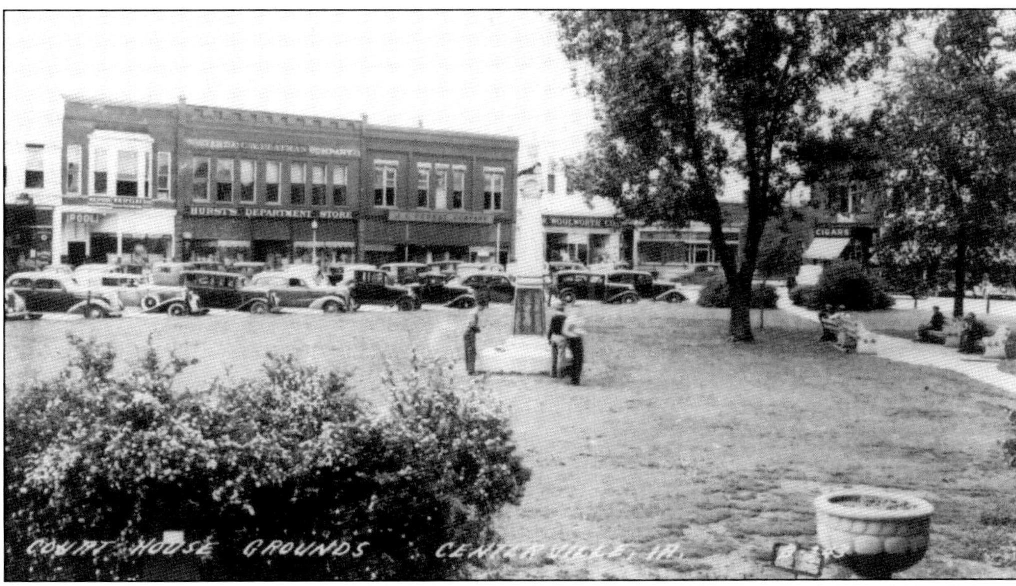

This view of the southwest corner of the courthouse lawn and businesses around the Square includes the Civil War veterans memorial. The memorial was erected in 1869 and dedicated on July 4 of that year. It is a monument to the memory of Appanoose County soldiers who died in the Civil War. Their names are inscribed on three sides of the monument. It still stands today.

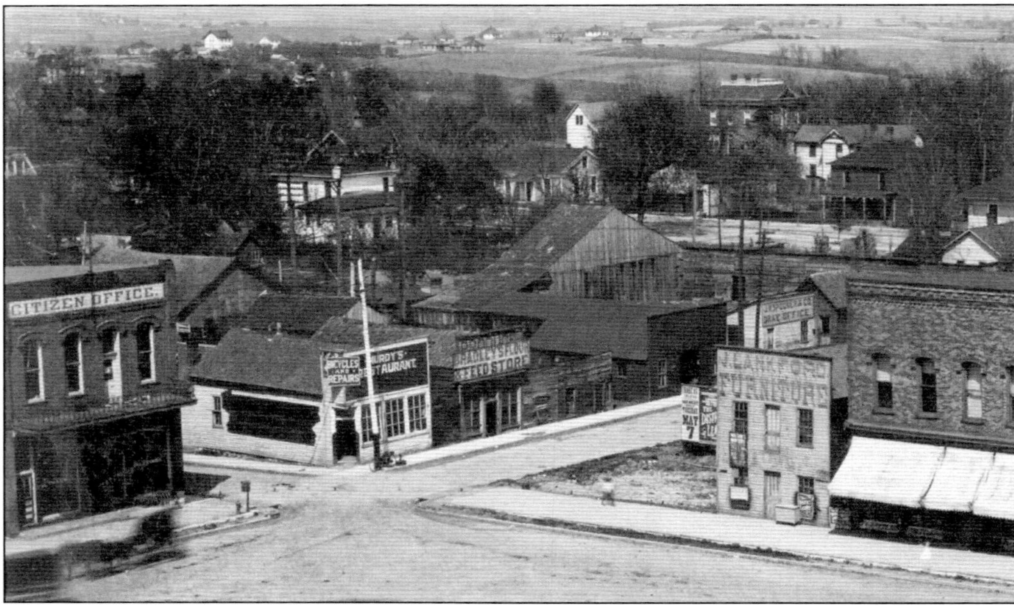

This bird's-eye view of the northeast corner of the Square was taken before all of the buildings had been completed on the east side. Lankford's Furniture was still a wooden structure, and so were all of the buildings on East Van Buren, just off of the northeast corner. Lankford's was also an undertaking parlor, not an uncommon combination in those days.

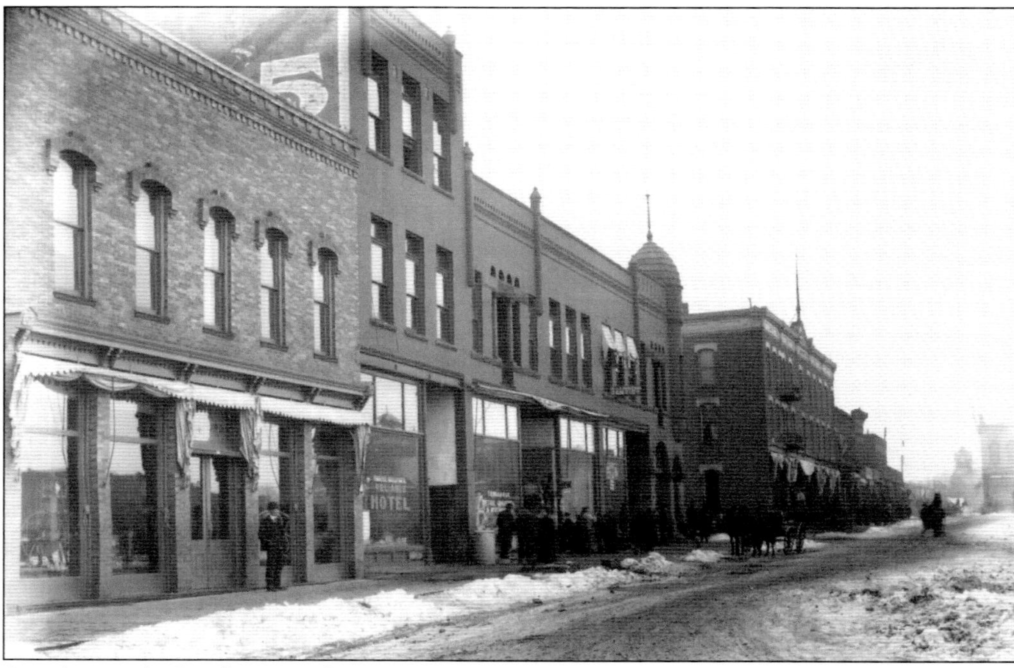

Seen here is the Bradley-Hamilton-White block, not long after it was built around the turn of the century. The tall building in the center was a hotel at the time of this photograph. It later became the Badger Hotel & Restaurant. After that, it was a pool hall for many years. Himie Voxman played for dances on the third floor of this historic structure when he was young.

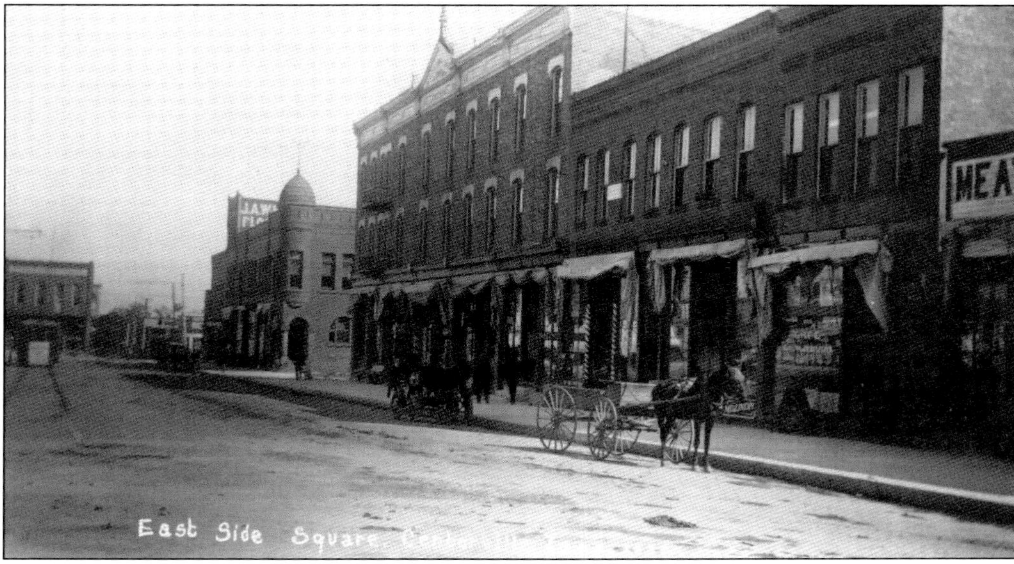

This c. 1900 photograph shows the east side of the Square. The city streetcar, visible at far left, went around the Square, its route taking it away from the Square on the south side. The streetcar then snaked its way to the levee via Drake Avenue, which explains the presence of a "pathway" from the Square to the levee.

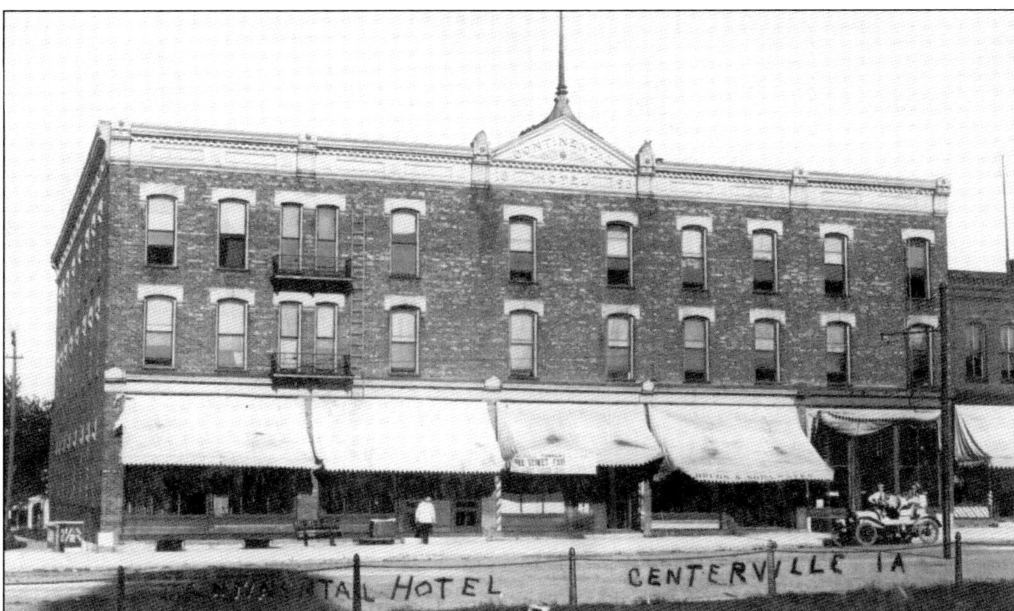

The new Continental Hotel was built in 1893, replacing the former Continental Hotel, which had burned down on February 9 of that year. One guest lost his life in the fire. The other death was that of the proprietor, Susannah McKee, who jumped from a third-story window to escape the fire. She died of her injuries from the fall.

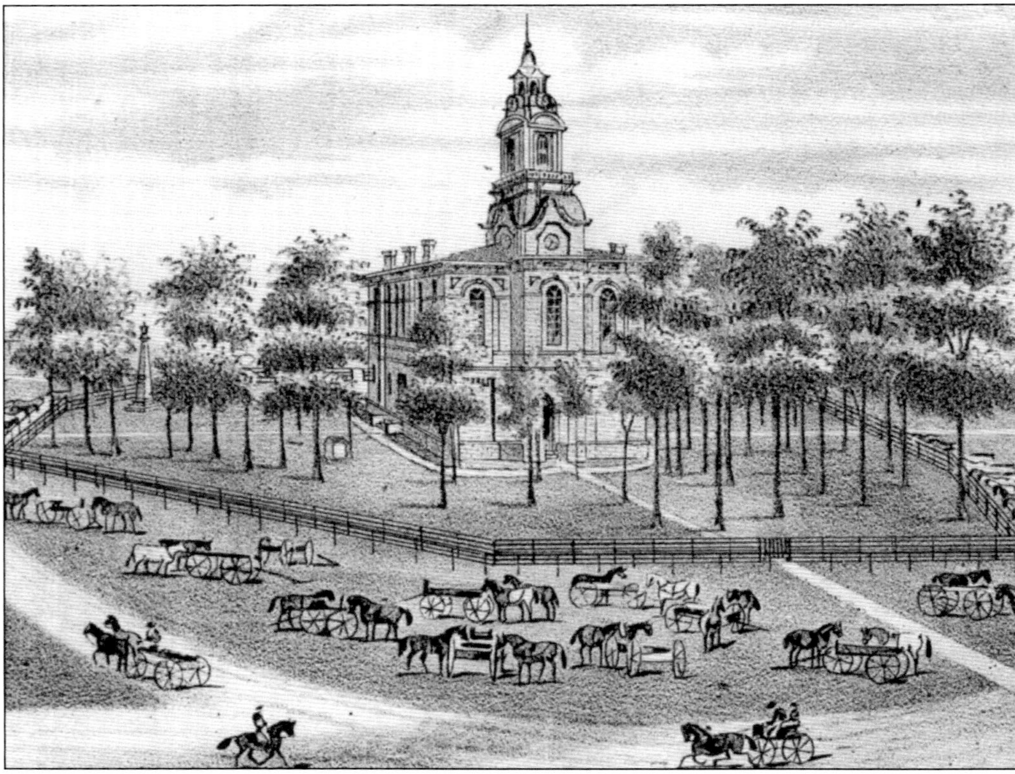

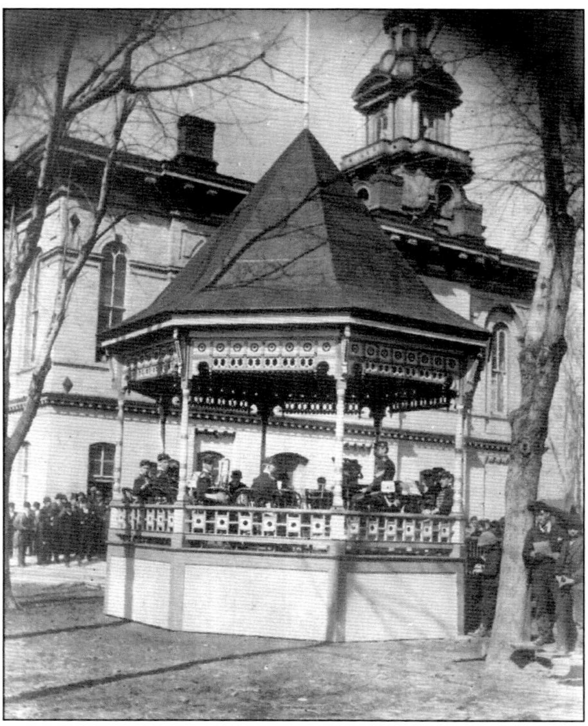

The first Appanoose County Courthouse was a log cabin on the south side of the Square. It measured 20 by 24 feet and cost $324 to build. Sadly, no pictures exist of that building. The second courthouse, pictured here, was a more substantial building. Built in 1863 in the middle of the Square, there are few pictures of it. This engraving comes from the 1875 *Illustrated Historical Atlas of Iowa.*

The second courthouse was approved and built in 1860–1863, the Civil War causing some interruption in its construction. It can be seen in the background of this photograph. The band pavilion pictured here was built in 1891 and would later be moved when the third courthouse was constructed. This pavilion remained in use until 1914.

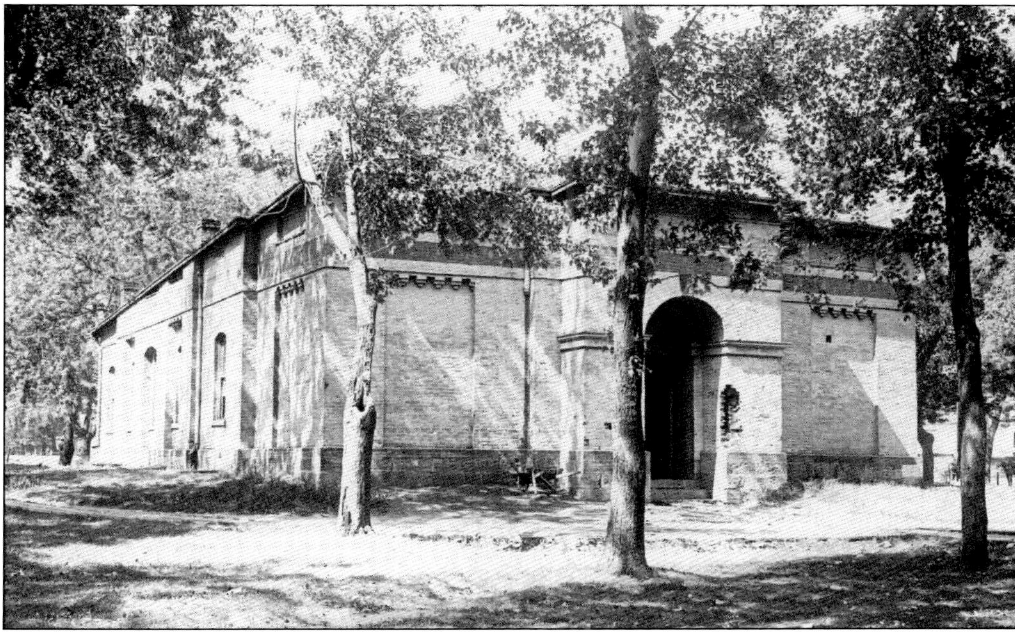

The second courthouse was used for several years, but in 1881, it suffered a fire in the upper floor and cupola area due to errant fireworks on Independence Day. It was used for another few years in its damaged state before the second story was removed in 1894, leaving an ugly remnant of a structure that earned the name "the Sheep Shed."

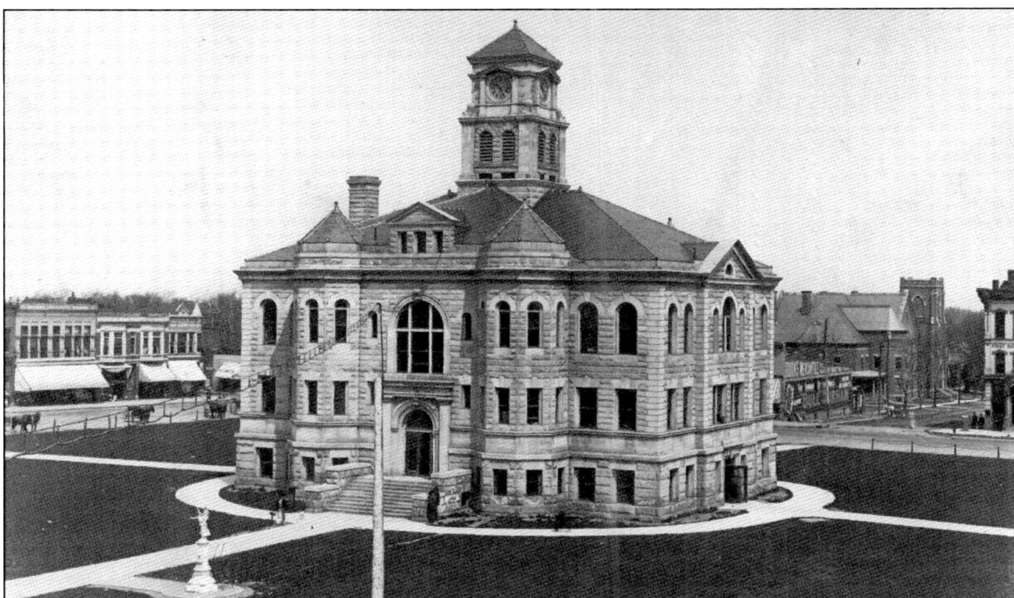

The construction of the current Appanoose County Courthouse was approved in November 1902. It was built in 1903–1904 and dedicated on September 12, 1904. The structure cost a total of $90,600 to build, the equivalent of $2.4 million in 2012. The courthouse clock was donated by James R. Wooden, and it rang for the first time at 8:00 p.m. on March 14, 1905.

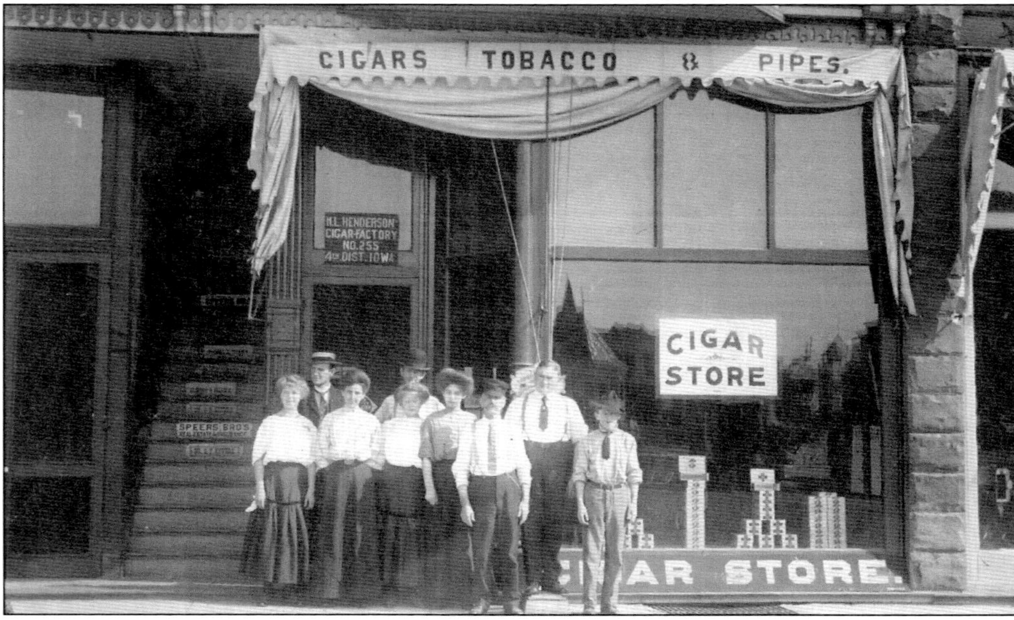

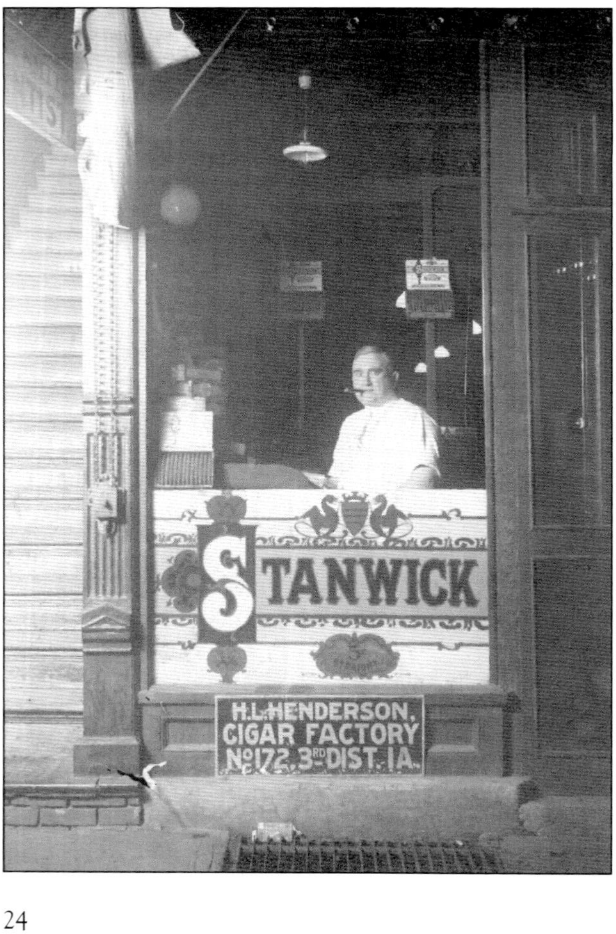

The Henderson families were premier cigar makers in Centerville. In the *Daily Iowegian*, mention is made of William, Ed, and, most often, Hal Henderson's Cigar Factory. Details are sketchy for the early days, but William Henderson sold his cigar factory to Ed Henderson in 1885. Eventually, it was Hal Henderson who was the main cigar maker in the family, designing a tobacco-processing machine that was patented in 1924.

The Henderson Cigar Factory moved several times and was variously located on the north, west, and east sides of the Centerville Square. The image above shows the factory and store during the period from 1902 to 1913 when it was located on the north side of the Square, at 113 West Van Buren. The photograph at left shows the storefront when the establishment had moved to the west side of the Square, at 210 North Twelfth Street.

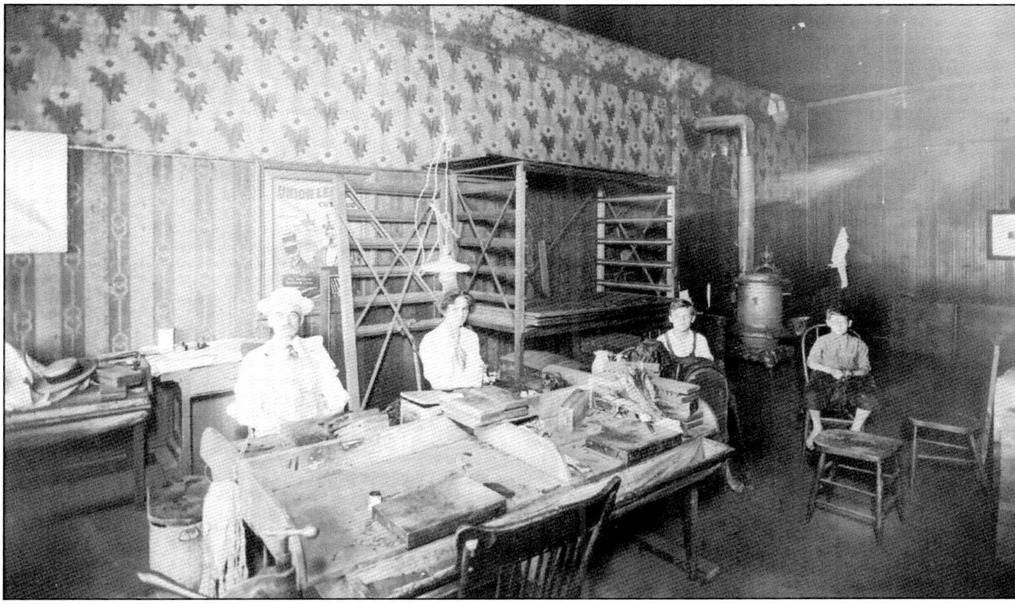

A scene from inside the cigar factory room shows a specially equipped table for four workers and an ample supply of cigar molds. Note the drying racks along the wall, and the young, barefoot boys who prepared the tobacco leaves before they were used in the cigars. The cigar factory rooms were usually upstairs, above the store.

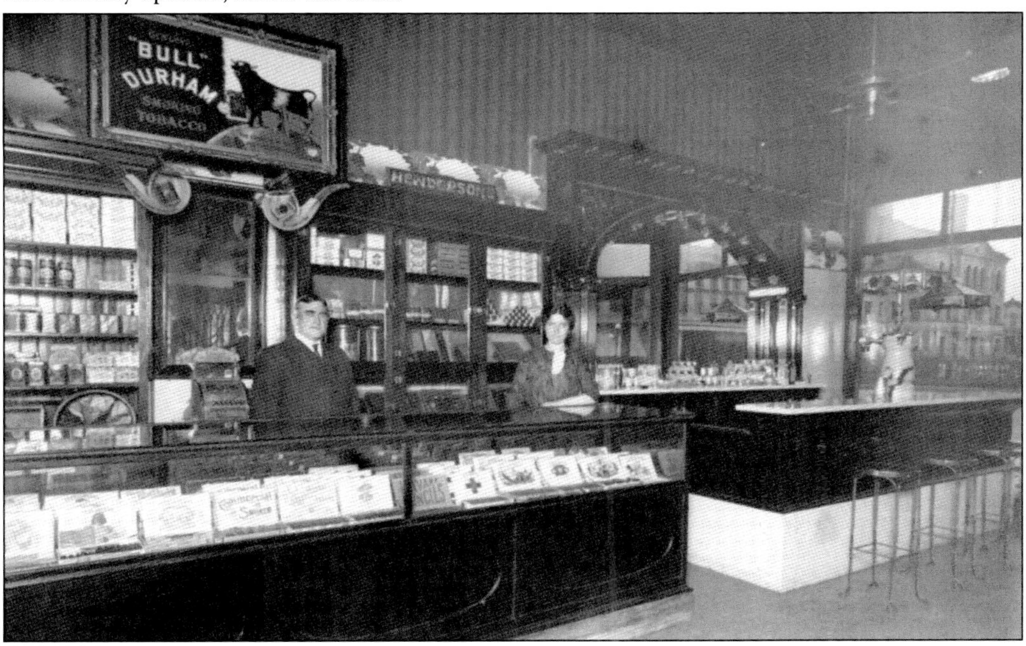

Over the course of time, Hal Henderson moved the factory to the White building, at 309-1/2 North Thirteenth Street, where it remained into the late 1920s. The store stayed on the west side of the Square a while longer. Evidence seems to indicate that Henderson engaged in an ongoing struggle to convince Centervillians to buy his cigars, as he wrote an opinionated article in 1909 appealing to customers to buy their cigars locally.

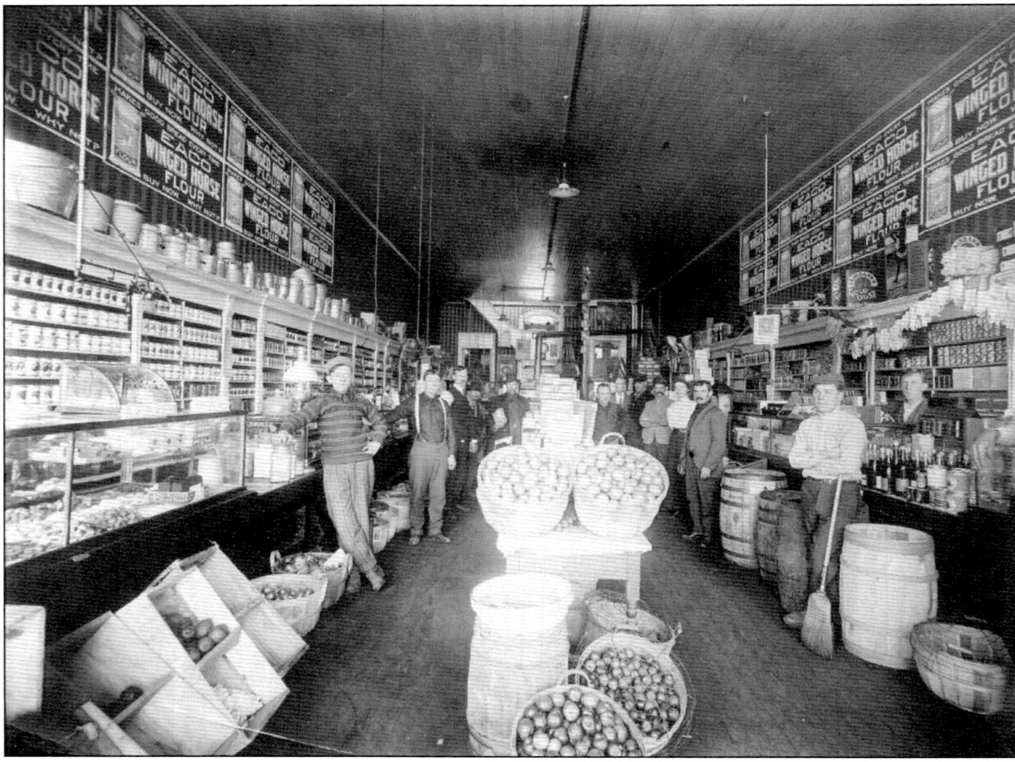

The J.M. Biddle Store was located on the south side of the Square. It originated in 1889 as Biddle & Riggs, selling groceries. In 1917, J.M. added his son to the management, making the store J.M. Biddle & Son. This c. 1910 photograph shows the great assortment of groceries available. The store closed in 1917, when it was sold to J.B. Wentz.

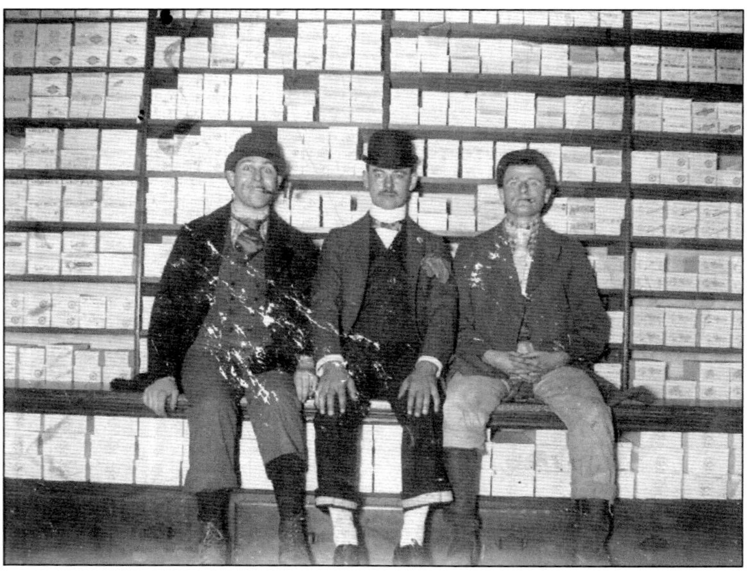

These fellows are hamming it up inside the Robert M. McKee Shoe Store on the west side of the Square around 1905. Robert McKee was the son of Susannah McKee, proprietor at the Continental Hotel. Robert bought the shoe store in 1896 and operated it until 1913, when he sold it to C. Ward Howell. McKee wanted to devote more time to managing his other business, the Sunshine Coal Mine.

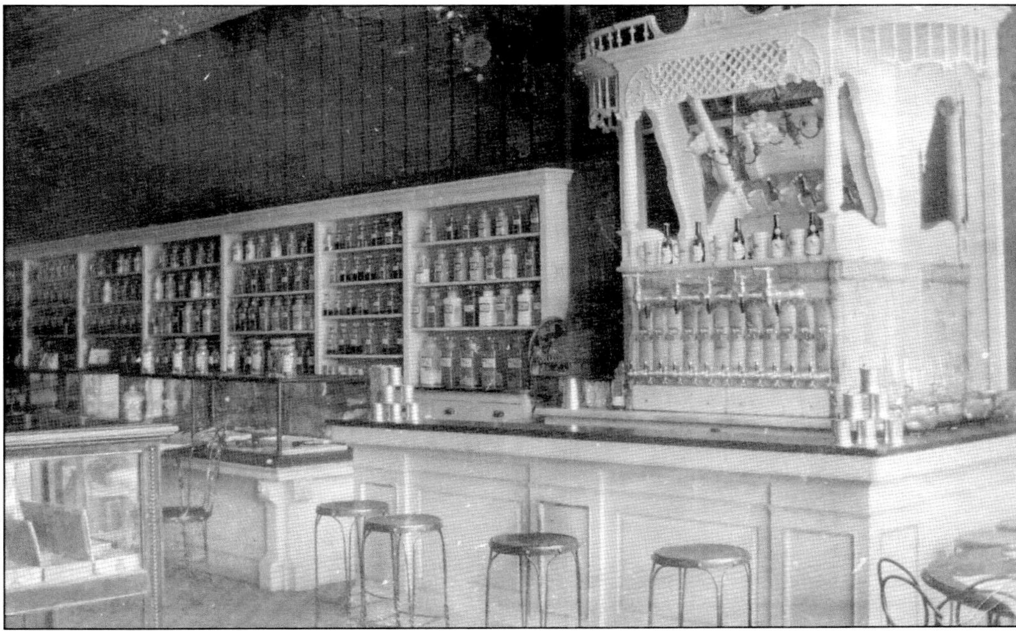

Nearly every drugstore in town featured a soda fountain. This ornate one was located in the Red Cross Drug Store in its early days. The first Red Cross Drug Store was opened in Centerville by Carl Weeks in 1900. Weeks moved to Des Moines and became very wealthy with his Armand Cosmetics product line, later building the famous Salisbury House.

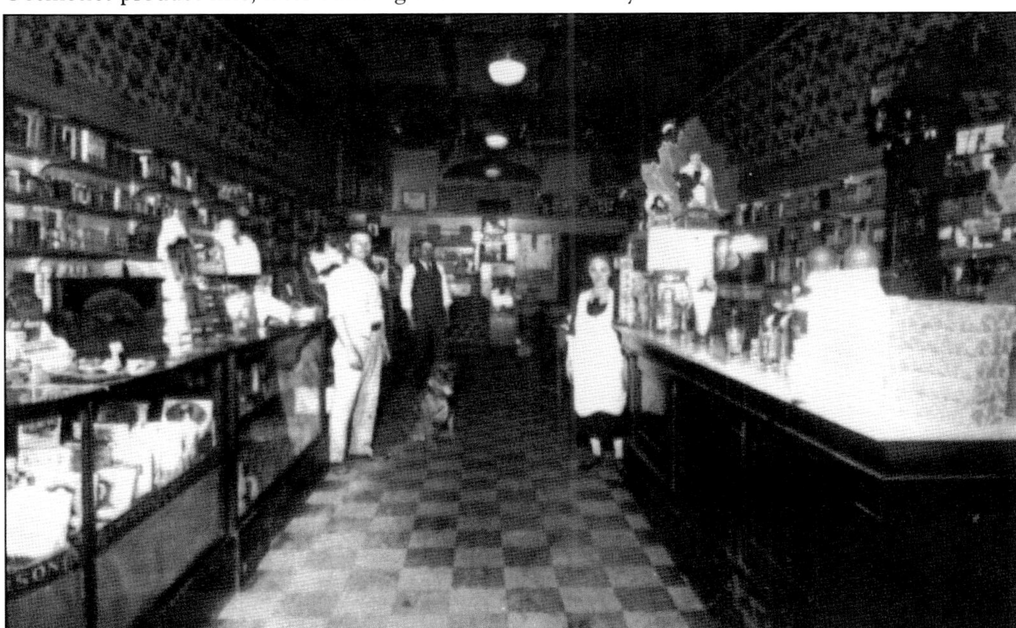

The Beer's Drug Store was a fixture on the west side of the Square from 1906 to 1955. The store was purchased by Mose Beer from W.M. McCreary in 1906. Beer retired in 1925, and his son, Paul, continued to operate the establishment until 1955. The building was destroyed by fire in 1968 while operating as Willier Pharmacy.

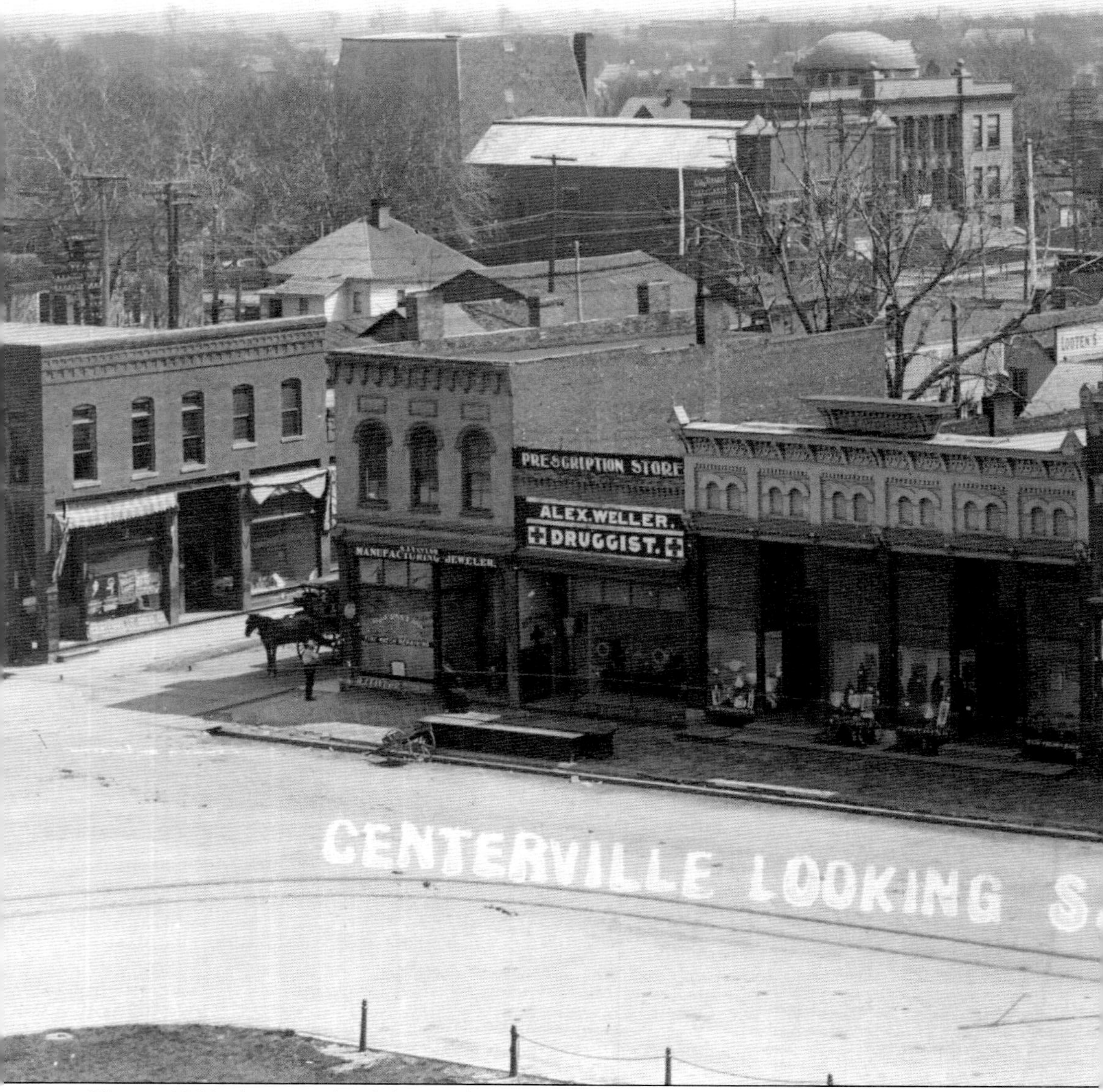

This c. 1900 photograph of the southeast corner of the Square reveals two candy factories on the same block. Two of the historic buildings in the background are Looten's Bakery on Pill Row and Citizen's Lumber on Maple Street. On Drake Avenue are the Drake Opera House, the Drake Library, the Central Church of Christ on the east side, and the old Centerville High School across

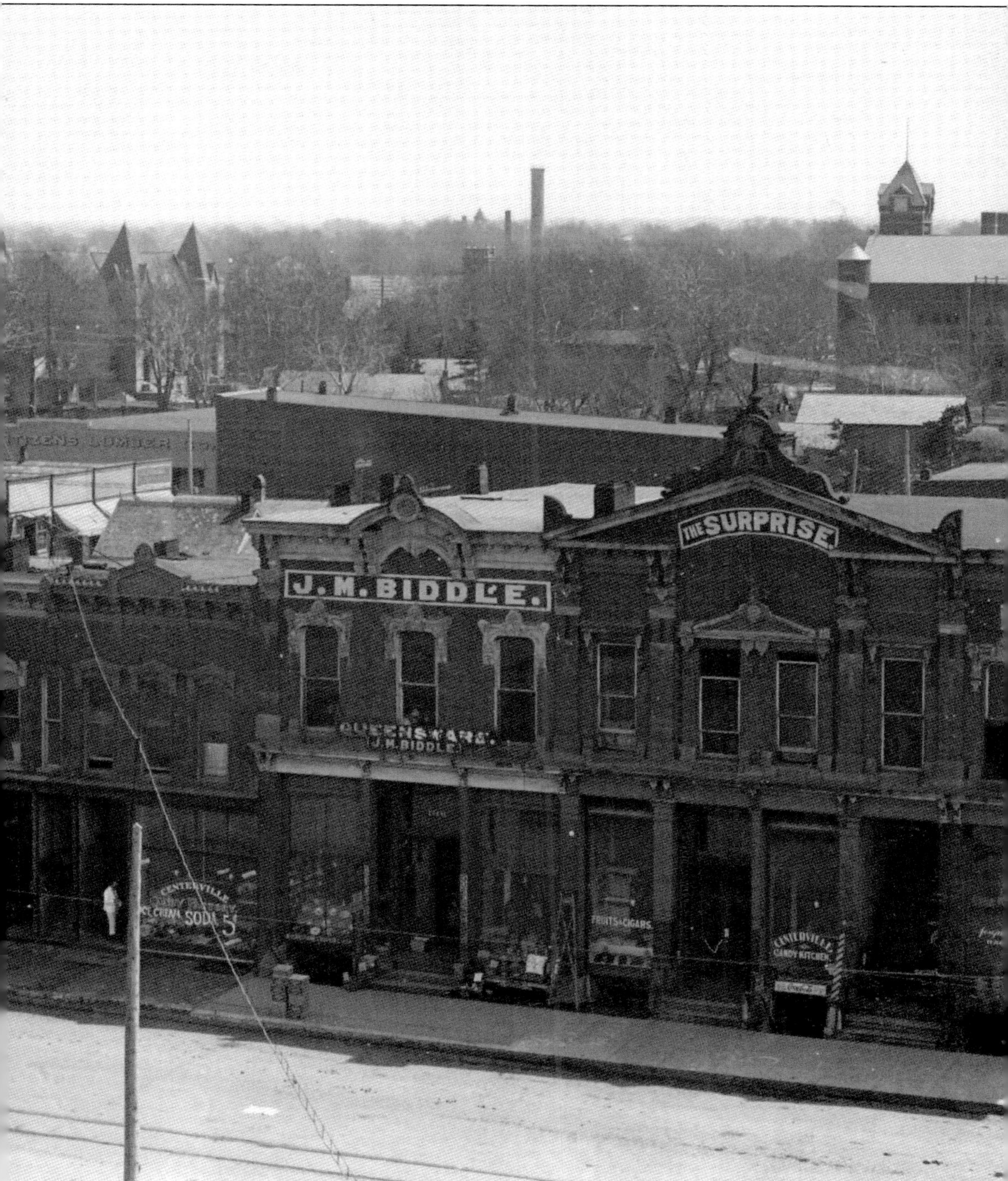

the street. The school building appears to be quite a distance off the street. A little farther south are the towers of the Centerville Water Works pump house at Sixteenth and Terry Streets. Even farther out is the bell tower of Garfield School on the city's south side.

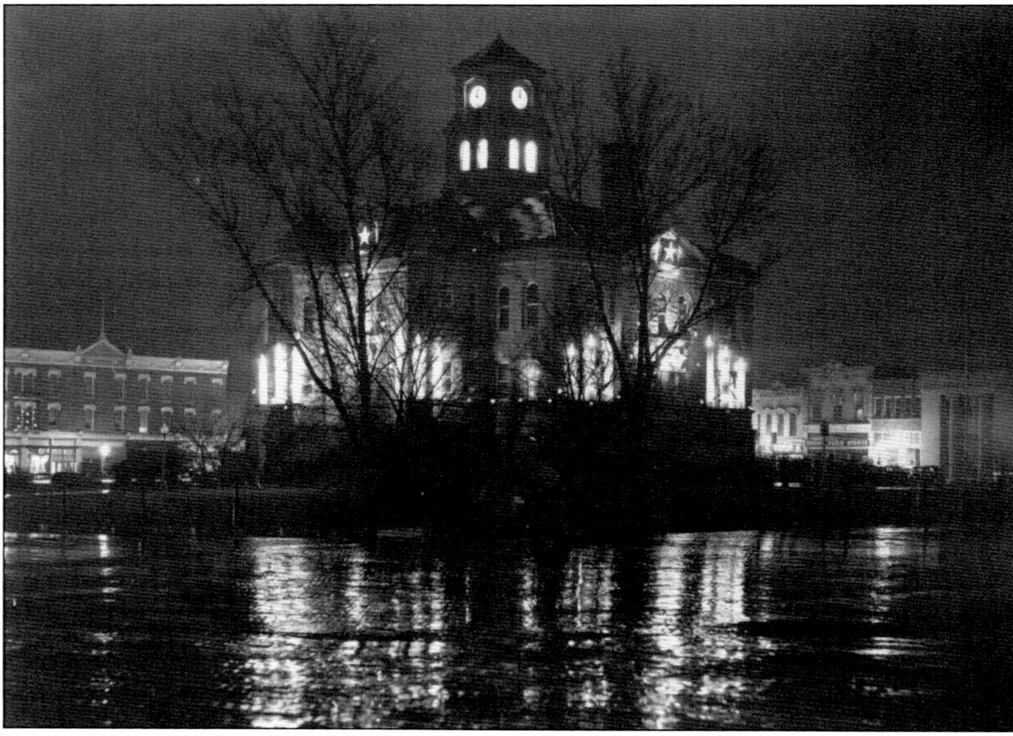

Harry Luther was a longtime merchant on the Square and an avid photographer. He took these two photographs after an ice storm in December 1940. It was reported that the holiday decorations on the Square, seen here reflected on the ice, were the best the town had ever seen, and amateur photographers from all over were coming to Centerville to capture their beauty. On each side of the courthouse was a Yule scene, six feet tall and twelve feet wide. Flanking each scene were six candles, eight, ten, and twelve feet tall. Huge stars were hung in each gable of the courthouse, and the lattices in the bell tower were removed, replaced with backlit cellophane windows. That year, Centerville was dubbed "The Christmas City."

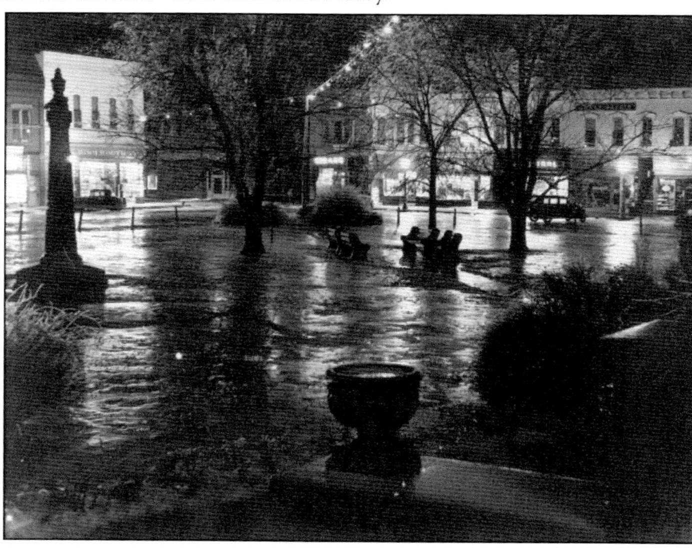

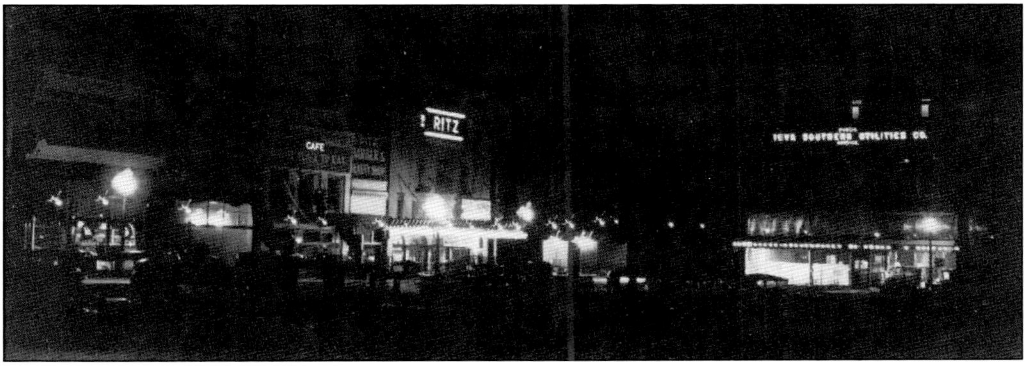

This nighttime shot of the northeast corner of the Square shows all of the "Ritz" businesses. The Ritz Theatre was opened in 1926 and was famous for its "Bank Nites," when people came to the theater in hopes of winning cash or prizes. No purchase was necessary to win, but the promotion did increase traffic into the theater during the Great Depression, helping it survive the lean times.

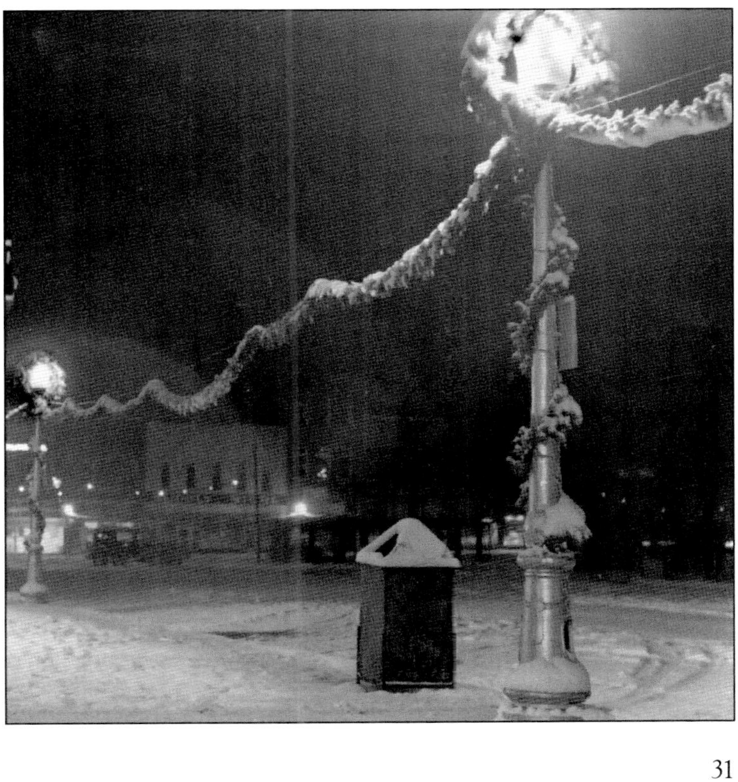

This Harry Luther Christmastime image of the Square was taken from the vantage point of Luther's store on the north side of the Square. Shown here is the east side, where the first Supply Store was located. The Supply Store, owned by the Hydes and Vredenbergs, was the predecessor to the present-day HyVee. For a time, the Supply Store had two locations on the Square.

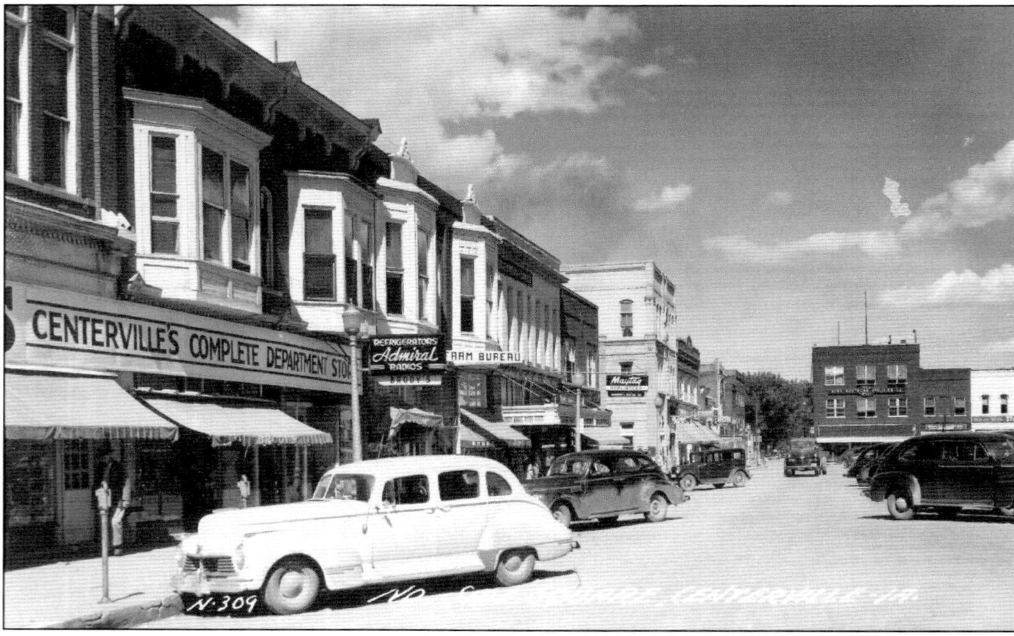

In 1948, this block included Brody's Department Store, Luther's Store, Tilton's Shoe Store, The Wood Brothers Barber Shop downstairs, Milani's Law Office, Milady's Clothing Store, Waughop Maytag, and the A&P store. In 1946, parking meters were installed. They graced the Square until being phased out in the 1970s. (Courtesy of Historic Preservation Corporation.)

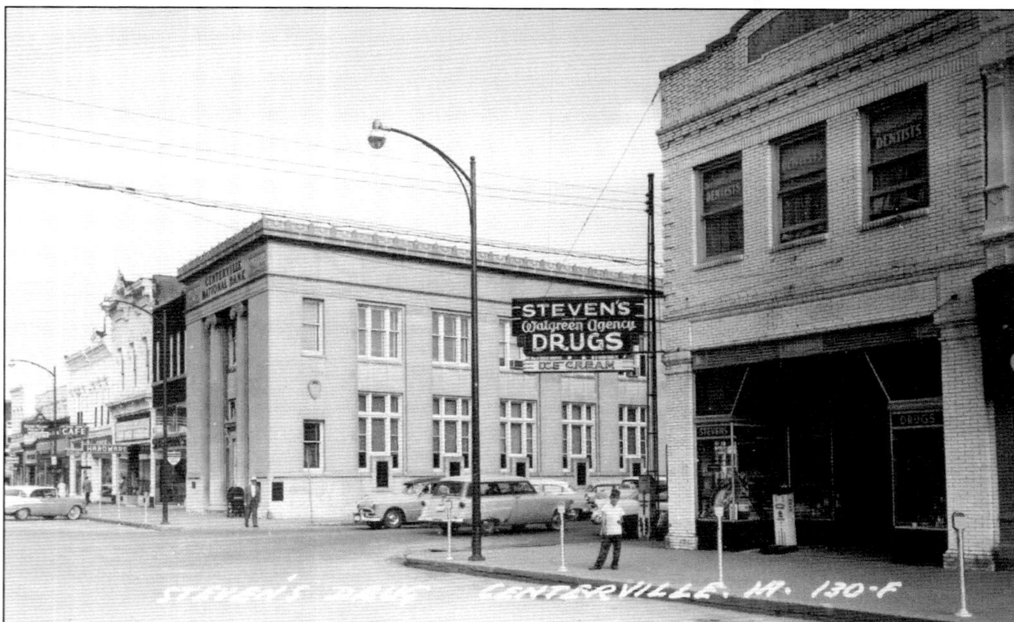

Steven's Drug Store opened in June 1936 and was known as Steven's Drug Store and Tea Room. In addition to pharmaceutical products, it had a full-service dining room. In 1945, the full dinner service was discontinued, and the room became known as a "luncheonette," where a full line of soups and sandwiches were served.

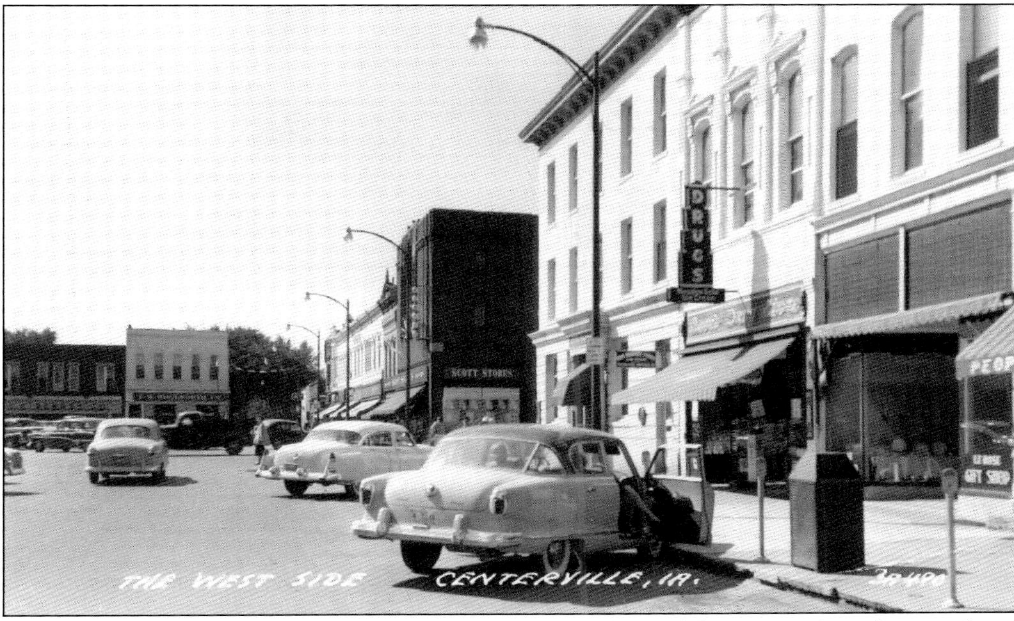

The building on the right was Mose Beer's Drug Store. It burned down in 1968 and was replaced with a one-story structure. The building next to it was the Wooden Savings Bank. The streetlights shown here were switched on for the first time on Pancake Day in 1951. (Courtesy of Historic Preservation Corporation.)

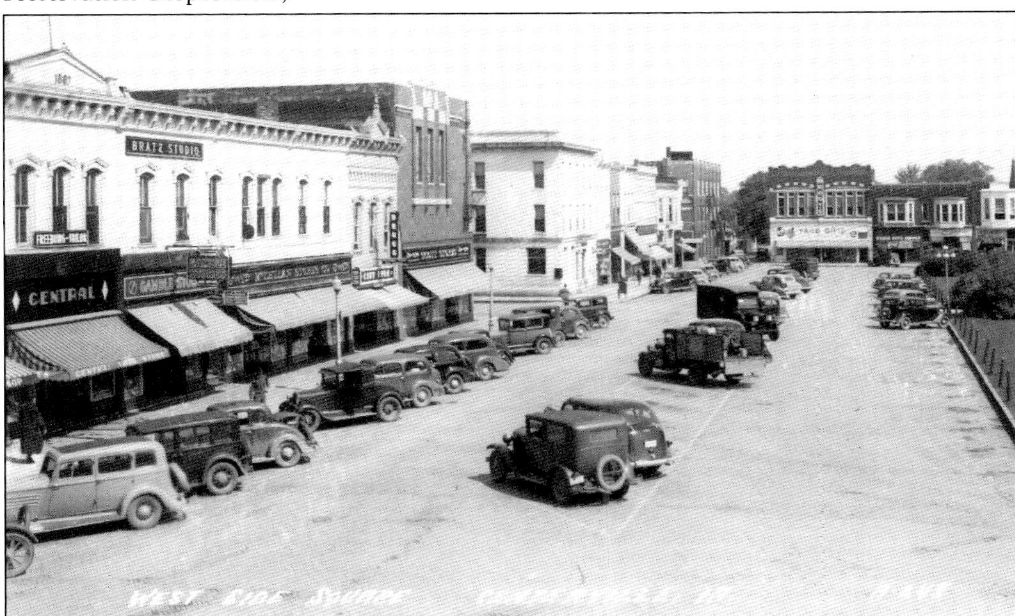

This 1930s photograph of the west side of the Square shows that there was only one row of parking between the two lanes of traffic. In 1949, the road was widened by cutting back the courtyard, adding an additional row of parking. In the late 1960s, both lanes of traffic moved counterclockwise. By 1970, clockwise travel was restored to the inside lane. (Courtesy of Historic Preservation Corporation.)

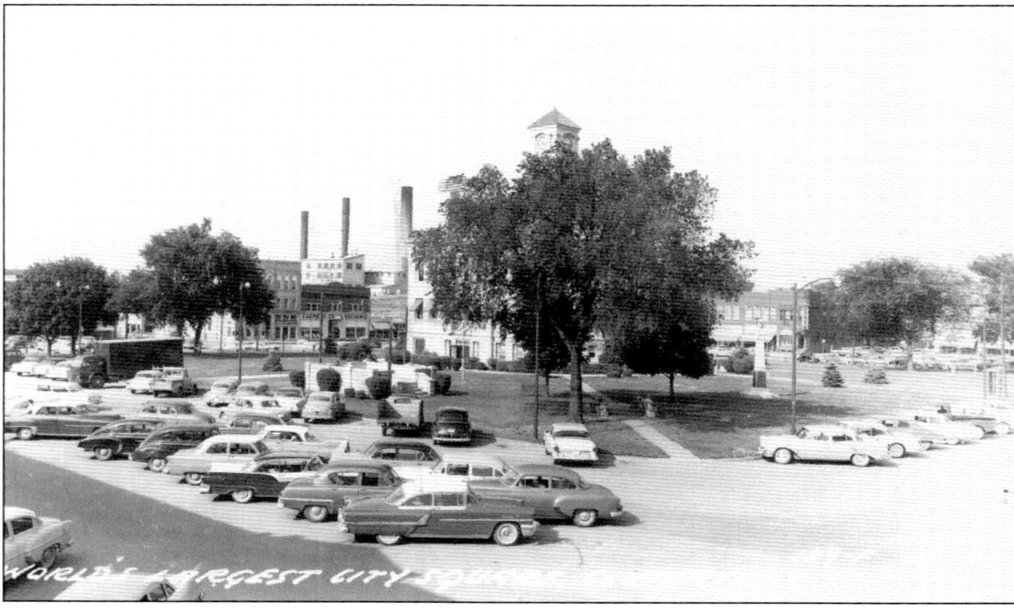

Taken from the southwest corner of the Square looking toward the northeast corner, this photograph shows two long-gone structures. On the courtyard is the square band shell that was in place from 1916 until 1959. Beyond that, off the northeast corner, are the smokestacks from the Iowa Southern Utilities (ISU) generating plant. (Courtesy of Historic Preservation Corporation.)

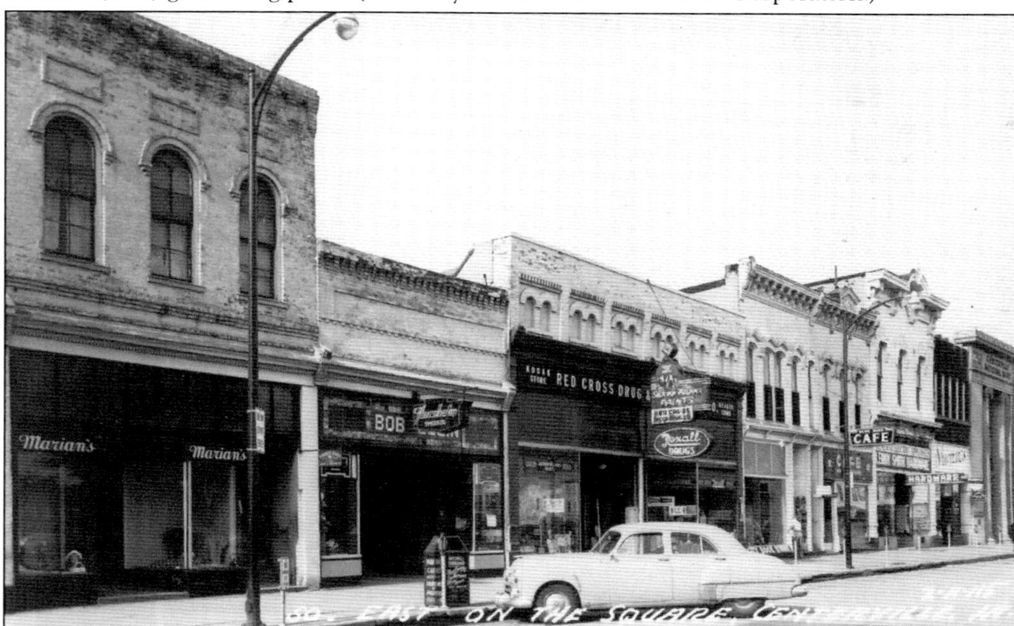

This postcard photograph of the south side of the Square was taken during the 1950s. The brick buildings were showing signs of their age, many years before Square revitalization was considered. Not long after this photograph was taken, many of the buildings on the Square had metal facades applied to cover the aging brick, to give the buildings a more "modern" look. (Courtesy of the Historic Preservation Corporation.)

Two

Beyond the Square

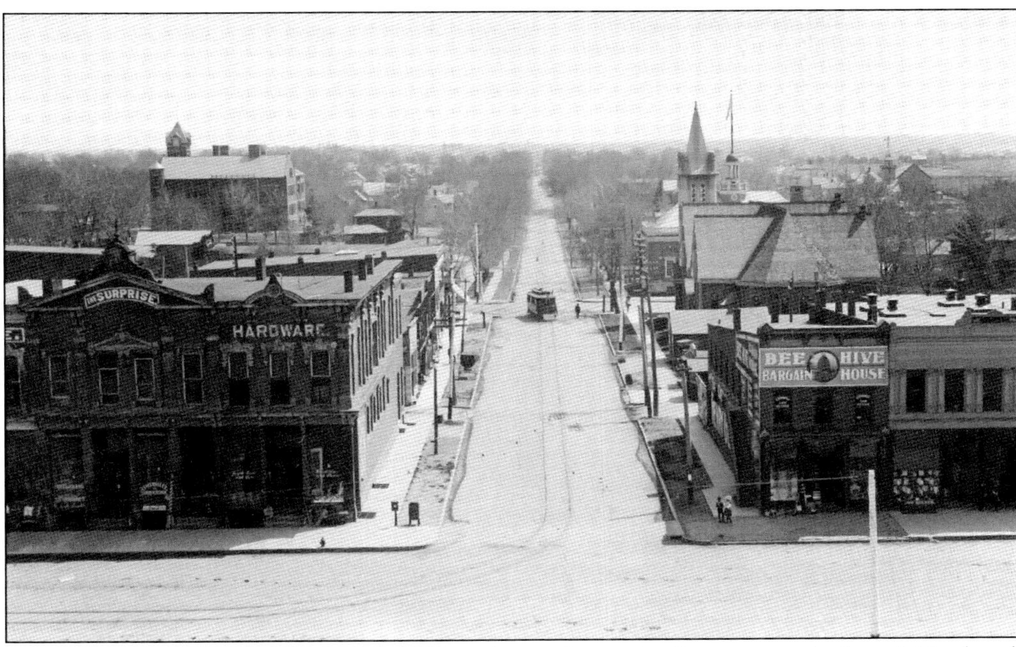

This chapter, like the streetcar in this photograph, now leaves the Square to reach the neighborhoods beyond. The streetcar is on North Main, going south, between the Bee Hive Bargain House and Joseph Goss & Sons Hardware.

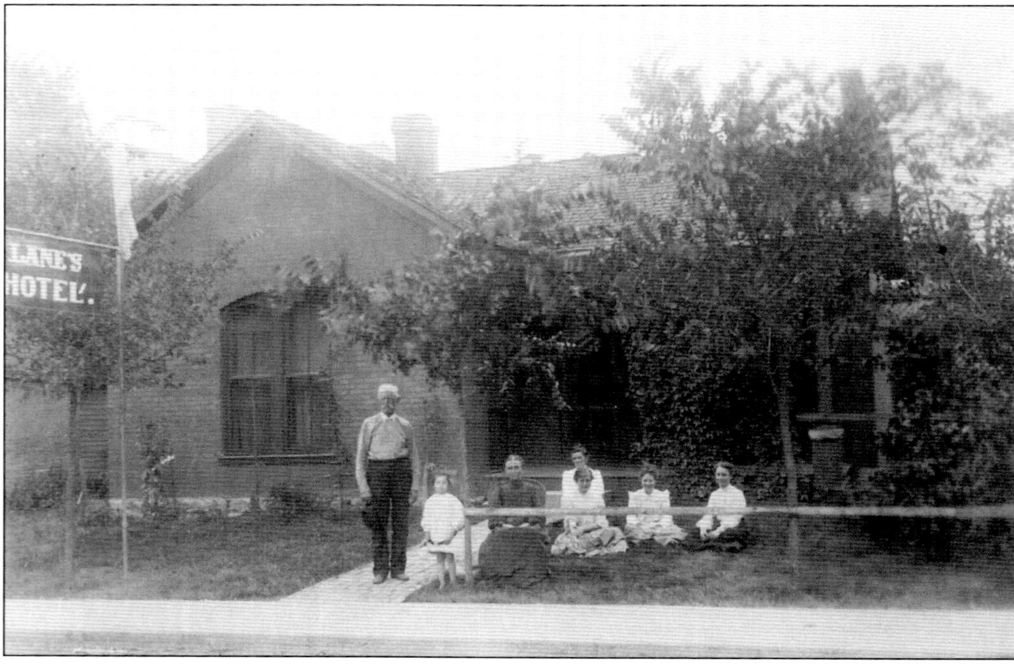

Lane's Hotel was located on North Twelfth Street, off the northwest corner of the Square. It had the appearance of a small house. Judging from advertisements for the hotel between 1906 and 1912, it appears that traveling businesses would set up shop here for a week or two. Clairvoyants, foot masseurs, knife grinders, and even a Zulu prophet did business in Lane's Hotel.

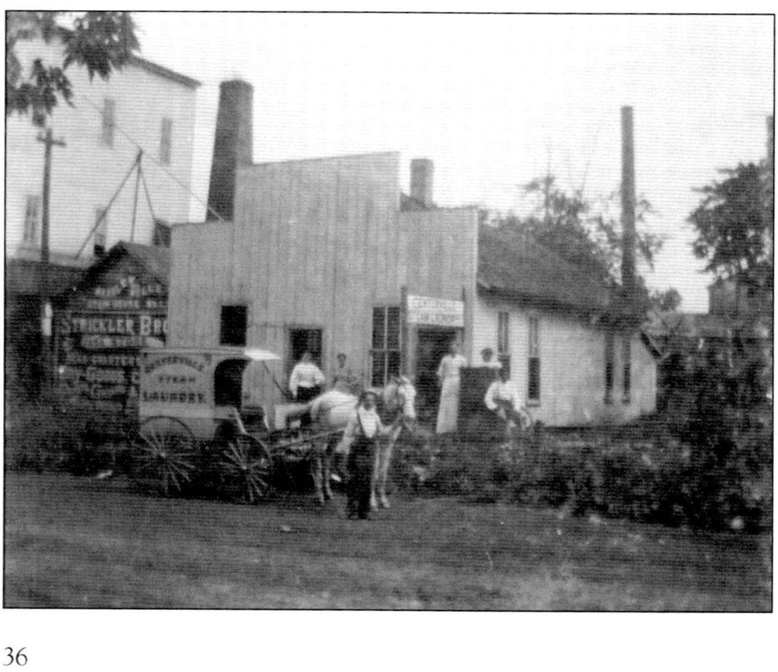

Centerville Steam Laundry was located at 303 East State Street in 1898, around the time of this photograph. Eventually, it was bought out by Regal Steam Laundry, which located its business on North Thirteenth Street, just north of the Square and next to the ISU power plant. Regal used the steam from the power plant to launder clothes.

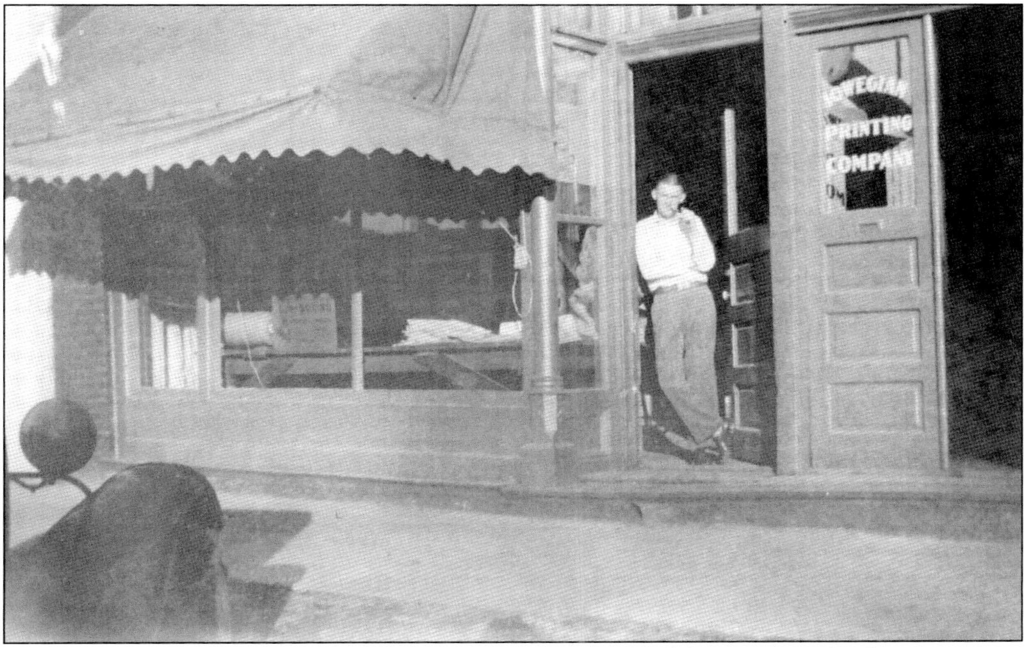

This is the Iowegian building on North Main Street, south of the Square. The first newspaper in Centerville was called the *Appanoose Chieftain*. In 1864, it became the *Loyal Citizen*. Its competitors were the *Times* and the *Journal*. In 1883, the first *Iowegian* was published. In 1912, the *Iowegian*'s competition came from the *Sun*, the *Citizen*, and the *Journal*. The *Journal* later became the *Southern Iowa American*, the newspaper of the Ku Klux Klan.

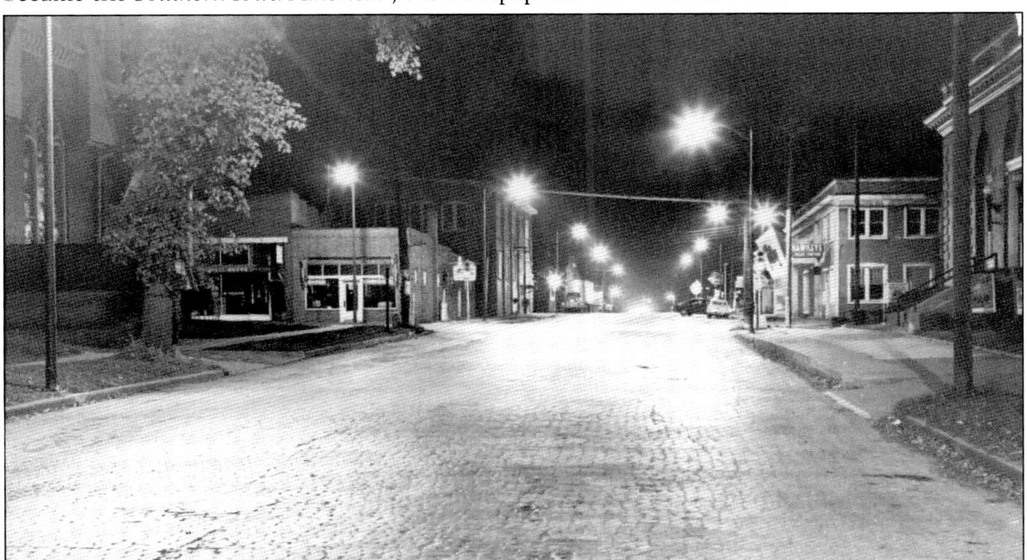

Prior to July 23, 1954, Maple Street was brick. In 1954, it was paved with concrete, and an official dedication of the street took place in front of the *Iowegian* office. Speakers recalled the street's earlier incarnation, the CHS band played, the CHS Cadettes performed, and the mayor dedicated the new, smooth highway. A street dance was planned as part of the celebration, but was cancelled due to rain.

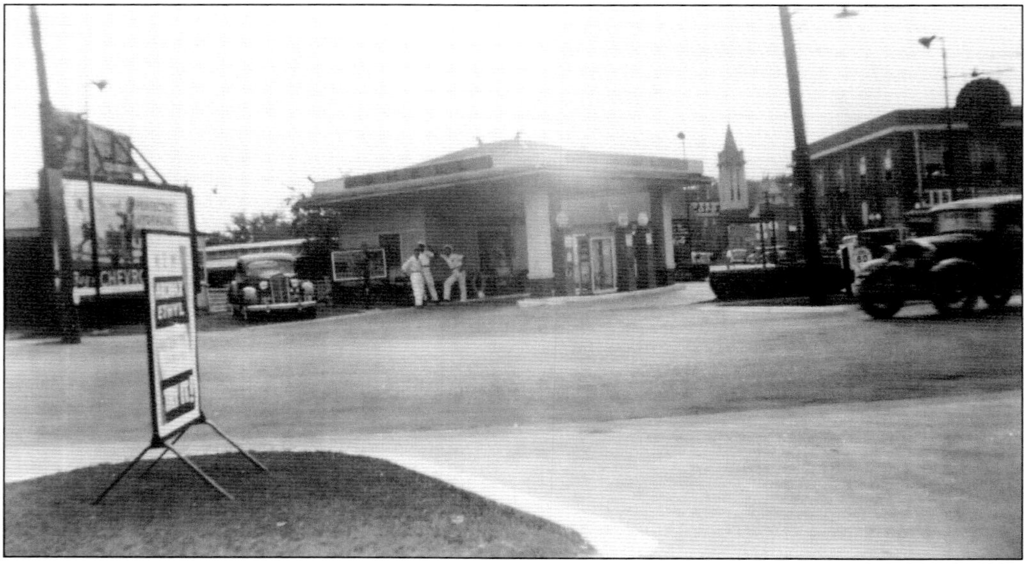

Twin brothers Harold and Gerald Carlson owned Carlson's Service Station on the corner of Maple Street and Drake Avenue in the late 1930s and early 1940s, until they were inducted into the service during World War II. Wearing all-white uniforms, they pumped gas, washed windshields, and checked oil. The station stood at an angle to the corner. (Courtesy of Helen Carlson.)

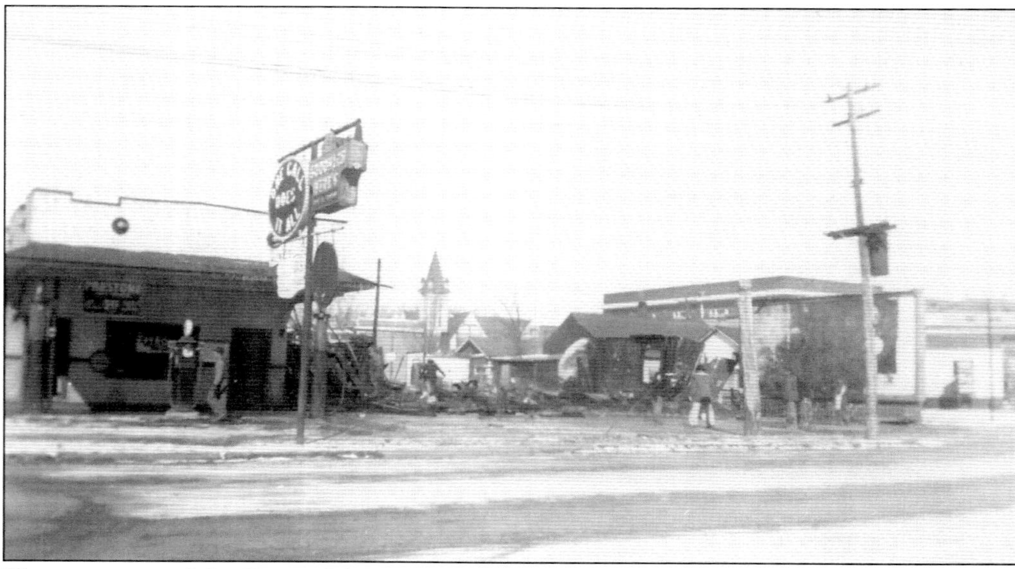

The proprietor of the Home Oil Station, next door and to the south of Carlson's Station, was W.O. "Oscar" Billberg, a well-liked man in the community. In 1940, an explosion rocked the establishment, throwing Billberg across the street to the Drake Library. Days later, Billberg was arrested for arson. He was tried, found guilty, and sent to the state prison in Fort Madison for the crime. (Courtesy of Helen Carlson.)

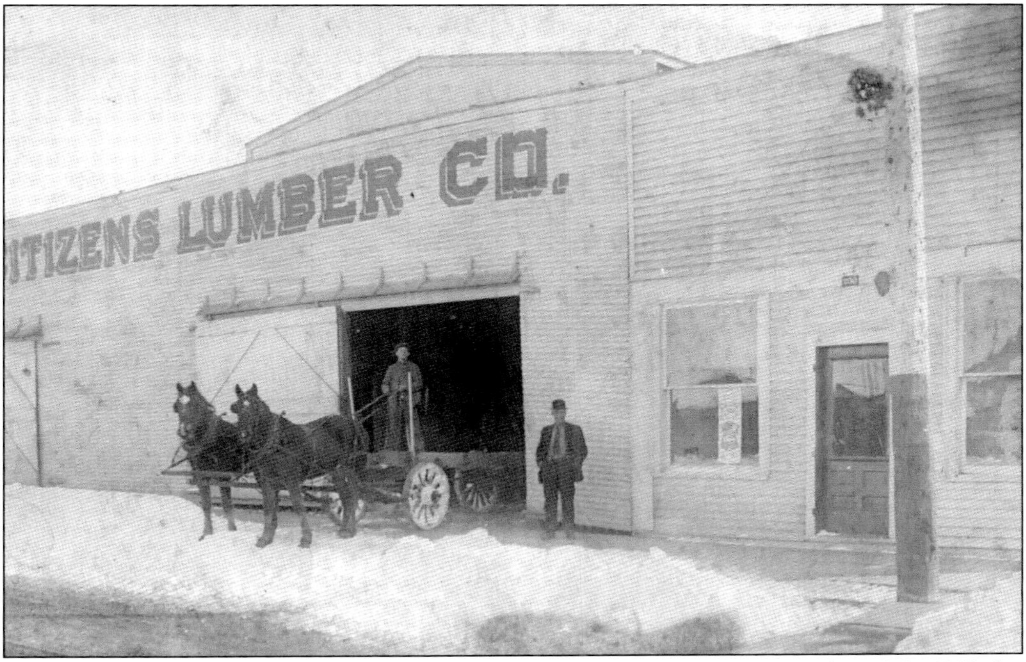

The Citizen's Lumber Company was located at 200 East Maple from 1903 until 1916. In 1917, the owner of the property, W.R. Krapfel, sold the buildings, with the exception of the small office structure, and announced that he and Majestic Theater owner Leo Moore would be building an ice-skating rink in its place.

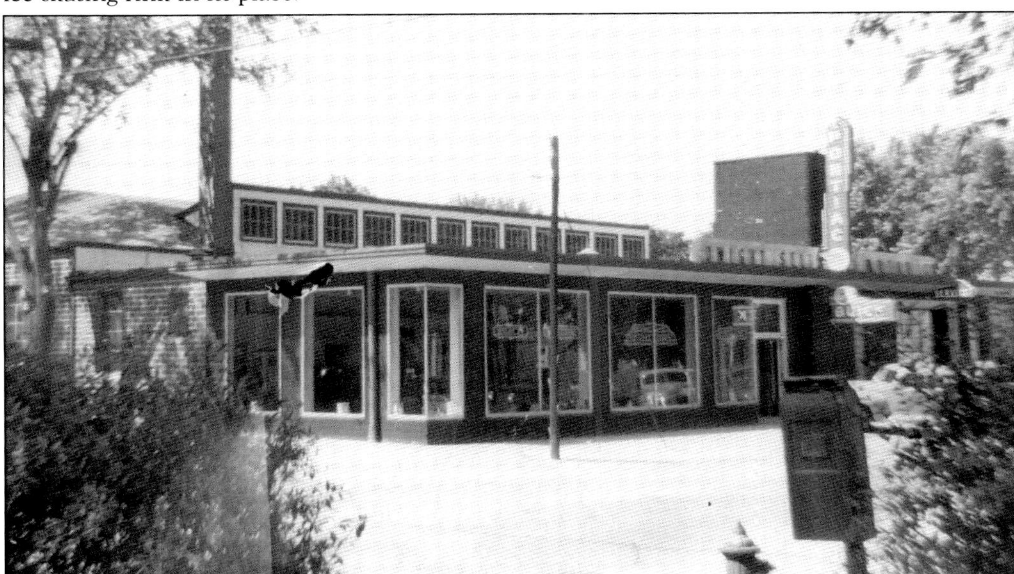

Dwight Selix Motors went into business in 1940; in 1946, the company built this new, modern building at the corner of Fifteenth and Maple Streets. In 1959, the building became home to Centerville City Hall, the fire department, and the community center. After a fire on October 28, 1977, the building was replaced by a new city hall and fire department complex that was dedicated in 1980.

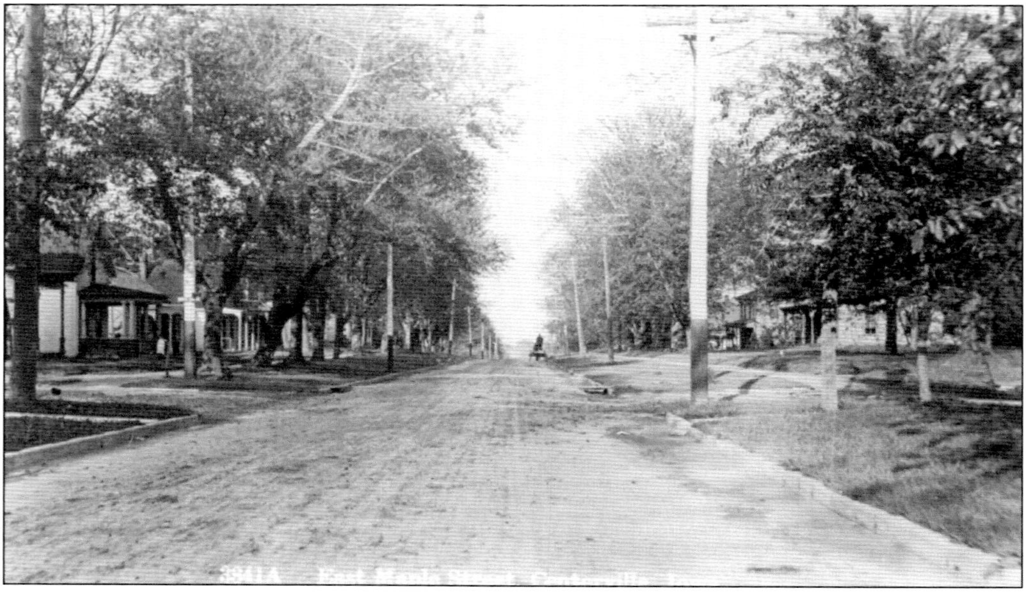

The neighborhoods in Centerville at the turn of the century looked much the way they do today, except for the dirt roads. Above is East Maple Street, and below is Maple Street, looking west. It is hard to determine where the photographer was standing in the above photograph, but in the image below, the Presbyterian Church is visible on the far right.

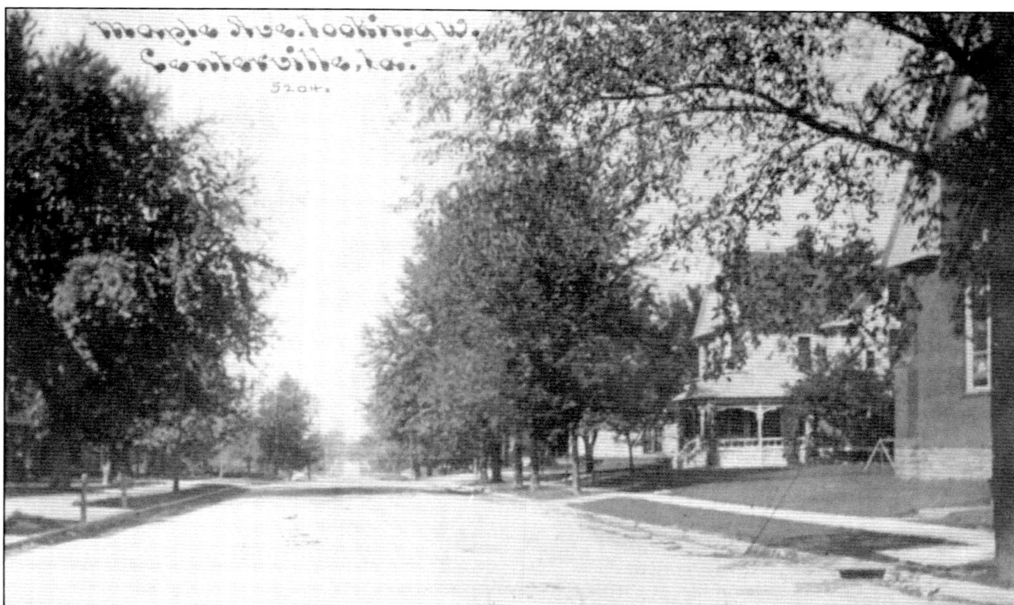

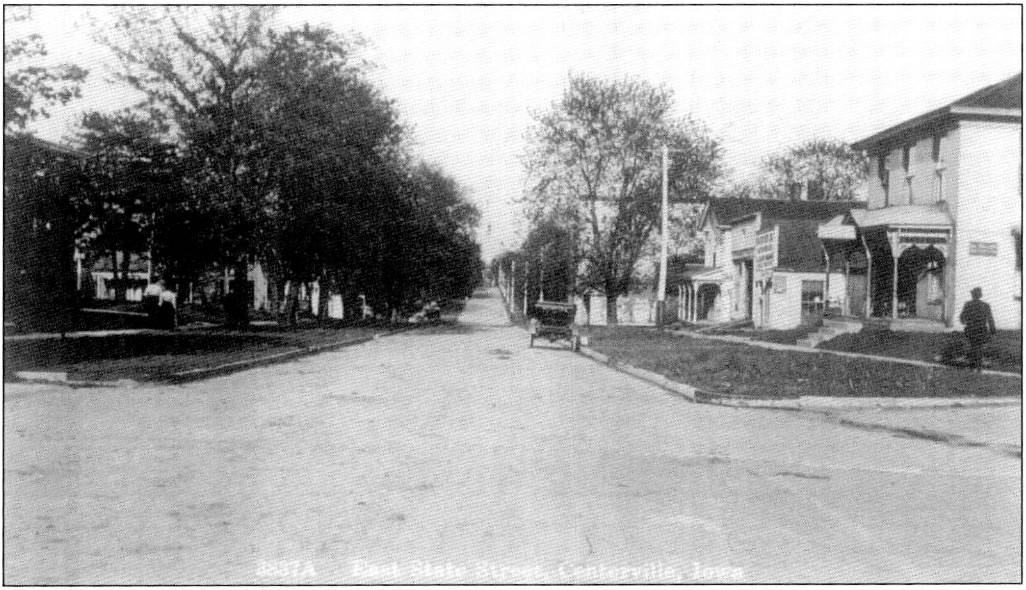

East State and West State Streets were the main gateways through Centerville. They were lined with businesses as the traveler approached the Square. In this photograph can be seen Dr. Dillon's office at 216 East State Street, just off the Square. The very tall building that was the Bradley & Wells Mill is visible in the distance.

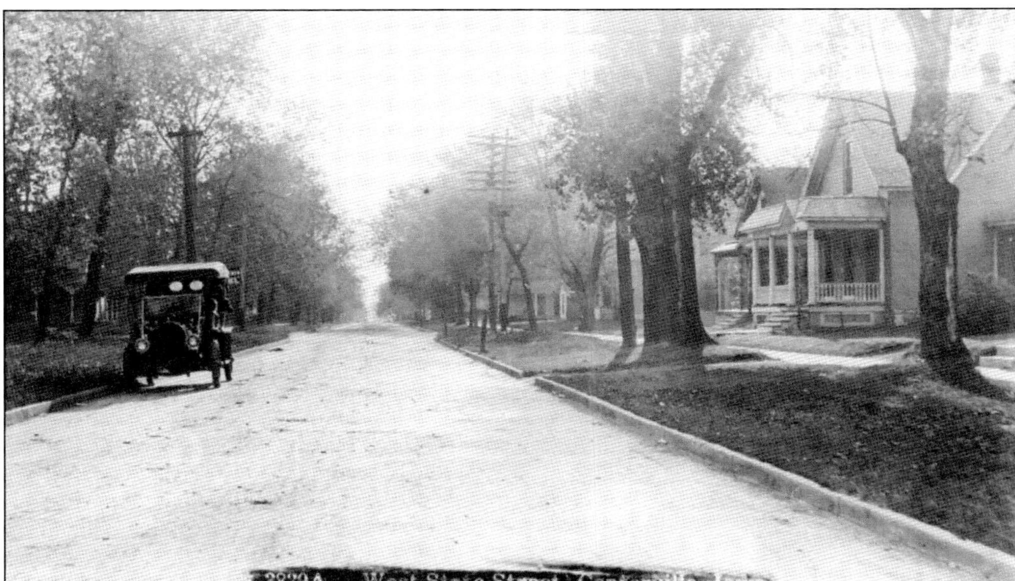

This photograph shows the 300 block of West State Street. Behind the car is a partially hidden sign that reads "Merchants Hotel." West State Street, the main thoroughfare in Centerville, was home to several hotels over the years.

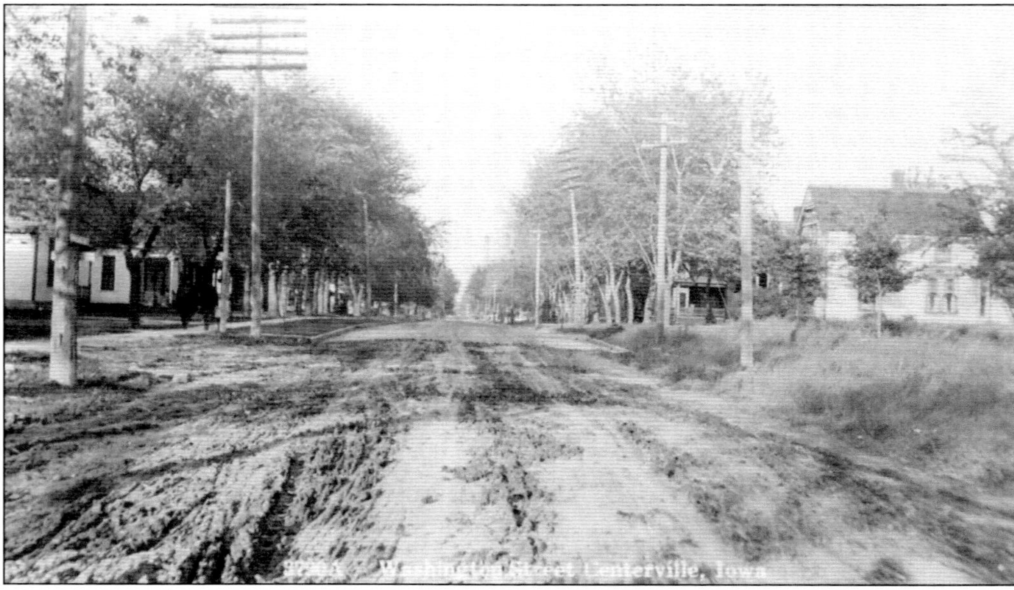

This photograph of Washington Street looks to have been taken from about Eighth Street, facing east. In the distance can be seen a smokestack from the Iowa Southern Utilities power plant near Thirteenth Street. Washington Street from Seventh Street to Fourteenth Street was paved with brick in 1905. The starting point of the brick surface can be seen here.

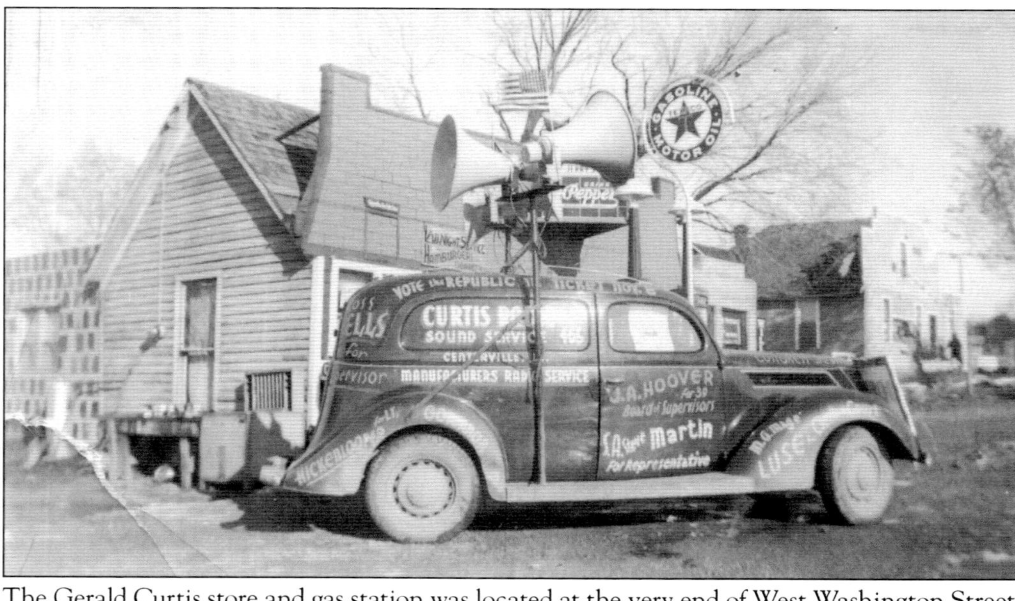

The Gerald Curtis store and gas station was located at the very end of West Washington Street. The Curtis Radio Sound Service truck was a 1936 Ford panel truck with speakers attached to the roof. The truck is being used to promote political candidates in this photograph. (Courtesy of Bob Curtis.)

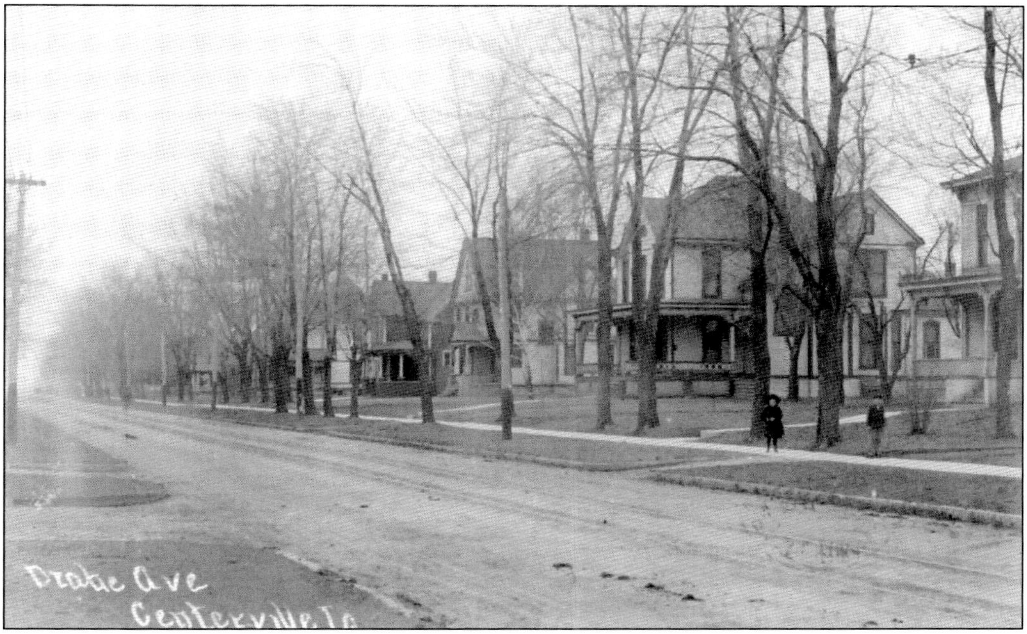

These houses on Drake Avenue are on the west side of the street and north of Sheridan Avenue, evidenced by the tracks in the road for the streetcar, which traveled this route. The street turning off to the left is East Bank, and the homes behind the photographer would have been the Bradley, Sawyer, and Drake mansions.

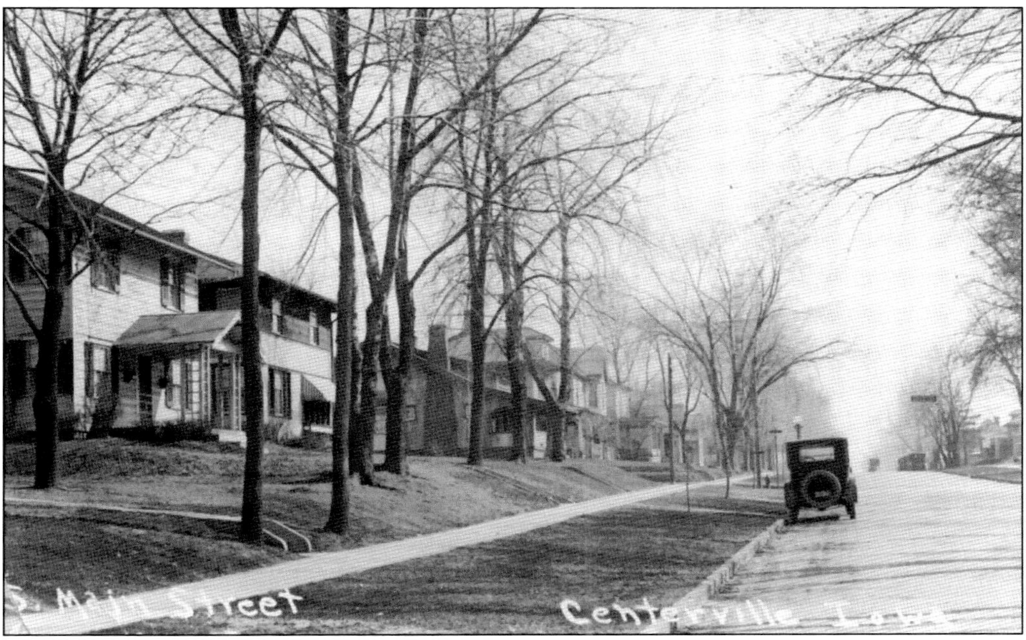

This 1924 photograph shows the 500 block of South Main, looking south. In the distance is an overhead sign that instructs motorists to slow down for the "hospital zone." St. Joseph's Mercy Hospital was located in the 700 block of South Main Street. Some of the houses pictured here are still in use.

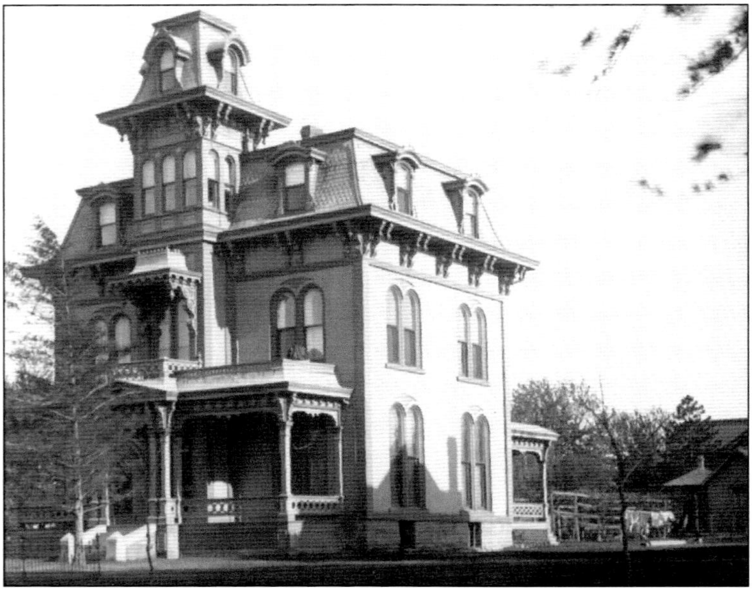

This stately mansion once stood in the space occupied by the current Centerville City Hall and fire department. It was built in 1871 by David C. Campbell, a local banker. Over the years, it had several owners, including Dr. Ephraim Reynolds, Dr. E.E. Bamford, and D.C. O'Neil. The structure, abandoned for many years, was dismantled in 1937 because it was an "eyesore" and a "menace to safety."

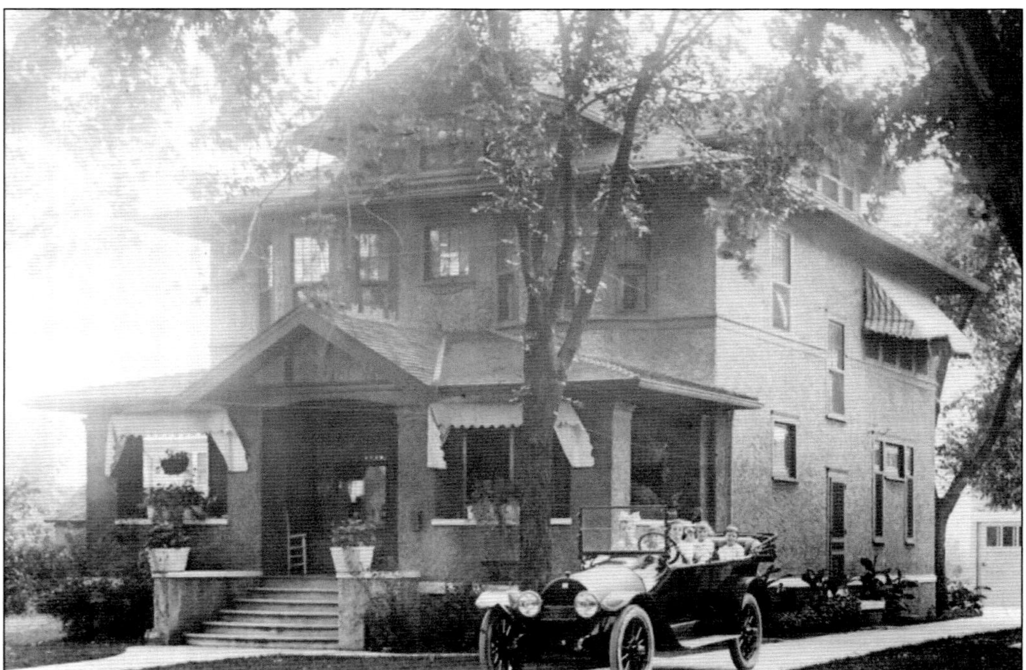

This lovely stucco home is located at 119 South Fifteenth Street. It was built in 1911 by Dr. Charles P. Tillmont. He and his wife, Catherine, lived here until his death in 1931. Dr. Tillmont was known for his "electric baths," which were popular in the 1920s. This home still stands today.

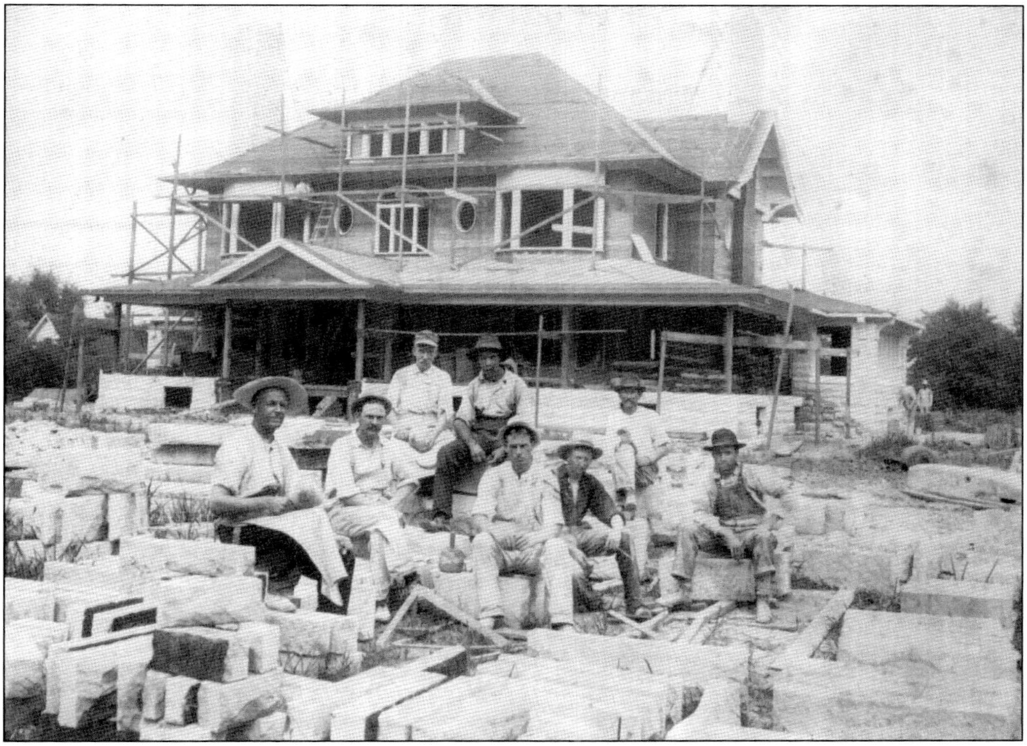

D.C. Bradley's mansion along Centerville's "Gold Coast" was built in 1909–1910. The home was designed by Wetherell and Gage, the same architects who designed the courthouse, the high school, Drake Avenue Christian Church, and the chapel at Oakland Cemetery. The interior boasts 16 rooms, including a ballroom and servants' quarters. As the Great Depression took hold, D.C.'s fortunes diminished. He died in 1928, his brother J.A. assuming some of his debts and the mansion. It remained in the family until 1955. From 1956 until 1963, it was a nursing home. From 1963 until 1970, it became Centerville Community College, and the Centerville School District used it for classes and administration from 1970 until 1999. In 1998, Morgan Cline purchased the home and restored the beauty of this grand structure.

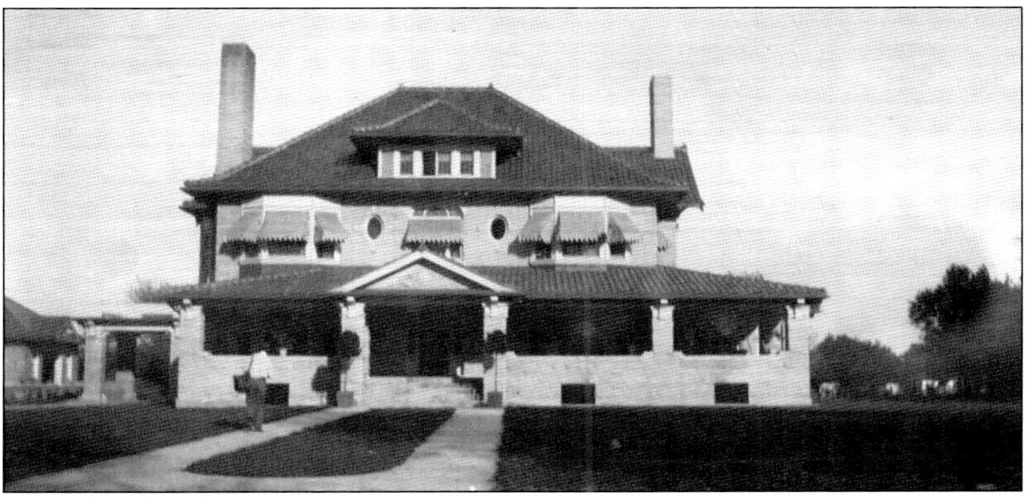

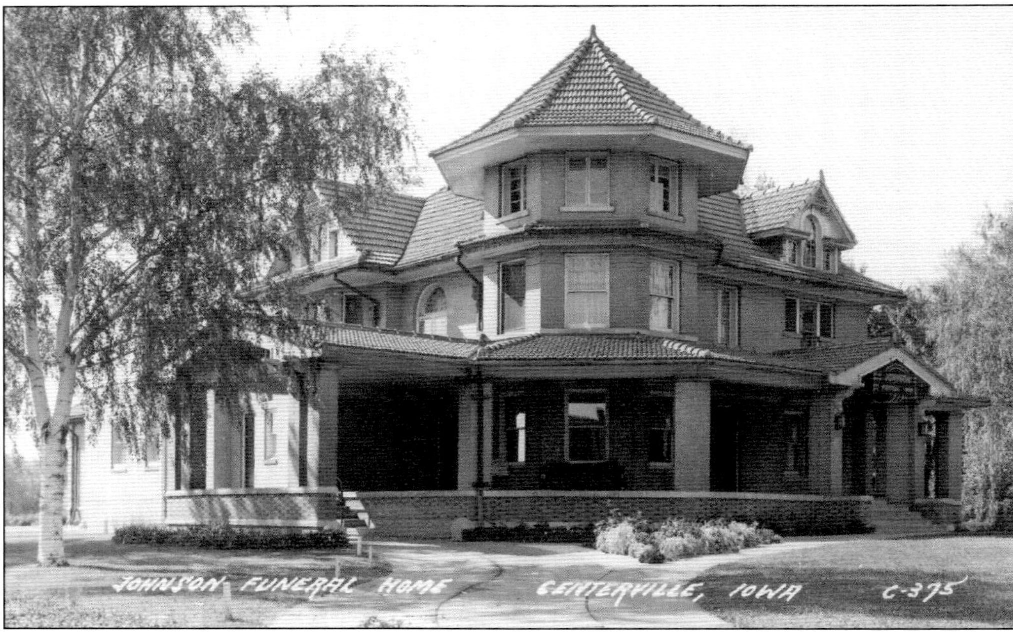

The picturesque home of J.A. White was built in 1911–1912. It is believed that White felt pressured to build a home as grand as D.C. Bradley's. White died in 1936, and his daughter, Della, sold the home to Hugh Johnson. It functioned as a funeral home until 2002, when it was purchased for use as a single-family residence once again.

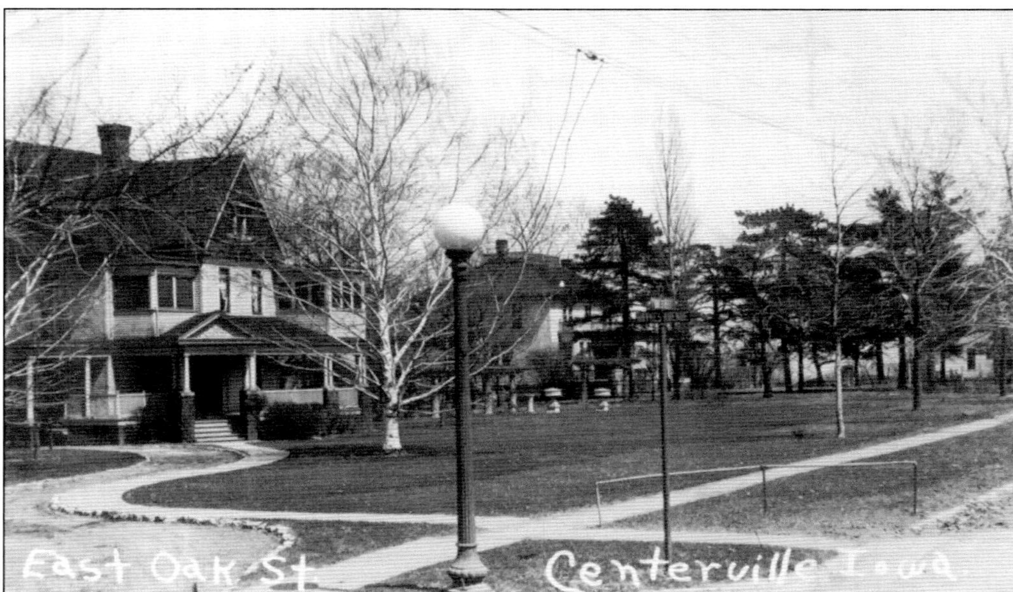

East Oak Street is only four blocks long, stretching from Haynes Avenue to Eighteenth Street. It would have been considered "out in the country" in Centerville's early days. Though the owners of these particular homes cannot be identified, several affluent families have had property on Oak Street, including Milton Vredenberg, Dr. E.A. Laurson, Dr. G.L. Richey, R.C. Link, the Bashaws, and Hale Greenleaf.

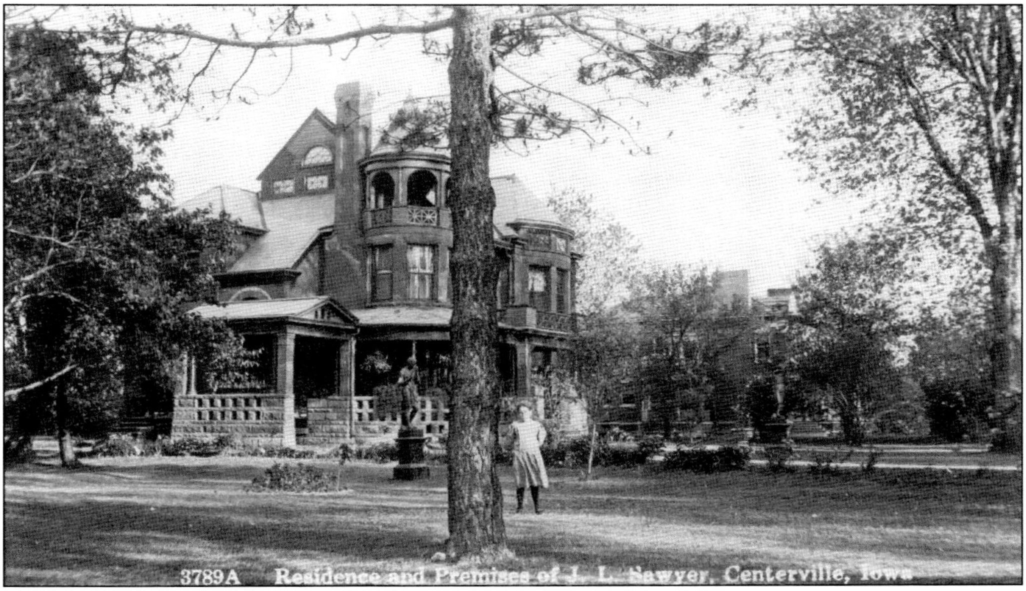

This beautiful residence was the second mansion built at 617 Drake Avenue by Gov. Francis Marion Drake. Governor Drake, whose wife had passed, lived here with his daughter's family from 1892 until Drake's death in 1903. The Dr. J.L Sawyer family moved into the home in 1907, and later his son Lazelle Sawyers and family lived there. The mansion was torn down in 1957.

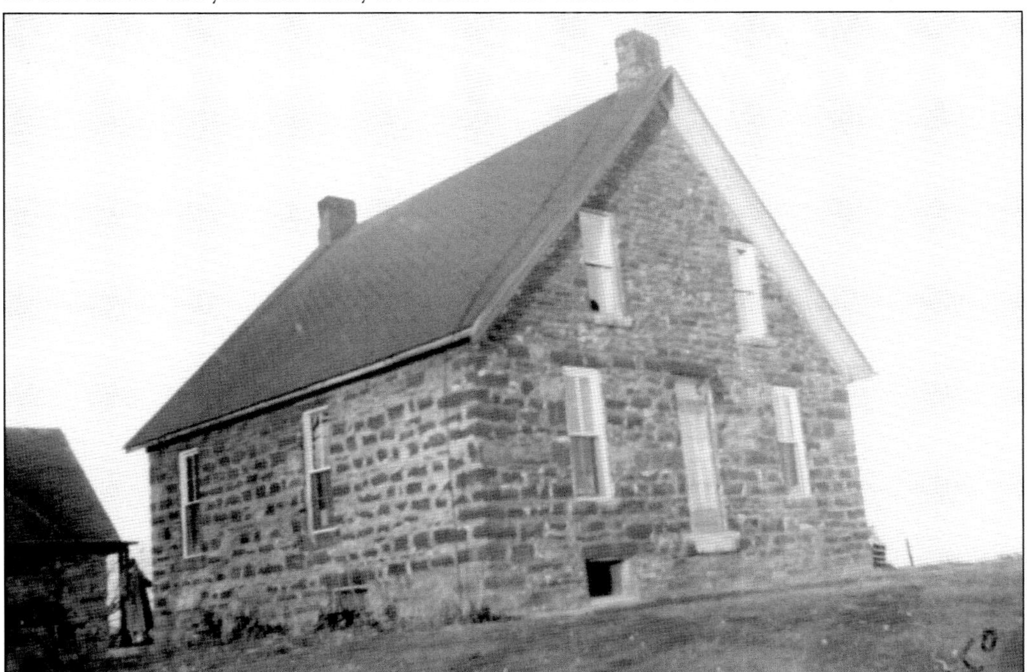

This photograph shows the "Old Stone House," also known as "The Lepper House." For a year prior to its construction in the spring of 1874, the building's materials were gathered at the location. It was rumored that the Jesse James gang spent a night at this home near Clarkdale. (Courtesy of Virginia Koestner.)

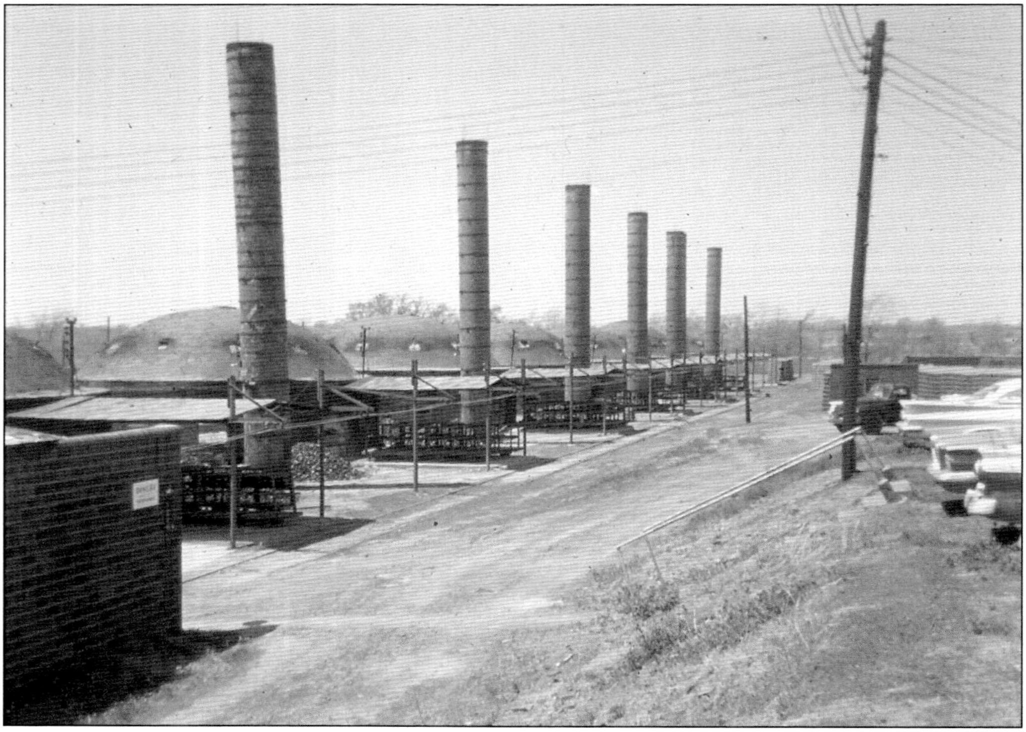

Commonly known as "the brick plant," this facility had several names over the years. Founded in 1904 as City Brick & Tile Company, it became Centerville Brick & Construction Company in 1912. By the time of this photograph, it was known as Iowa Clay Products. The plant was located at 1500 West Van Buren Street, on the south side of Highway 2 on the west edge of town.

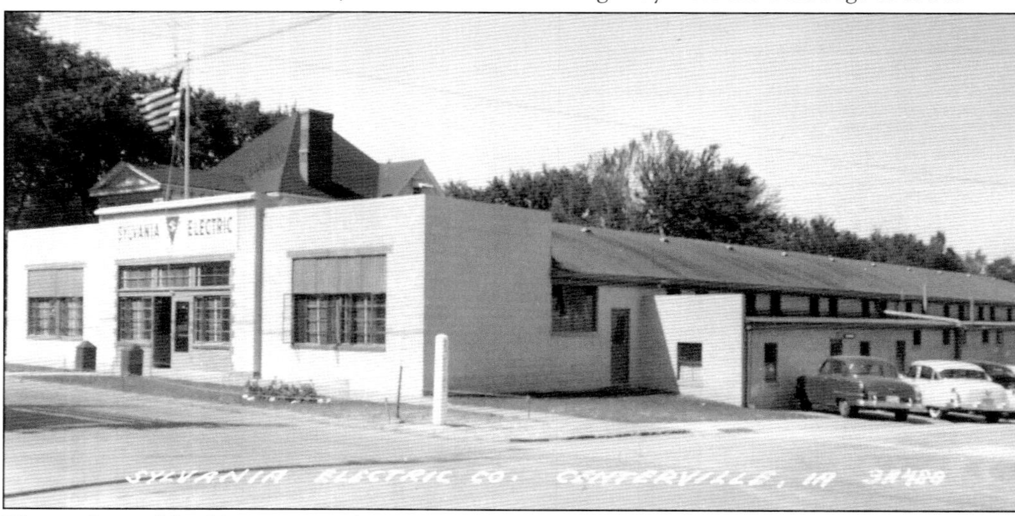

This industrial building on Washington Street was built by Centerville Industries, a group of local investors, and was used by the Sylvania Electric Company in August 1953. Sylvania was in business for less than a year. Luckily, another business, Uniform Printing & Supply, a printer of insurance forms, occupied the building until September 1963. It was then used by the community college as a science and technical laboratory.

Three

The Levee, Walsh, and South Centerville

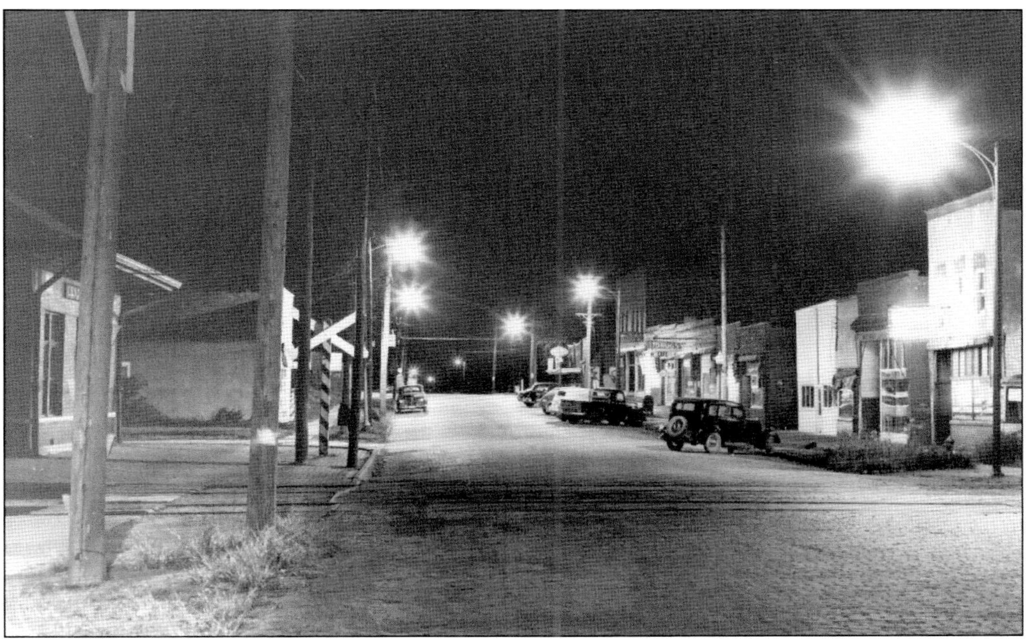

No one knows for sure why this part of town is called "the Levee," but it is rumored that the moniker was first used by Centerville tailor George Armour, who arrived in town in the 1880s. He said that Centerville's south-side business district reminded him of the area around the levee in Keokuk that was home to many establishments for men to indulge in various vices.

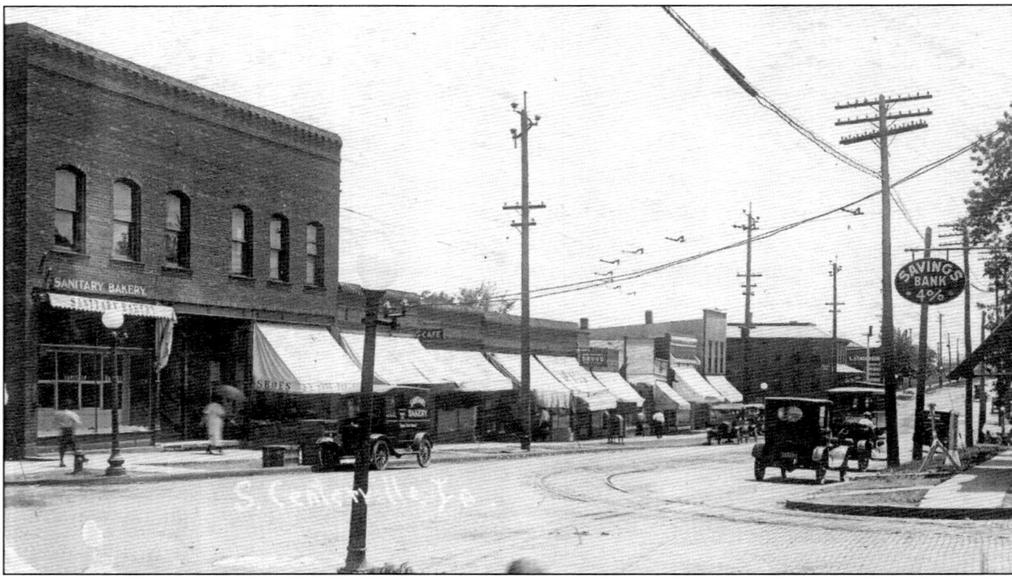

In 1922, the east side of the 1100 block of the Levee included no less than 12 businesses: Sanitary Bakery, Long Dry Goods, Saddle Rock Café, Pete Milani's Pool Hall, Gold & Chapman Grocery, Jim Shank's Drug Store, South Side Confectionery, South Side Café, Morris Barber Shop, Electric Shoe Repair, Long Brothers Grocery, and Samuel Sax Dry Goods & Shoes. Several of these buildings still stand today.

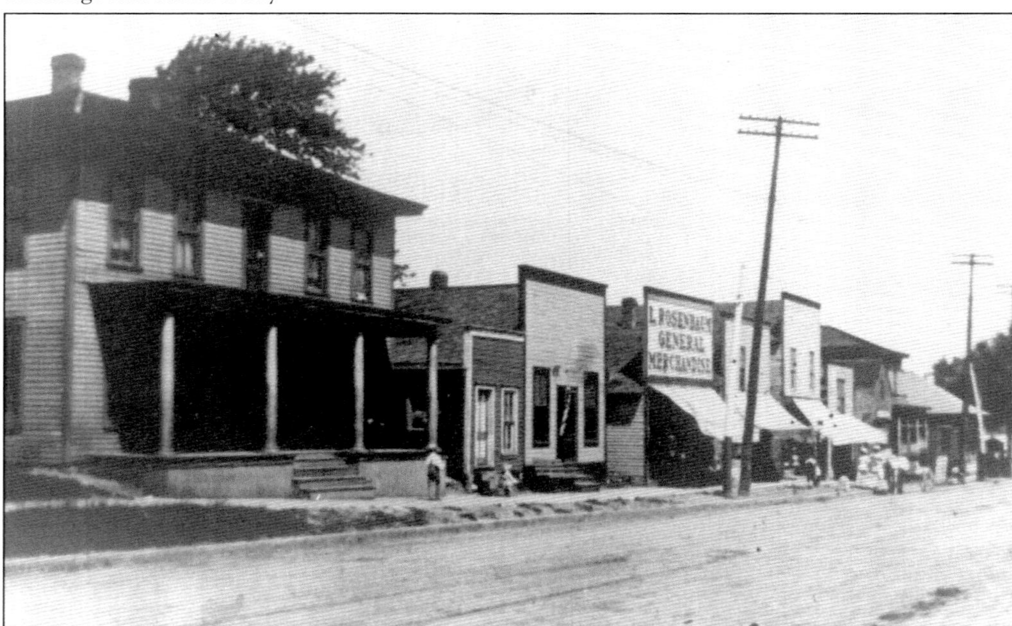

In 1880, the corporate limits of Centerville were expanded to include the Levee. Most of the businesses and residents of the area had immigrant names, and the residents were not as wealthy as the business owners around the Square. Many of the buildings were made of wood, like these on the west side of the Levee. The Chicago, Burlington & Quincy (CB&Q) depot can be seen at far right.

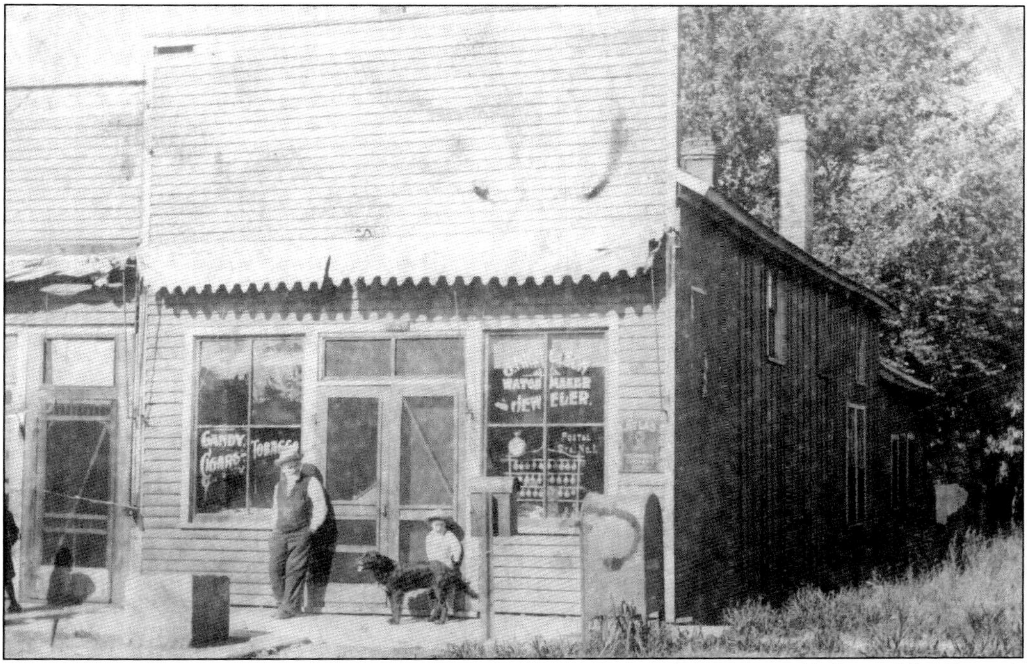

On turn-of-the-century railroad maps, there is a mail stop on the Levee called "Walsh." Patrick Walsh was an early shopkeeper who had a business at 1219–1221 South Eighteenth Street, south of the CB&Q tracks on the east side. His son, Edward Walsh, became the first postmaster of "Walsh" in 1888. The post office was inside his shop. The south side of the two-building unit was occupied by John Nicholson, a jeweler, who took over as postmaster in 1893, as shown in the above photograph. In 1897, both buildings were occupied by Carl Polson, who became postmaster until service was suspended in 1903. The wooden buildings were eventually replaced by the brick building shown below, which was occupied by Lawrence Henderson as a meat market from 1916 until 1937. This building still stands and is occupied today.

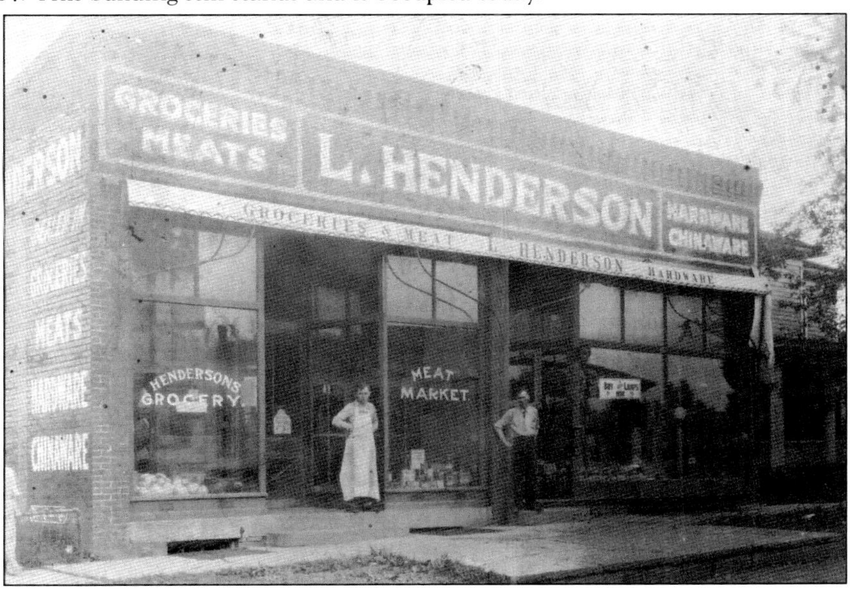

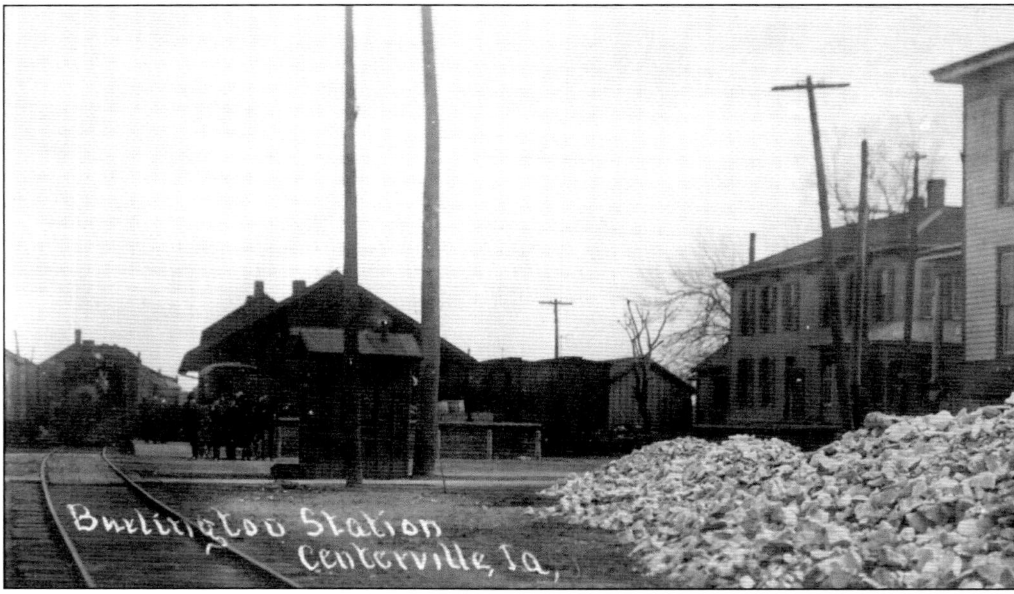

Benjamin Adamson donated 20 acres in south Centerville to the Rock Island railroad for its yards, and sold two lots to Thomas Fleming, who headed up the crew that built the Rock Island tracks through town. Fleming built a boardinghouse, seen at right, for his crews. He later built the first CB&Q depot, shown here, on the east side of Eighteenth Street.

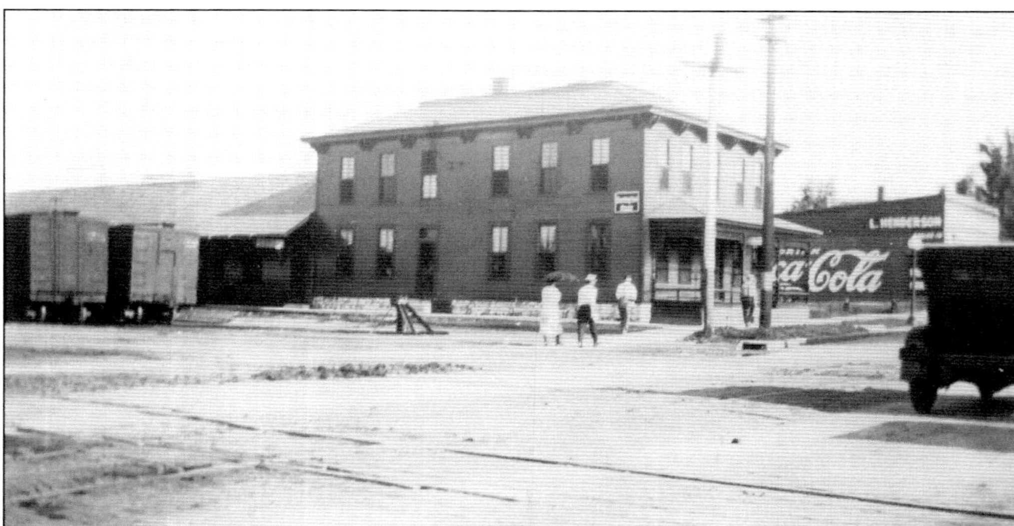

The boardinghouse became the Clinton Hotel for several years. When the new CB&Q depot was built on the west side of Eighteenth Street in 1911, the old depot became a freight storage building. In 1913, it was moved behind the two-story building, which, by that time, had become the district office for the CB&Q.

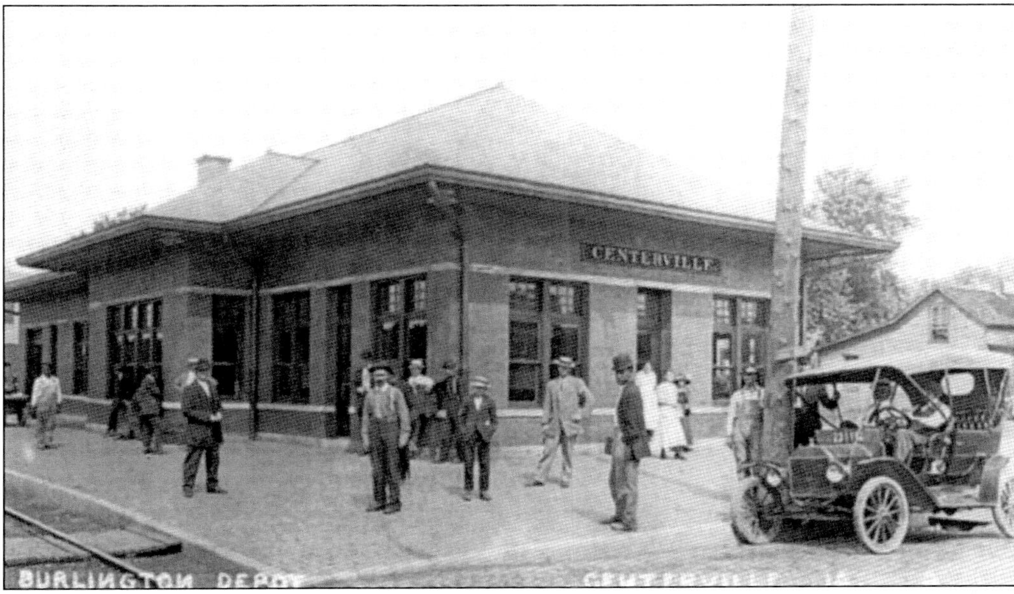

The brick depot in the Levee was built in 1911. It had two waiting rooms, one for men and one for women. This depot served the CB&Q line until the tracks were taken up in the early 1980s. The 1921 silent movie *The Wonderful Thing*, starring Norma Talmadge, features footage of a train leaving this station.

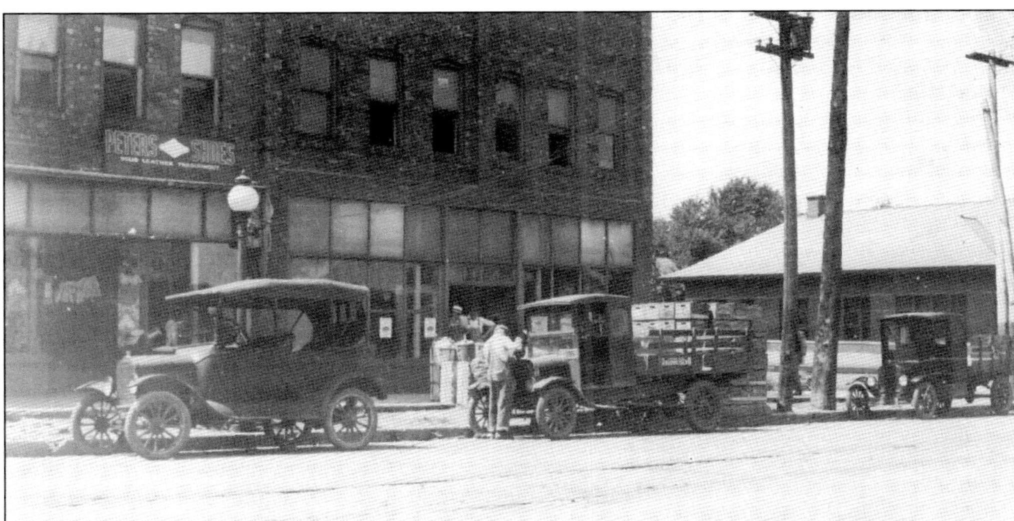

This building was erected by the Lagomarcino-Grupe Company in 1916 as one of its wholesale fruit distribution houses. It was later occupied by the Horne Fruit Company, and in 1943, the McKee Button factory located its business here. This building still stands today.

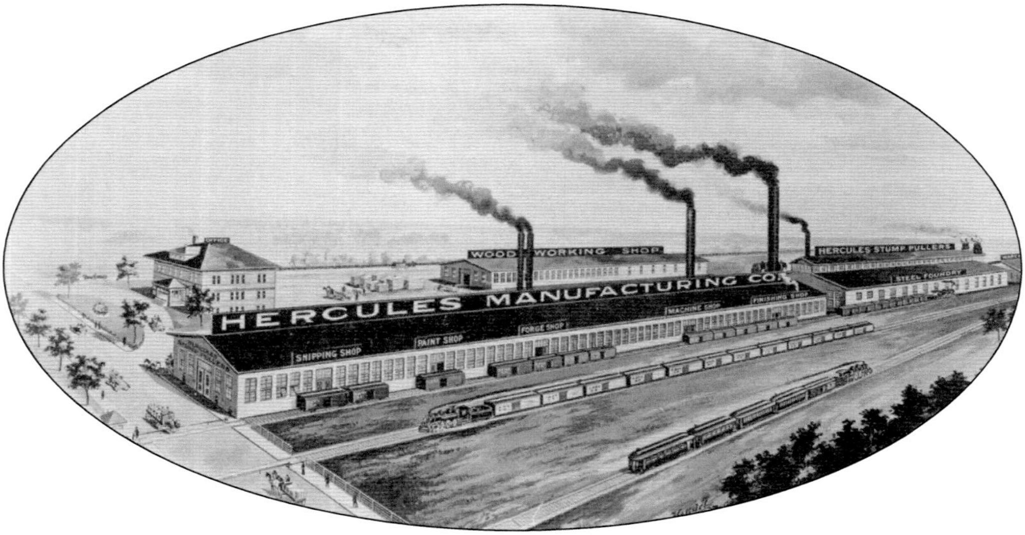

The Hercules Manufacturing Company was formed by Miles Bateman and Bernard Fuller, workers from two different foundries in Centerville who had collaborated to design a stump puller. They had the parts cast by local foundries and sold them commercially in 1898. The invention was named the Hercules Stump Puller in 1900. In 1903, the company built its own foundry. Due to increasing domestic and worldwide sales, it was replaced in 1912 by a larger factory complex near the railroad (above). The office (below), a handsome two-story building adjacent to Twenty-first Street, was home to the administrative offices, accounting department, engineering department, and metallurgical lab. The success of Hercules can be attributed to its investment in worldwide advertising. In 1912, the firm's advertising bills totaled $75,000.

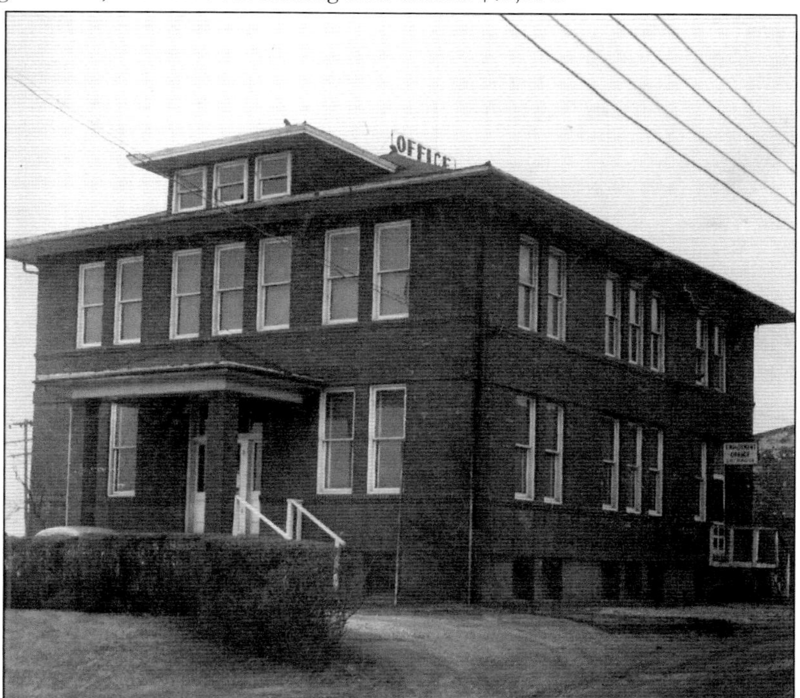

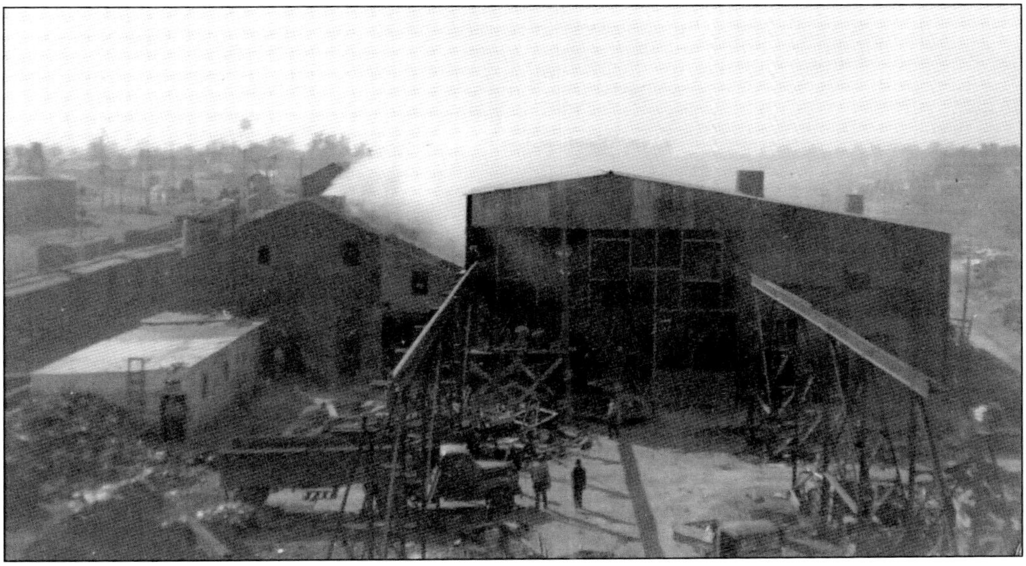

Pictured above are Steel Foundry No. 1 and Steel Foundry No. 2 of Hercules Manufacturing. The pattern and woodworking shop is shown below. Items manufactured by Hercules went beyond the scope of the stump puller. The firm made cast-iron wheels for mining carts, both for area coal mines and for coal mines in the eastern United States. It also made castings for bridges, carnival equipment, and, eventually, parts for the war effort. Defense contracts enlarged the business to the point that it employed up to 600 people during World War II. Shortly after the war, Batavia Metals Products purchased Hercules Manufacturing. Not long after the sale, the president of Batavia Metals, Dr. Henry Garson, was charged with wartime tax evasion. All equipment, machinery, and inventory were auctioned in 1946.

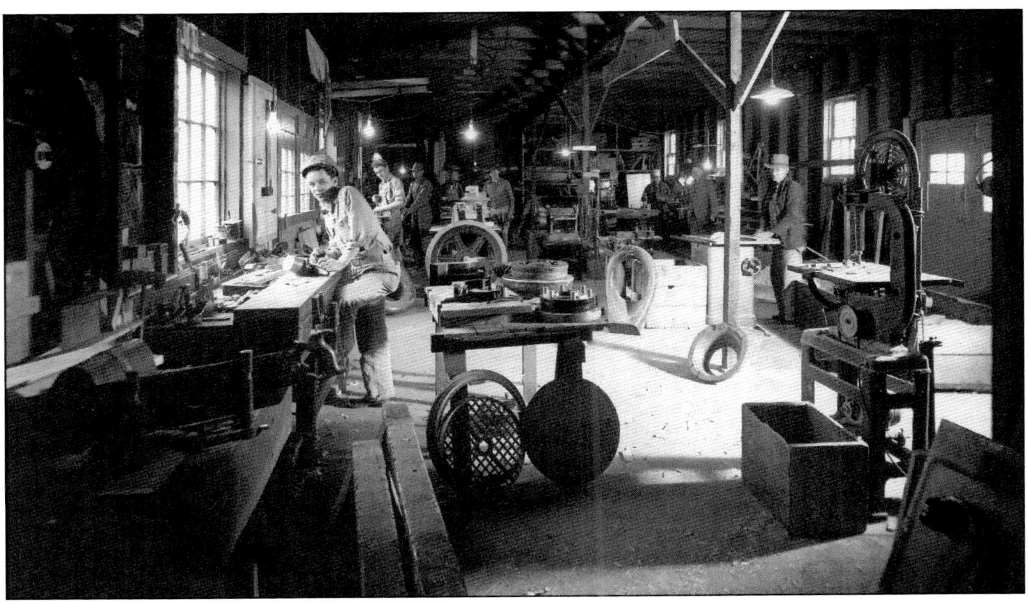

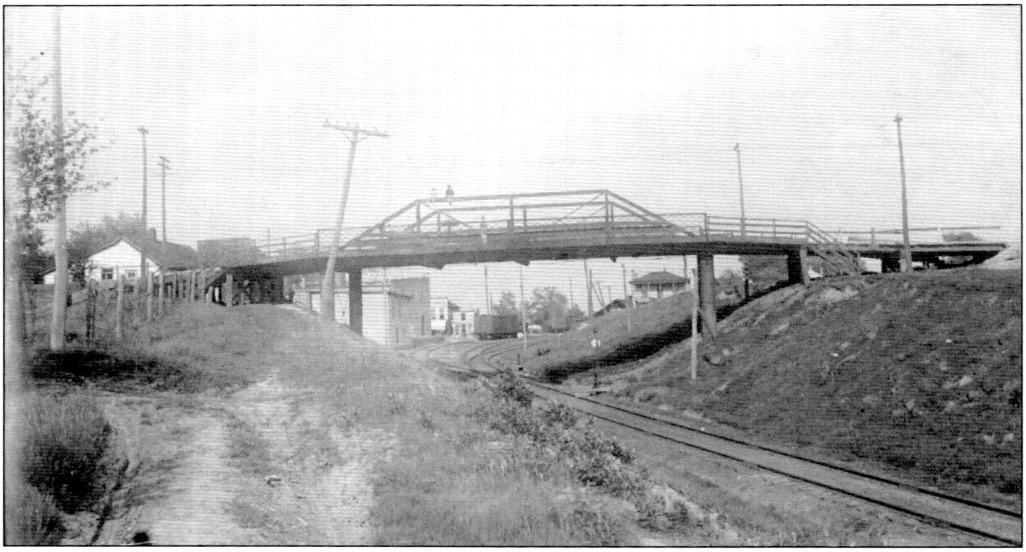

For over 100 years, a bridge spanned the CB&Q tracks on Sixteenth Street. An agreement was made that it was "to be maintained by the city until such a time that the population of Centerville reached 7,500," at which time the railroad company would take over the maintenance of the viaduct. Centerville reached that milestone in February 1916. The bridge was removed in 1996.

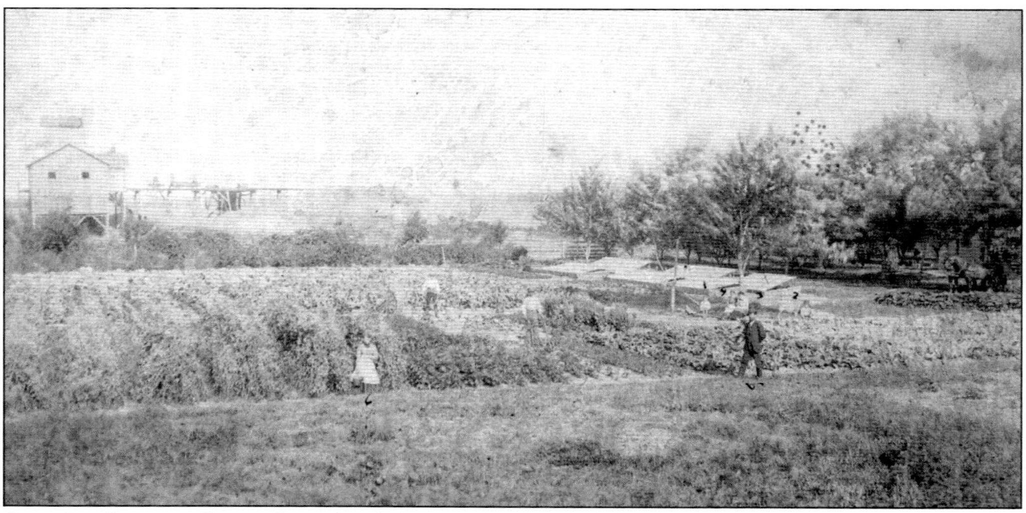

City Gardens was located south of the Levee, in the location where Golden Age Manor later built its facility. It opened in 1883 and was owned and operated by T.J. Greene for nearly 50 years. The business sold fruit, vegetable, and flower plants to residents, and wholesale produce to businesses all over southern Iowa and northern Missouri. Visible in this photograph is the tipple of the Watson Mine. (Courtesy Bob Greene.)

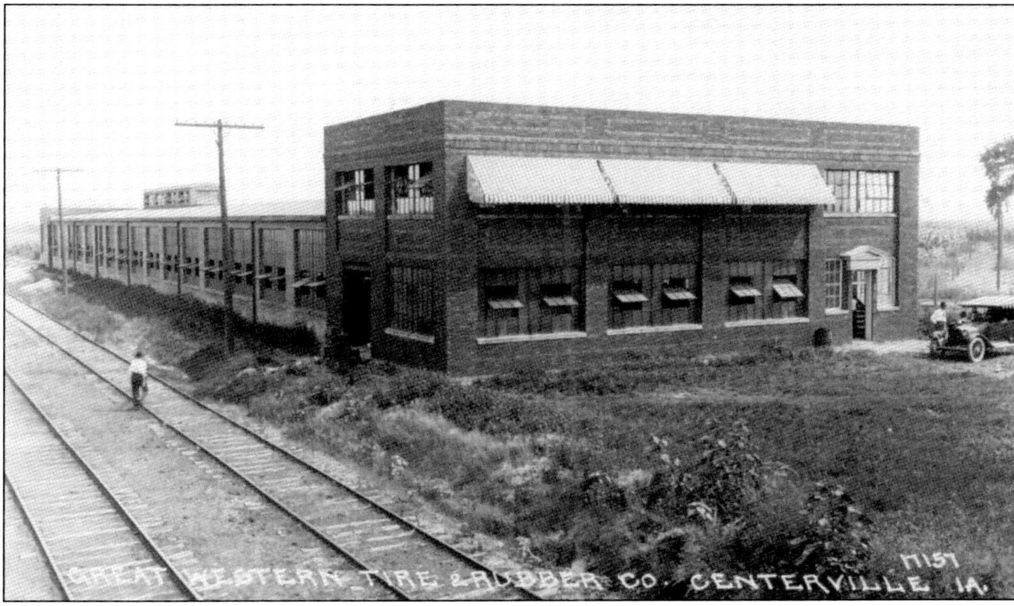

This building was erected at Cottage and Twenty-fourth Streets for the Great Western Tire & Rubber Company in 1920, but the company failed within a year. In 1929, the Standard Soybean Mills moved in and built a large elevator and silos for its beans. Pillsbury bought out Standard in 1943 and upgraded the facility in 1958. It produced soybean oil to be used in paints and varnishes, cooking oil, margarine, and soup, and produced soybean meal that was used in feed for livestock. Pillsbury was sold to Cargill in 1964, which continued the same operations until 1979, when railroad service into Centerville was discontinued. Ingredients to manufacture feed were dependent on rail service, and the Appanoose Community Railroad had not yet been established. Feed company MFA purchased the building shortly thereafter, but abandoned it in 1985.

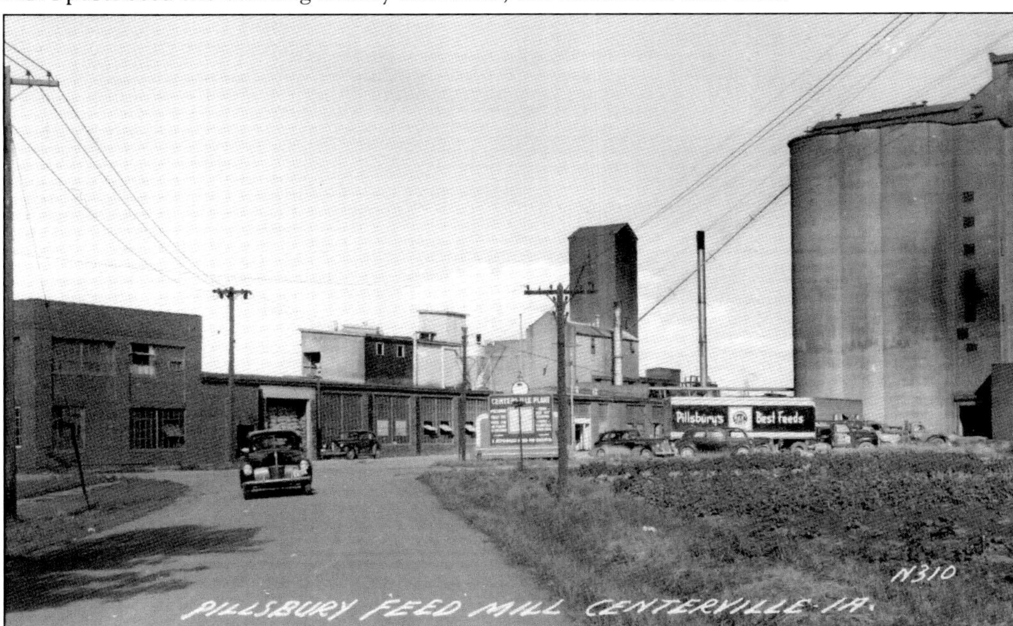

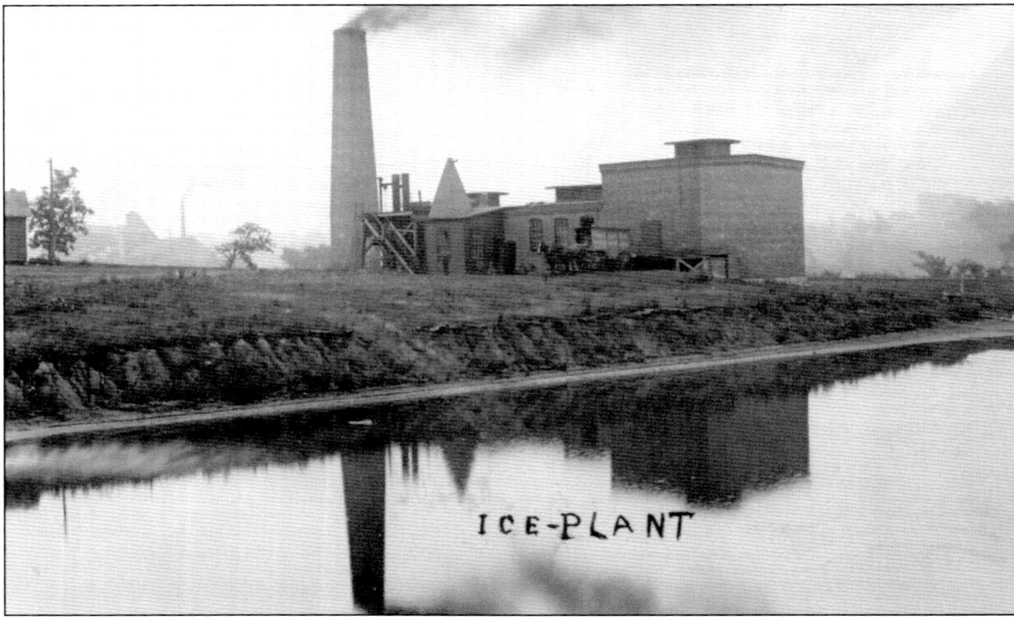

In early years, keeping perishables cold in the warmer months could be a challenge. Putting food in a well or a spring were the only ways to keep food cool. In 1882, William McKee started an ice business on West Garfield Street. Ice was cut from ponds in the winter and stored in sawdust for use in warmer months. In 1897, Steve Martin and Bolar Bryant purchased McKee's business and expanded it. In 1906, Martin bought out Bryant's share. In the same year, Martin founded the Pure Ice Company, which produced ice by a process using anhydrous ammonia, which created a cleaner product than cutting it from ponds. Ice was a thriving business up until the 1950s, when refrigerators were found in most households. Martin closed the business in 1956. He died in 1957, and the buildings burned in 1958.

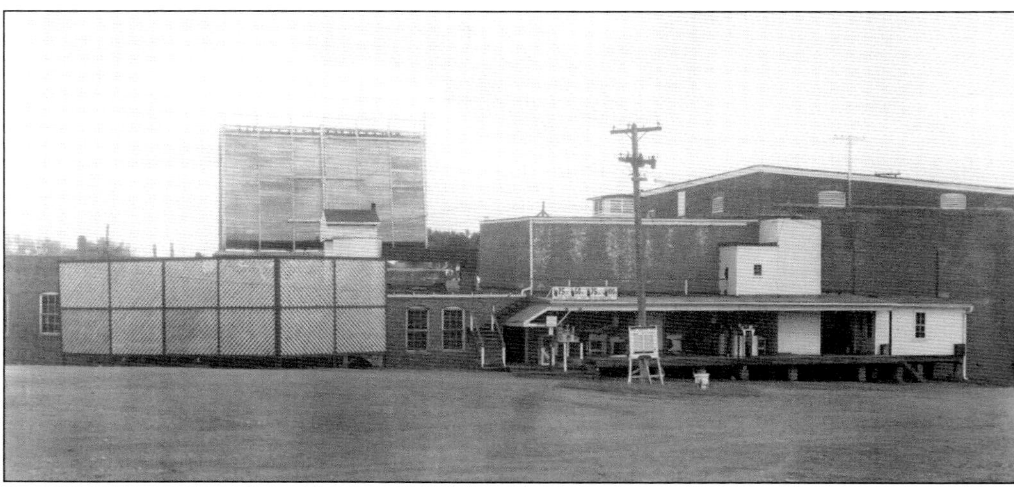

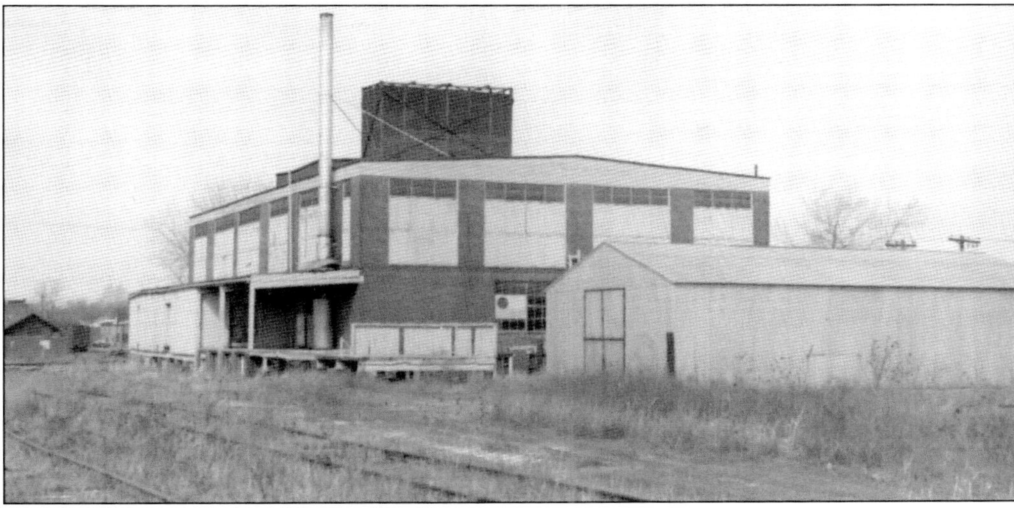

In 1912, a poultry feeding and finishing station was built at Twentieth and Keokuk Streets in the south part of Centerville, just west of the Hercules plant. In the 1920s, it was occupied by Swift & Company. A 57-foot sign erected on top of the building read, "Brookfield Butter." The sign was lit with 200-watt bulbs and could be seen for miles. The business closed in 1950.

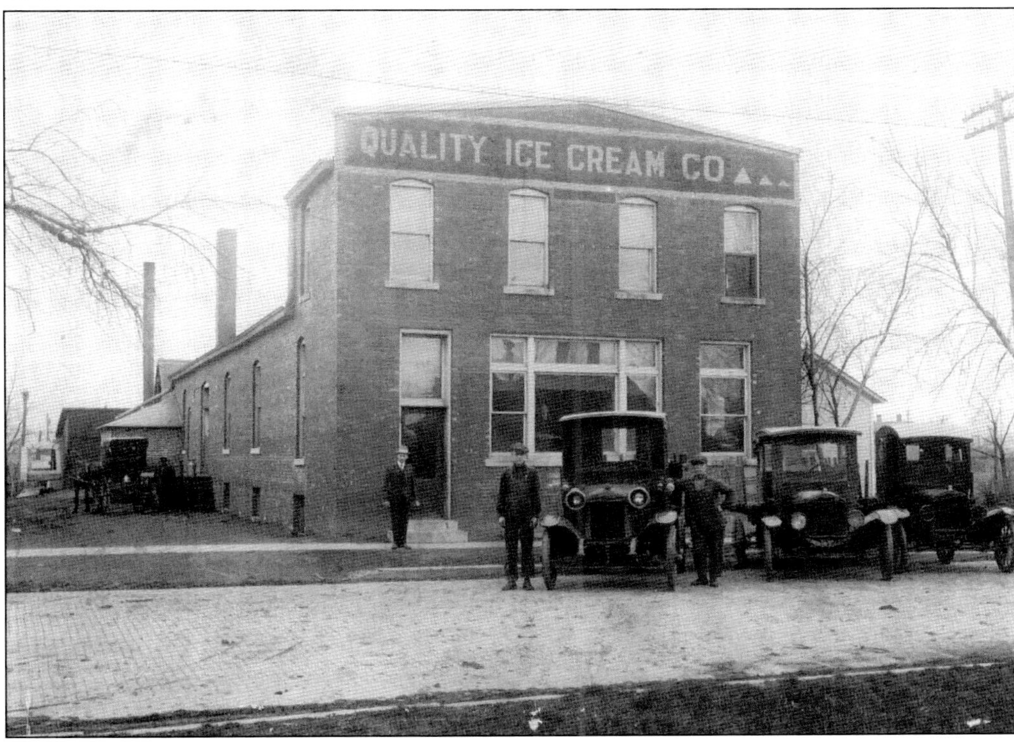

Founded in 1915, the Quality Ice Cream Company was originally located at 801 East Van Buren Street. In 1918, the company traded buildings with the Chapman Bottling Company and moved to the structure seen here, at 1115 South Sixteenth Street. In 1919, the Douglas Ice Cream Company purchased Quality Ice Cream, later selling out to Centrox Dairy. Centrox was in turn purchased by Beatrice Creameries, the owner of Meadow Gold brand dairy products.

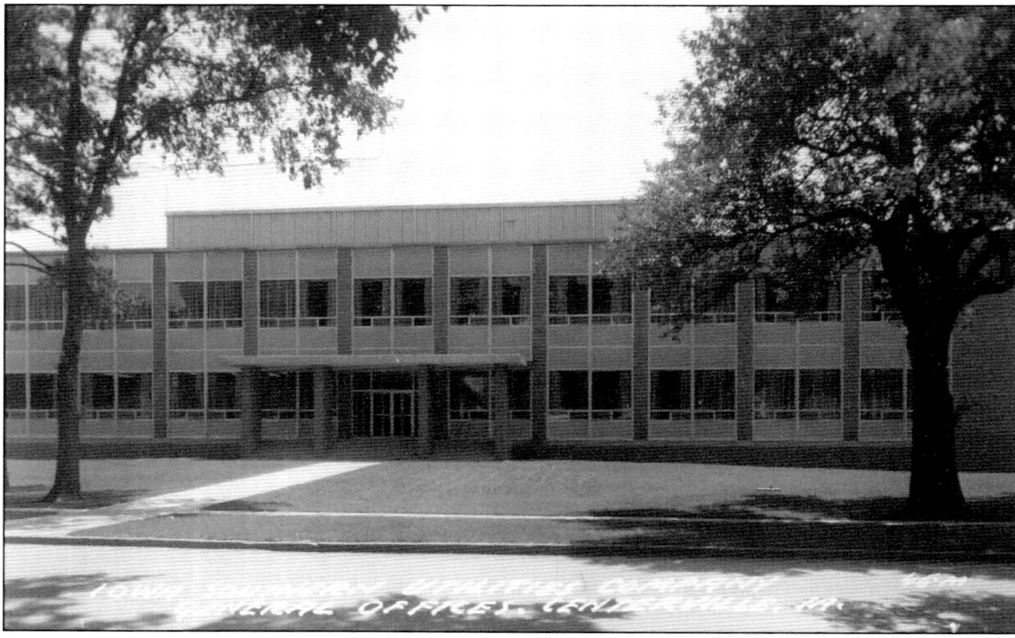

In 1957, fire devastated several offices of the ISU complex just off the northeast corner of the Square. In 1958, groundbreaking for a new general office building was held. It was completed in 1960.

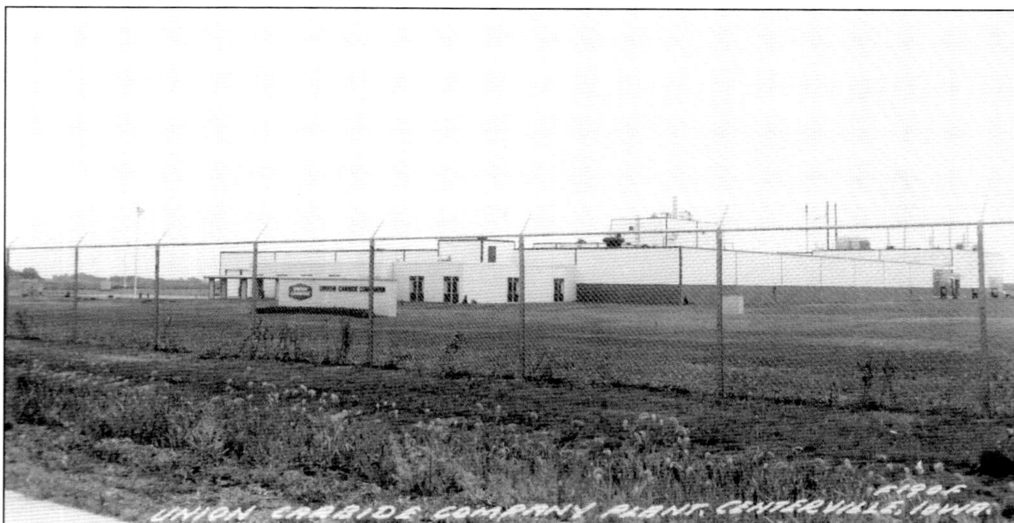

Appanoose County attempted to become an industrial community during the 1950s, and Union Carbide completed that mission. The community was elated when the Visking Corporation of Union Carbide announced it was coming to Centerville in November 1962. The factory's dedication was held on March 24, 1964, with 8,000 people in attendance. Consistently manufacturing meat packaging products since 1964, the company transitioned to Viskase, then Curwood.

Four

GIVE US GUIDANCE

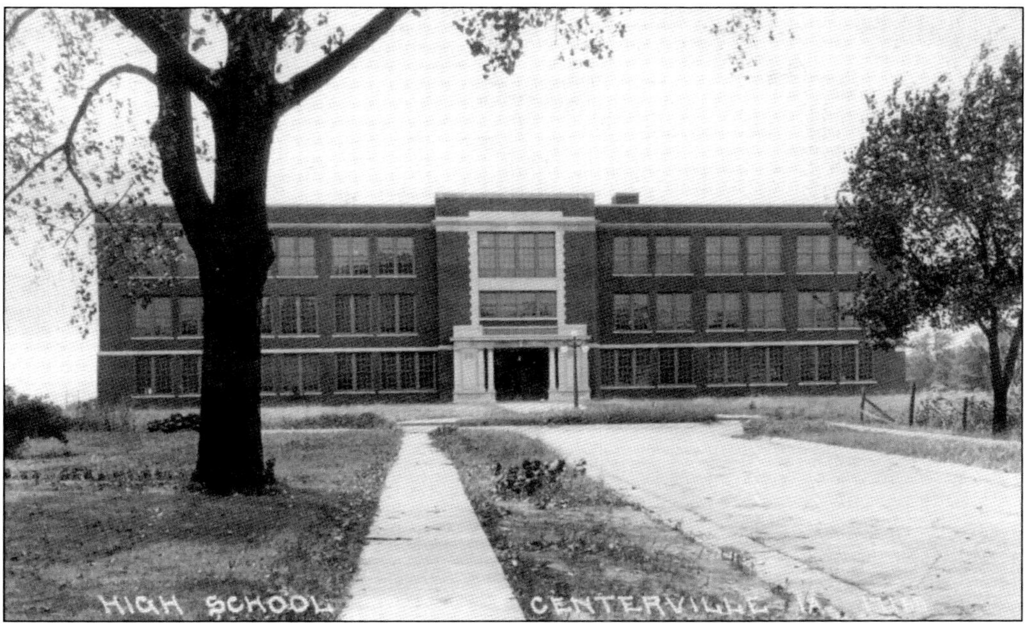

The Centerville High School that we know and love today was originally built in 1917, but was gutted by fire in 1938. It was rebuilt, retaining three of the walls that were still standing after the fire. The new structure was completed and dedicated in April 1940. Several layout changes were made in the new building, including the location of noisier activities to locations less intrusive to classroom study. Thus, the auditorium, band room, gymnasium, and shop room were constructed on the far ends of the new building. In the original building, pictured above, these areas were located back-to-back on the west side of the building.

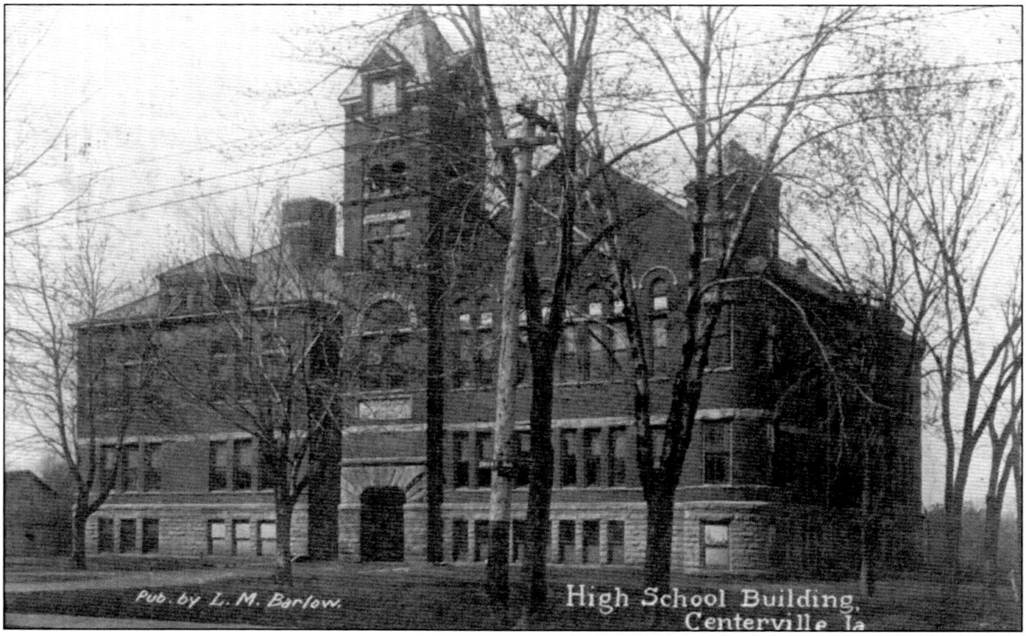

This Centerville High School building, erected in 1894, was located on the same lot where Central Ward sits today. This structure replaced another large school building that was erected in 1869. Originally built in 1868, it was destroyed by fire before the carpenters had even removed their tools. The principal, Rev. S.A. Holt, considered insane, was accused of purposely setting the fire and was run out of town.

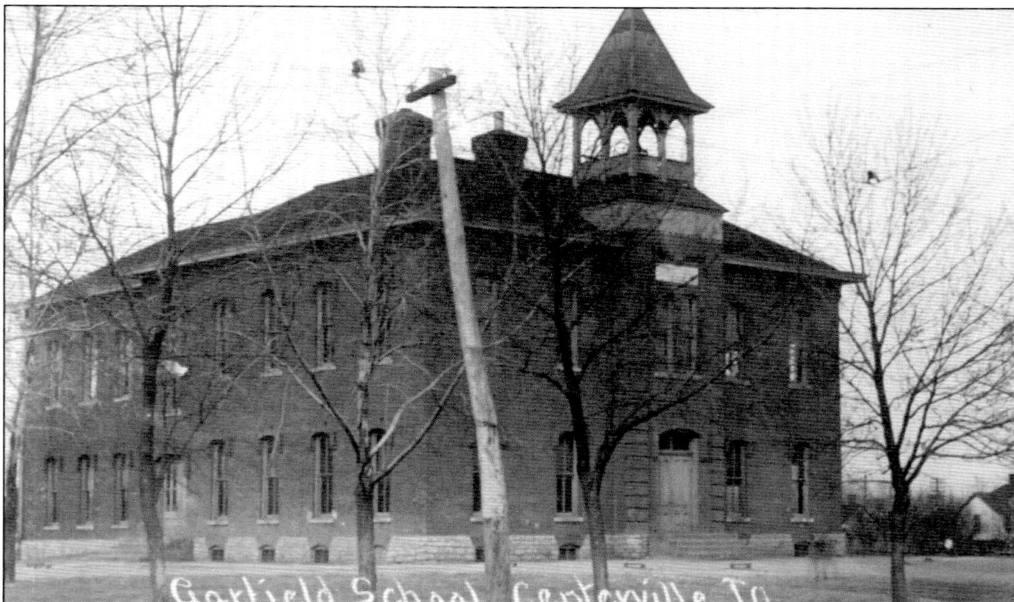

The Garfield School was located in the south part of Centerville, near the Levee. Garfield was also known as the South Ward School. This building and its twin, the Lincoln School, were built in 1882. An addition was constructed at the back of this building in 1892.

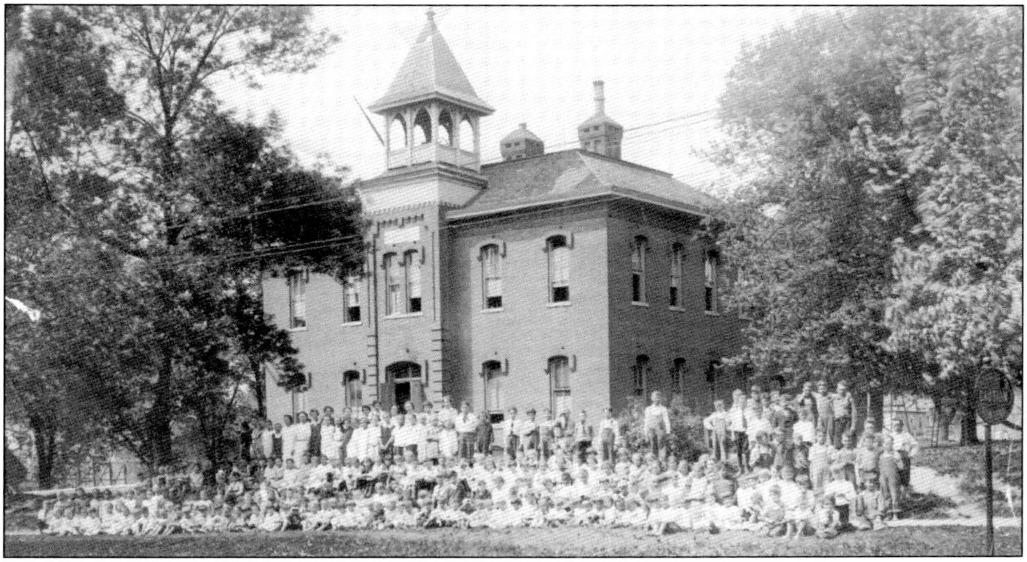

Lincoln School was also known as the North Ward School. An addition was built onto this school in 1903. At the same time, an additional school, McKinley, was built in south Centerville to accommodate the ever-increasing population in that part of town.

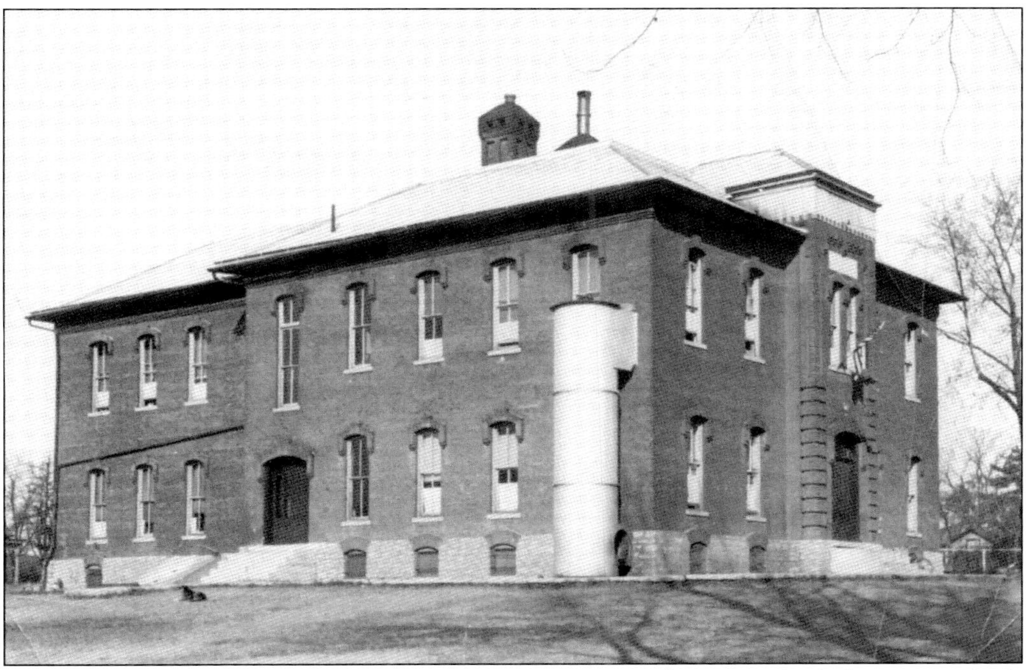

In 1908, fire escapes were added to Lincoln and Garfield. By the 1940s, the bell towers on both had been removed. After 80 years of productivity, the buildings were condemned in 1970. Students were then bused to Cincinnati and Mystic schools, and Fannon Hall was used to conduct classes. By 1973, the new Lakeview, Garfield, and Lincoln schools were ready for use.

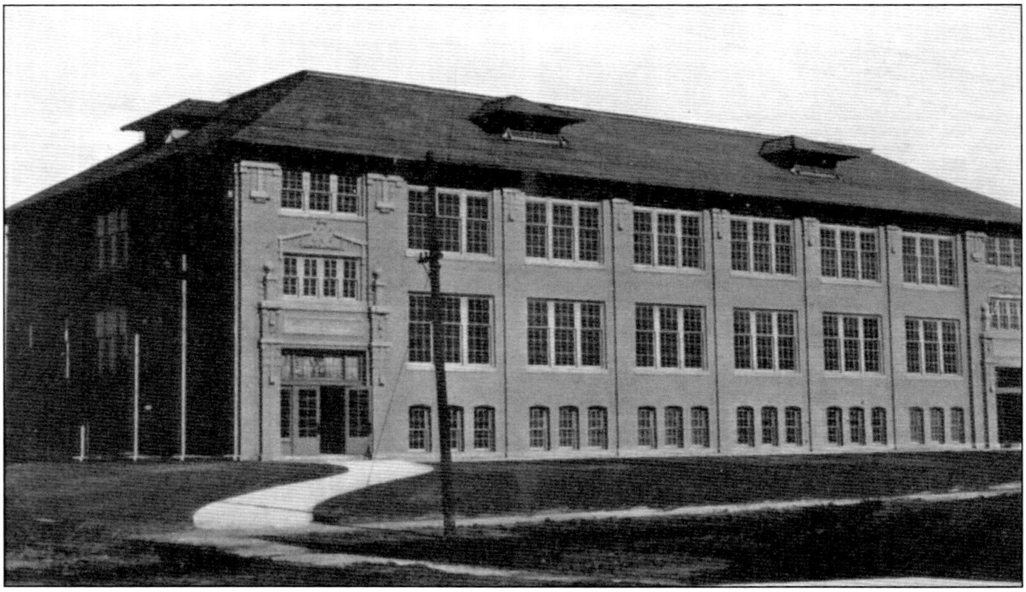

The enrollment boom in the first decade of the 1900s foretold the necessity of more space for high school students in the 1910s. In 1911, a new high school was built behind St. Joseph's Mercy Hospital. It would serve as a high school for only five years before another new high school was built. The structure was transformed into Washington Jr. High. It was condemned and demolished in 1957.

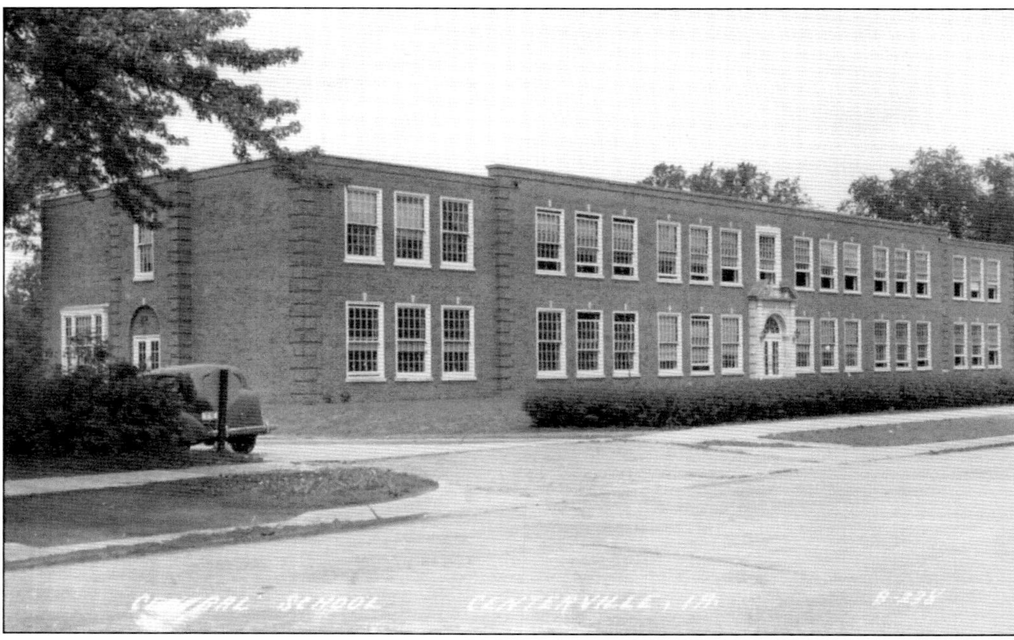

The Central Ward building pictured on page 62 was condemned as a fire hazard in 1935. During its demolition, the brick was saved for use in the new building, not as face brick, but as reinforcement. The cornerstone for the new Central Ward building was laid on June 10, 1936, and the new building was completed and dedicated in December of that year.

This schoolhouse in Rathbun was built around the turn of the century, but was quickly outgrown as coal-mining families, mostly from Croatia and Italy, filled the area. In 1905, records show that 40 students were enrolled. The building received a two-story addition on the south end, and a few years later, another two-story addition was built on the north end. By 1920, more than 200 students were enrolled here.

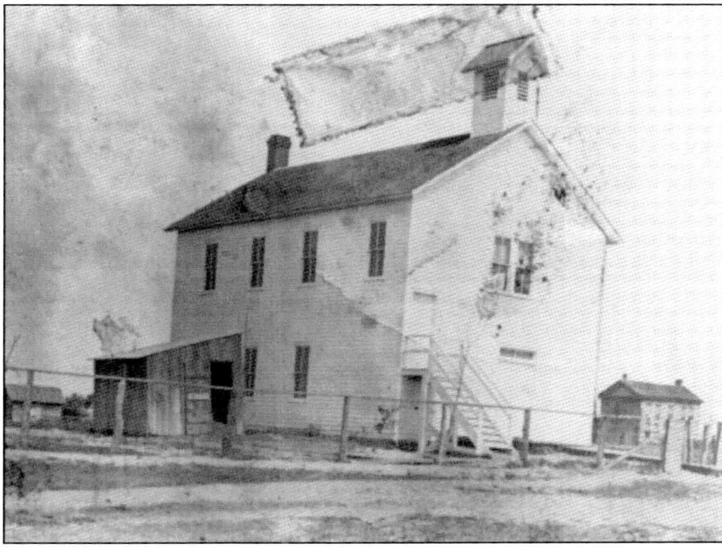

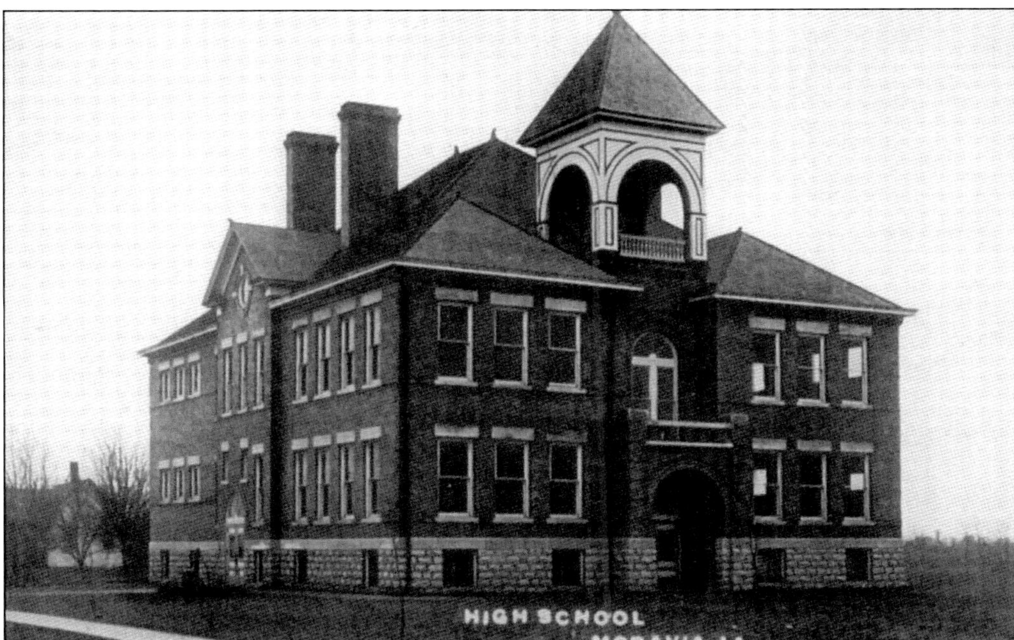

Moravia has always boasted a great school system, and this grand eight-room schoolhouse, built in 1904, possessed many improvements, including chemical toilets. Sadly, it was in service for only 20 years, burning down in 1924.

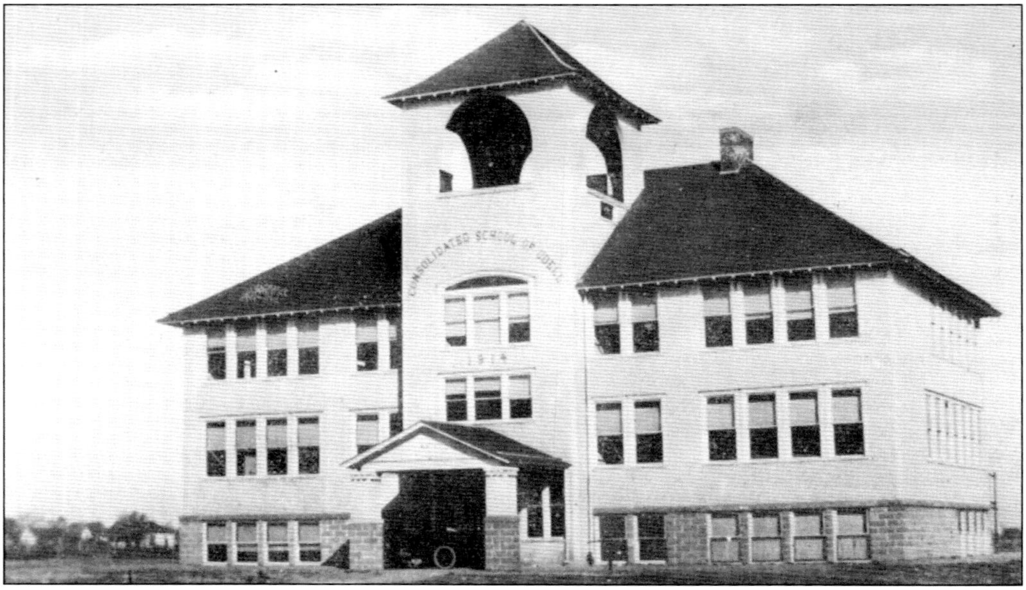

This Udell Consolidated Schools building was erected in 1914, replacing one that had been built in 1907 that served students through the eighth grade. This new school could accommodate high school students as well. It was the first school building in Iowa finished with Kellastone, a durable, waterproof, fireproof, and acid-proof material that was touted as being as strong as cement.

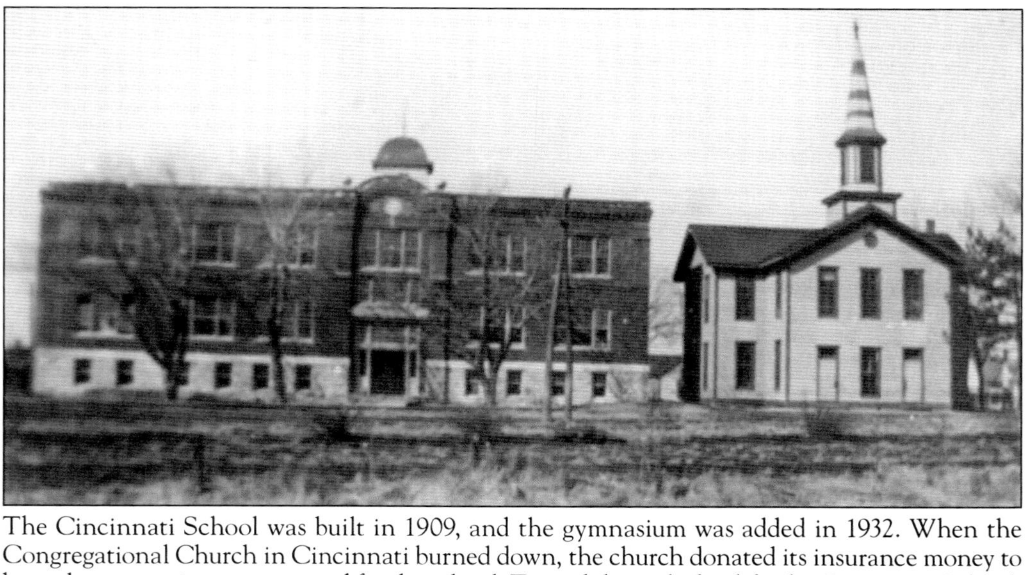

The Cincinnati School was built in 1909, and the gymnasium was added in 1932. When the Congregational Church in Cincinnati burned down, the church donated its insurance money to have the gymnasium constructed for the school. Toward the end of its life, the Cincinnati School, as well as the school in Mystic, became home to fifth- and sixth-grade students from Centerville while the new Garfield, Lincoln, and Lakeview schools were being built.

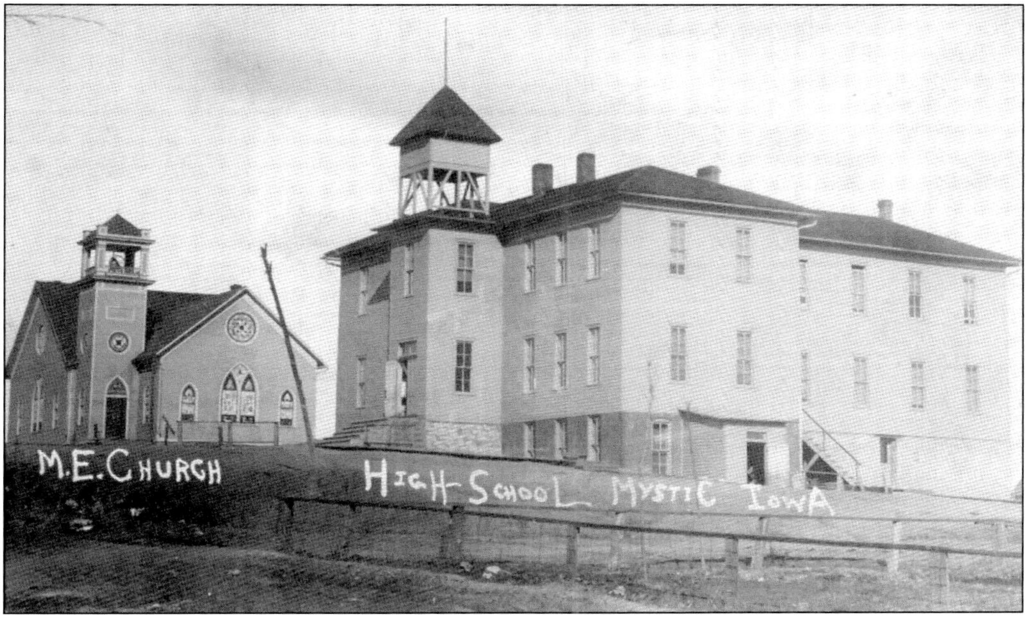

Until 1889, children in the burgeoning town of Mystic attended various country schools. This Mystic School building was erected in 1889 and served until 1914. In 1916, the building was replaced with a larger, modern brick structure. The Mystic Methodist Church is on the left.

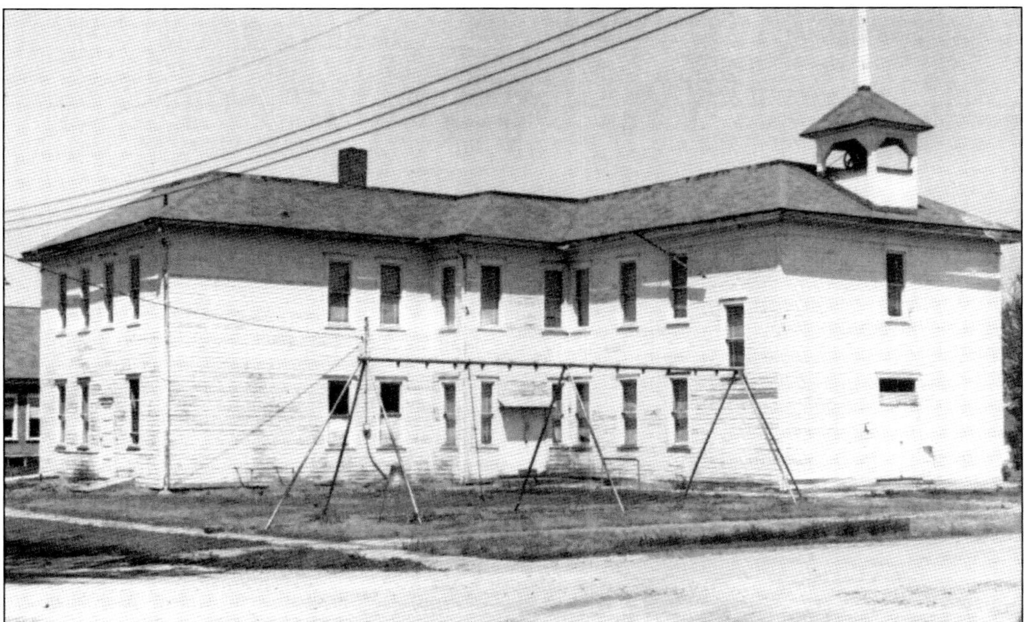

Built in 1897 and expanded in 1913, the Exline School served families in the Exline area until 1949, when it celebrated its last graduating class. Included in that class was Morgan Cline, a stellar student who graduated from Exline High School as valedictorian at age 16. Cline went on to become one of the most successful businessmen in America, founding the advertising agency of Cline, Davis, and Mann Inc.

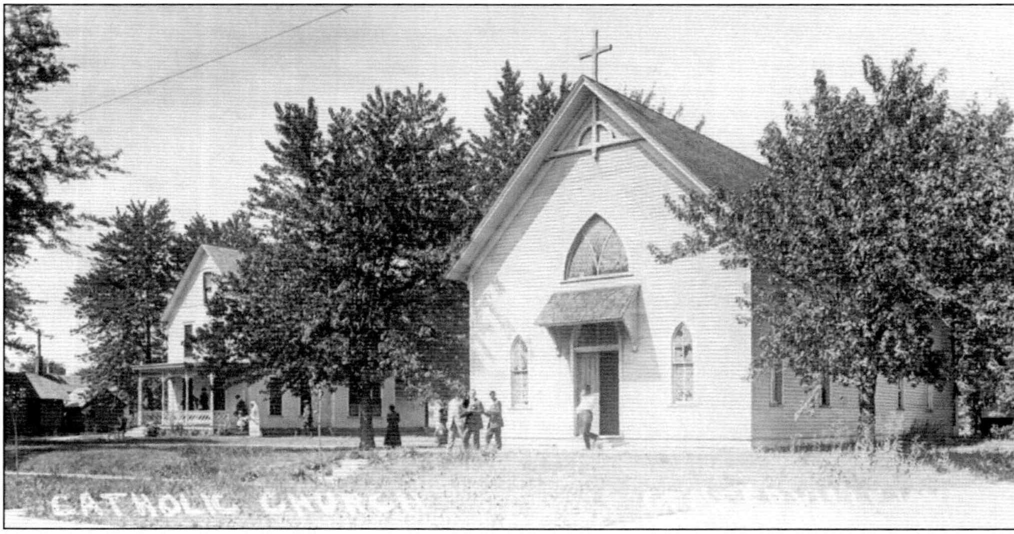

St. Mary's Catholic Church, shown above, was built in 1878 and included living quarters in the rear of the building. In 1898, a rectory was built nearby. The photograph below shows the church, which had been remodeled in 1931; the rectory, built in 1957; and the new St. Mary's school, built in 1959. This school replaced the one that had been built as an addition to the church in 1916. The church shown here was razed in 1967 after the new church, adjacent to the old one, was dedicated.

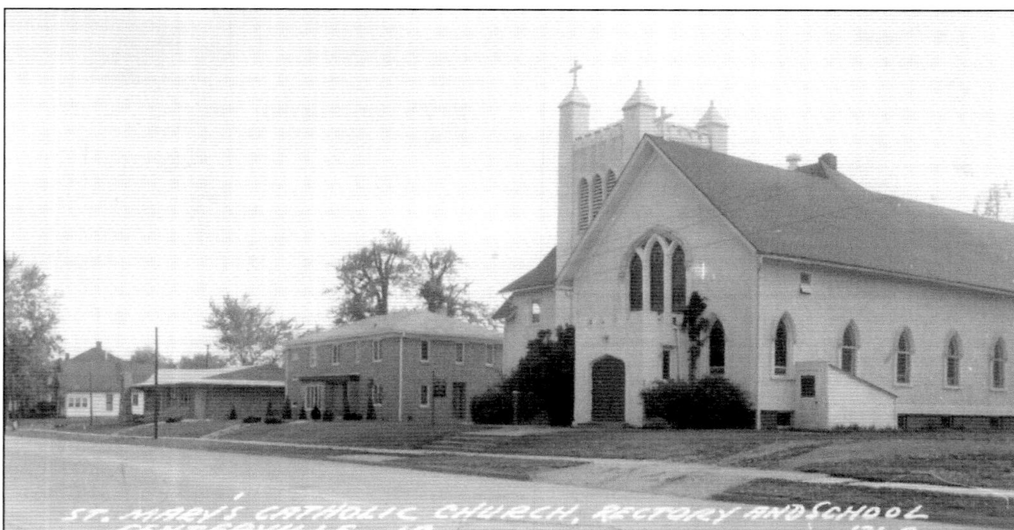

The Christian Church was organized in 1867; by 1872, the congregation had decided to erect its own building (right), which was completed the following year. Gov. Francis M. Drake, a member of the church, donated the bronze bell. When a new Christian Church (below) was built in 1903, the old building was sold to the Reorganized Church of the Latter-Day Saints. The new building was known as the Central Church of Christ; its name was officially changed to Drake Avenue Christian Church in 1953. Governor Drake's family donated the fine pipe organ for the church. This building was demolished in 1965. The 1872 building was eventually purchased by the Second Baptist Church and is still in service today.

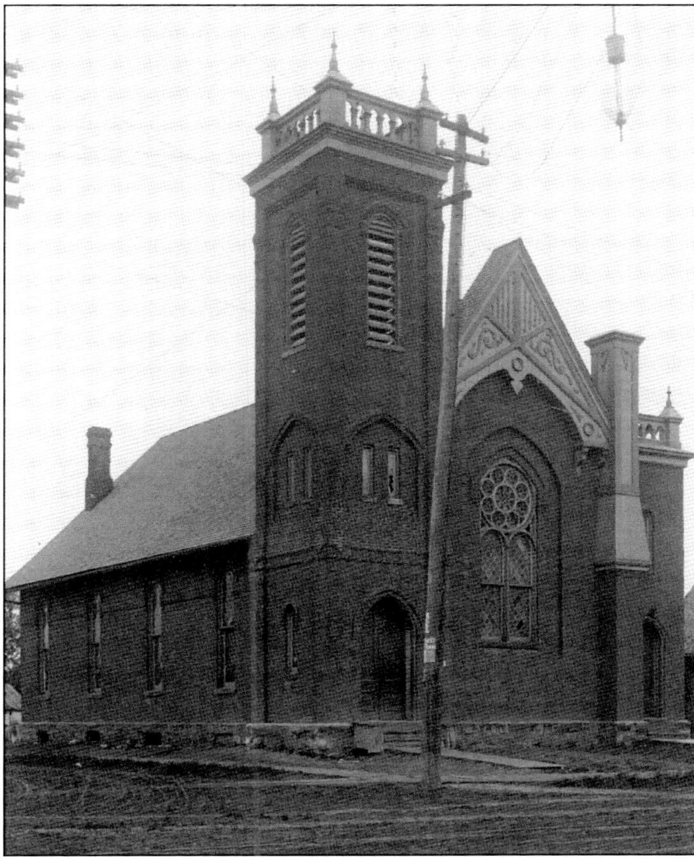

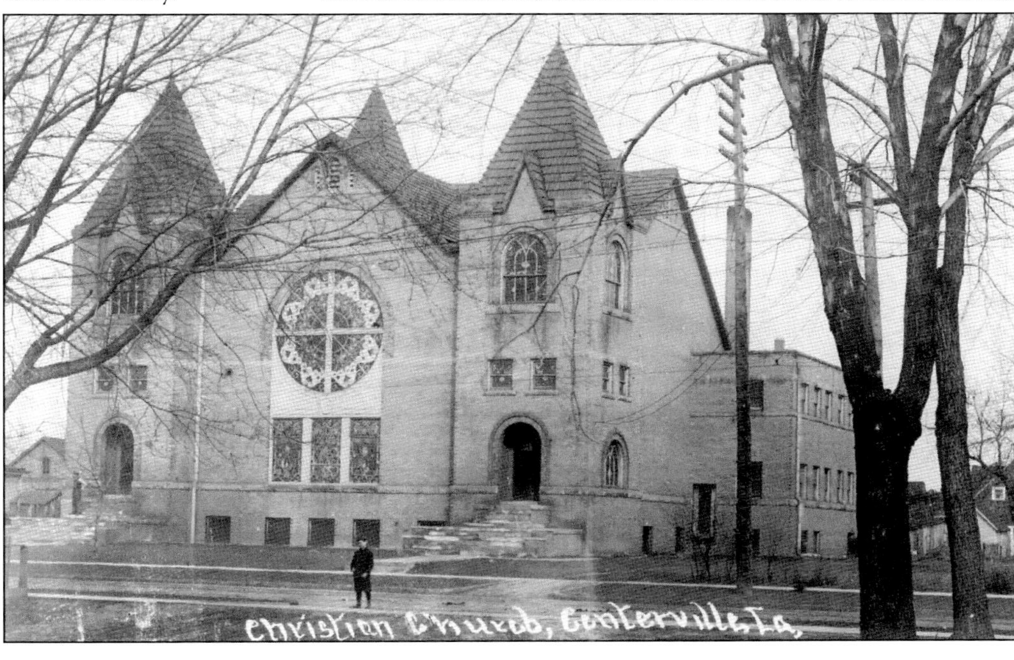

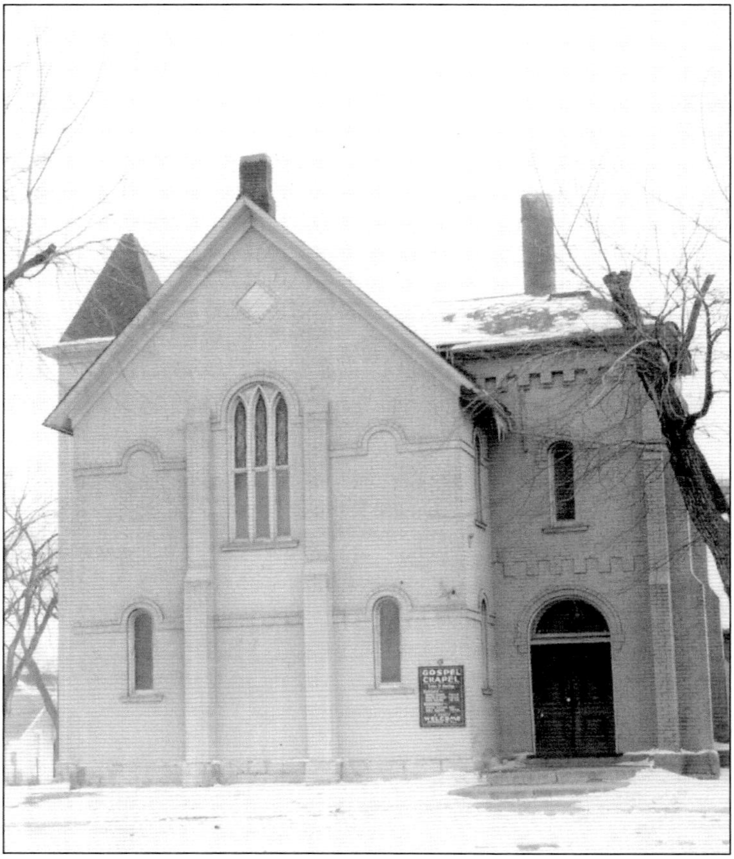

The Methodist Church, shown at left, was built in 1877. It was located on the corner of North Main and Washington Streets, across from the current First United Methodist Church. The elegant church included a gallery, and the bell alone cost $400, equivalent to nearly $9,000 in 2013. The newer, magnificent First United Methodist Church, shown below, was built in 1905 and seated 500 people, plus 200 more in its galleries. A unique feature was the inclusion of the parsonage under the same roof as the church, a situation that lasted until 1962. At that time, a home on North Eighteenth Street was donated by Dr. and Mrs. Frank Leffert to be used as the parsonage.

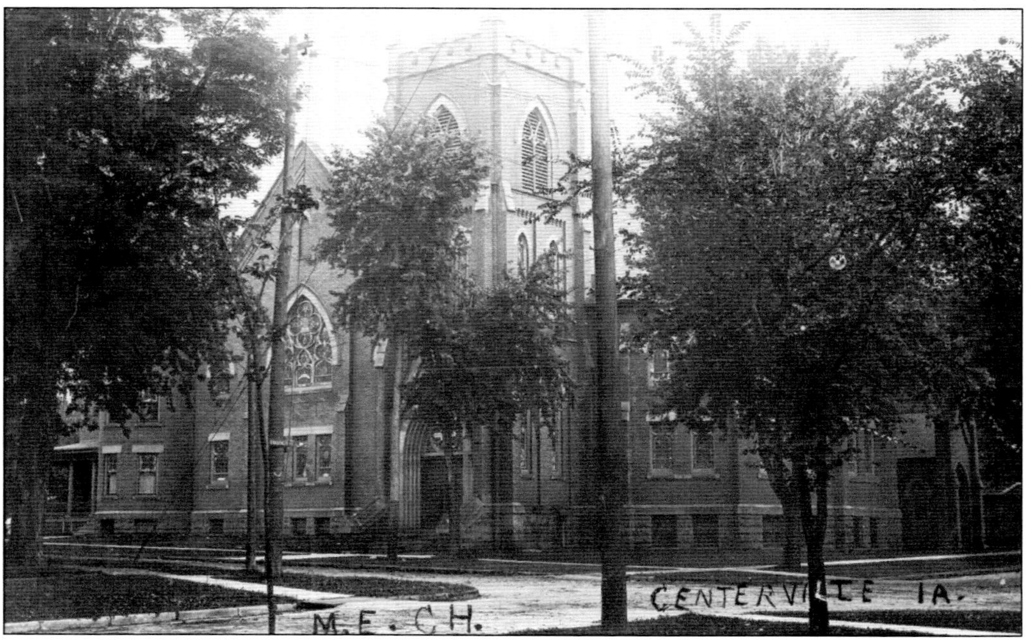

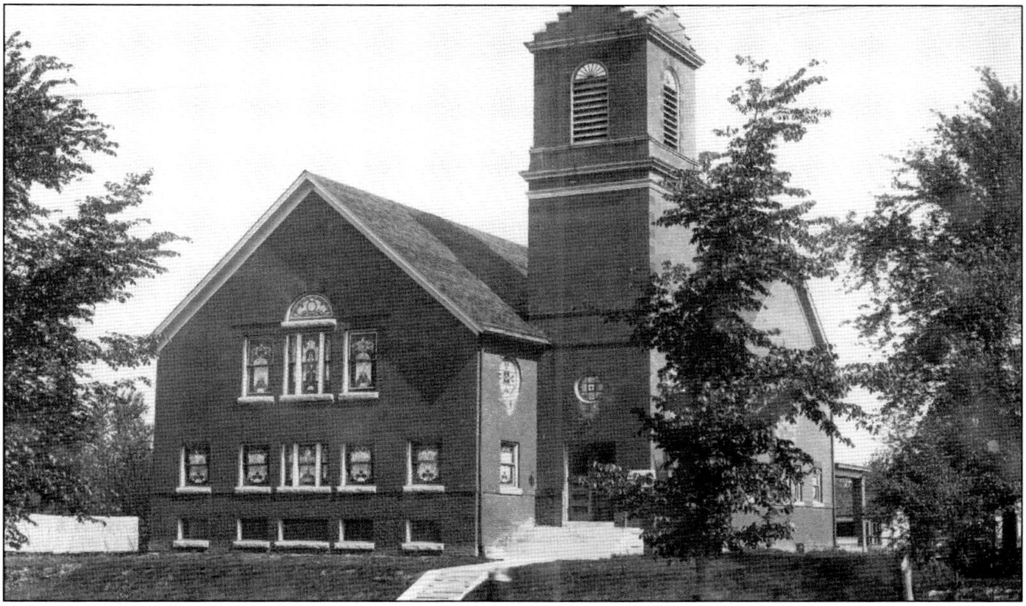

The congregation of the Baptist Church was organized in 1851 and built two different frame structures, one in 1856 and the other in 1875. The current First Baptist Church, built and dedicated in 1905, was made possible by an increase in membership following a 1902 revival at which evangelist Billy Sunday spoke. In the 1950s, part of the congregation split off and formed the Grace Tabernacle Baptist Church.

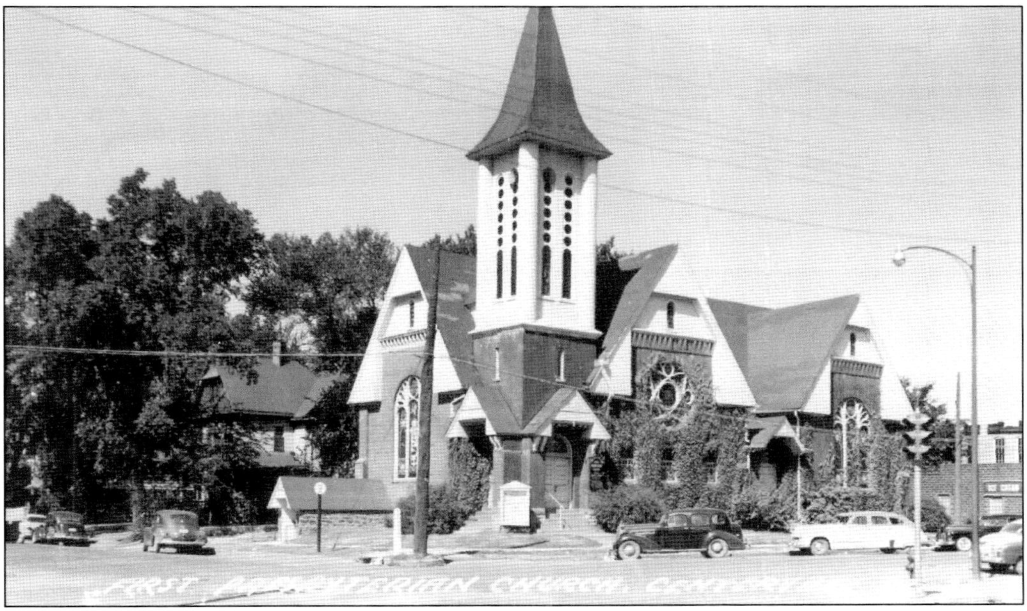

The Presbyterian Church, organized in 1851, erected its first building in 1857, one block south of the Square. It was replaced by a larger building in 1870, which in turn was replaced by the building shown here in 1893. The Reverend Mott Sawyers was a prominent church leader, civic leader, and author who served the church from 1919 to 1940. He was one of the few ministers who rejected the Ku Klux Klan in the 1920s.

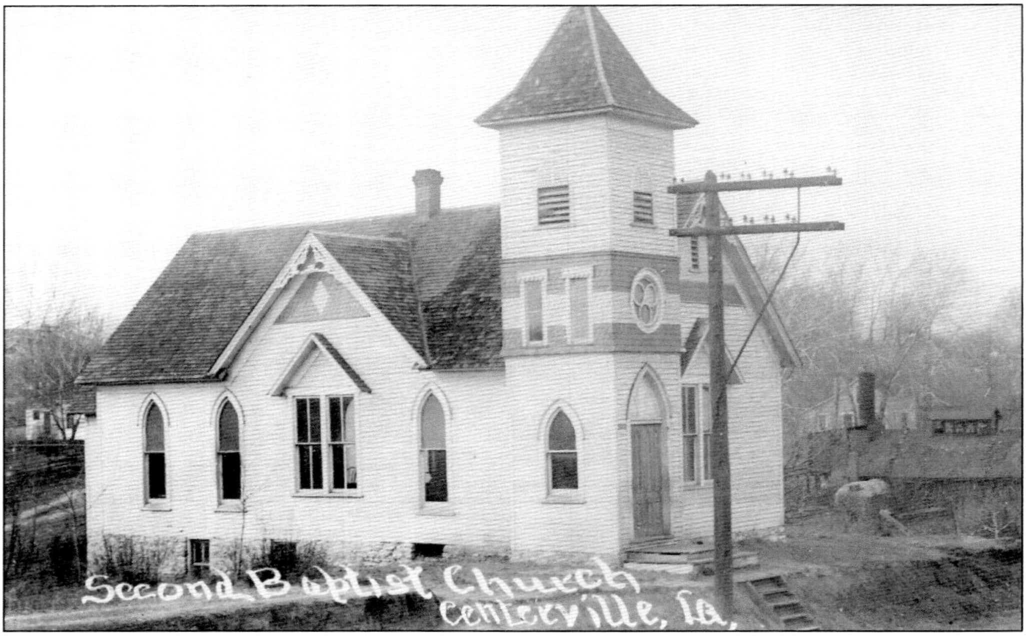

Over the course of time, more than one church served the African American population in Centerville. The cornerstone for the Second Baptist Church was laid in 1902, and the building was dedicated sometime later. Future world-renowned opera singer Simon Estes sang here while he was growing up in the 1940s and 1950s. This building is now listed in the National Register of Historic Places.

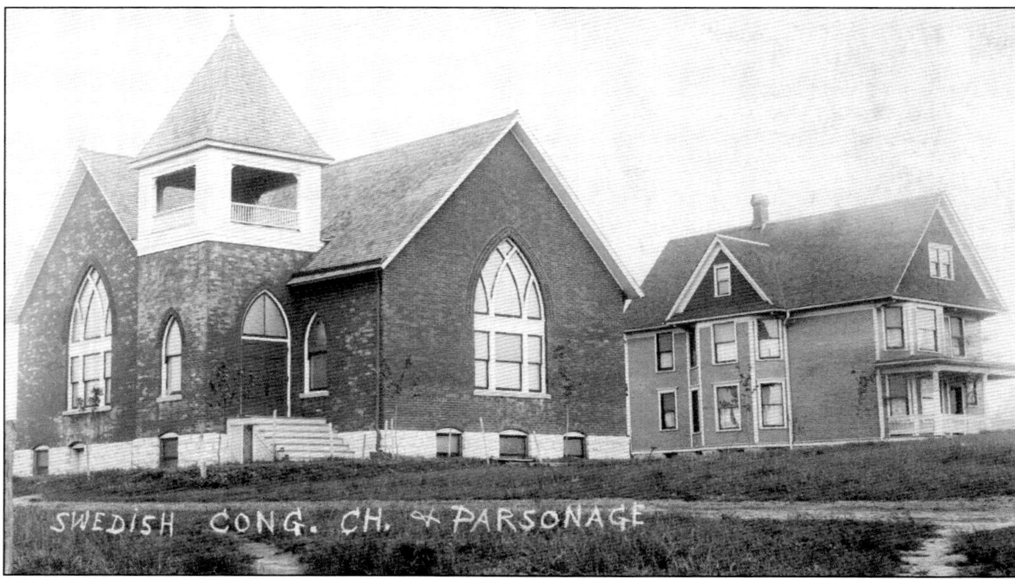

The building that is now home to the Evangelical Covenant Church was erected in 1906 as the Swedish Congregational Church. The Swedish immigrants living in Appanoose County had multiple congregations. In 1899, the Swedish Free Mission congregation merged with the Swedish Congregational group. In 1941, the name of this combined organization was officially changed to the Evangelical Mission Covenant Church.

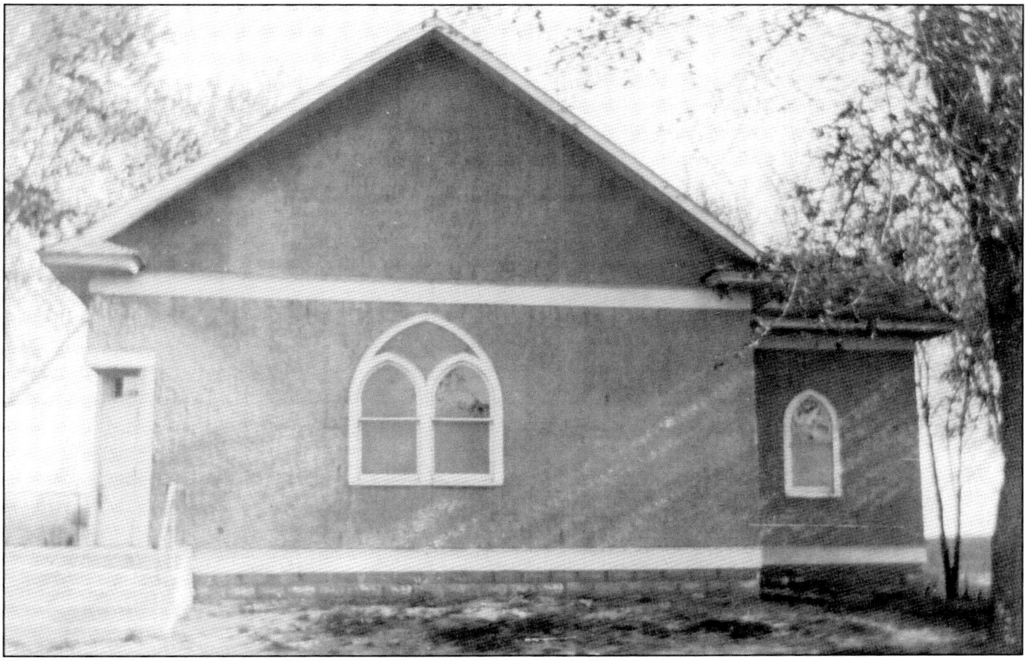

The Little Flock Baptist Church, organized in 1859, held services in the Little Flock School until 1873, when its first church building was erected. The building shown here was constructed in 1916 on the same location, and was dedicated in January 1917. It enjoyed over 100 years in service to the community, but was closed in 1966 and later destroyed. The Little Flock Chapel was later erected in its place as a memorial.

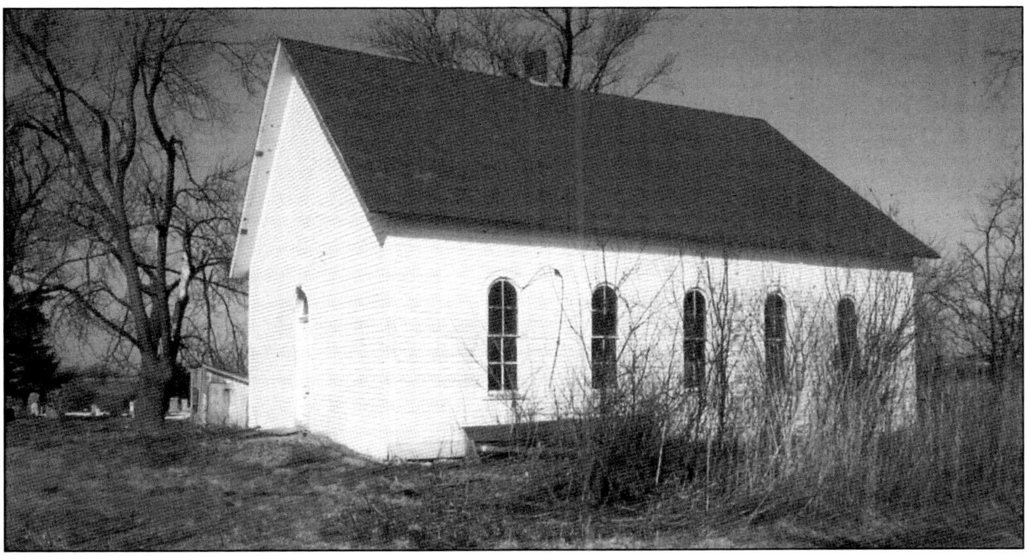

Johns Township was named for the many residents who shared the first name of John. One of these, John Hudson, organized the Concord Church. Originally meeting in the Hudson home, the congregation eventually built a structure in 1871. A newer structure replaced it and was torn down in the early 1970s. The tiffany-glass nickelodeon piano of the Concord Church is on display at the Appanoose County Historical and Coal Mining Museum.

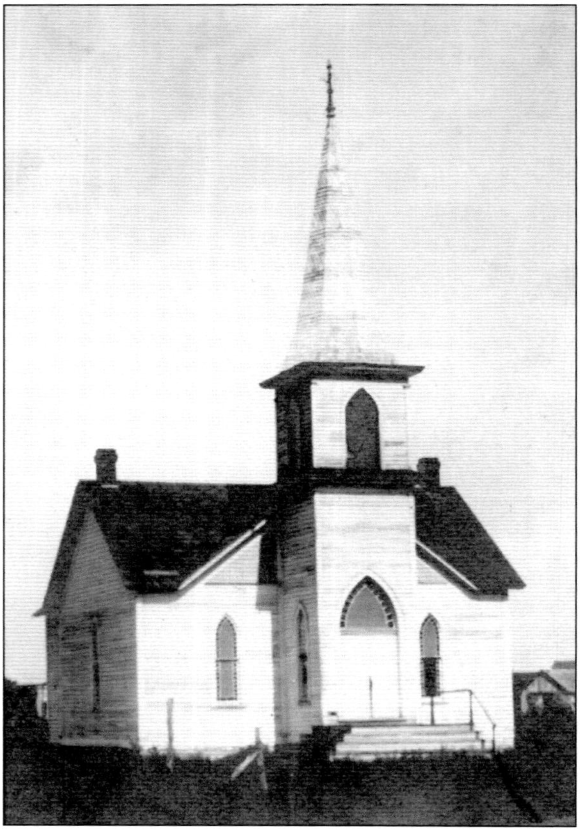

The Udell Christian Church, organized in 1867, erected its first building in 1873. In 1901, it was moved two blocks to the east, enlarged, remodeled, and dedicated in December of that year. It is shown at left in December 1908. This church burned down in 1912 and was replaced by the church pictured below, which was dedicated in July 1913.

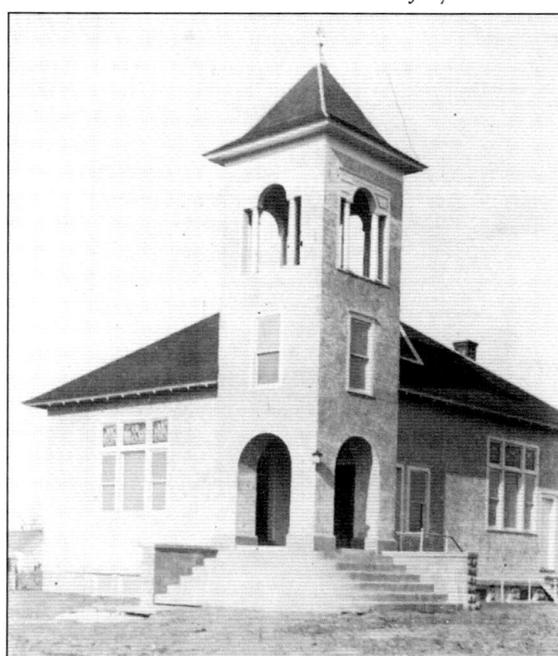

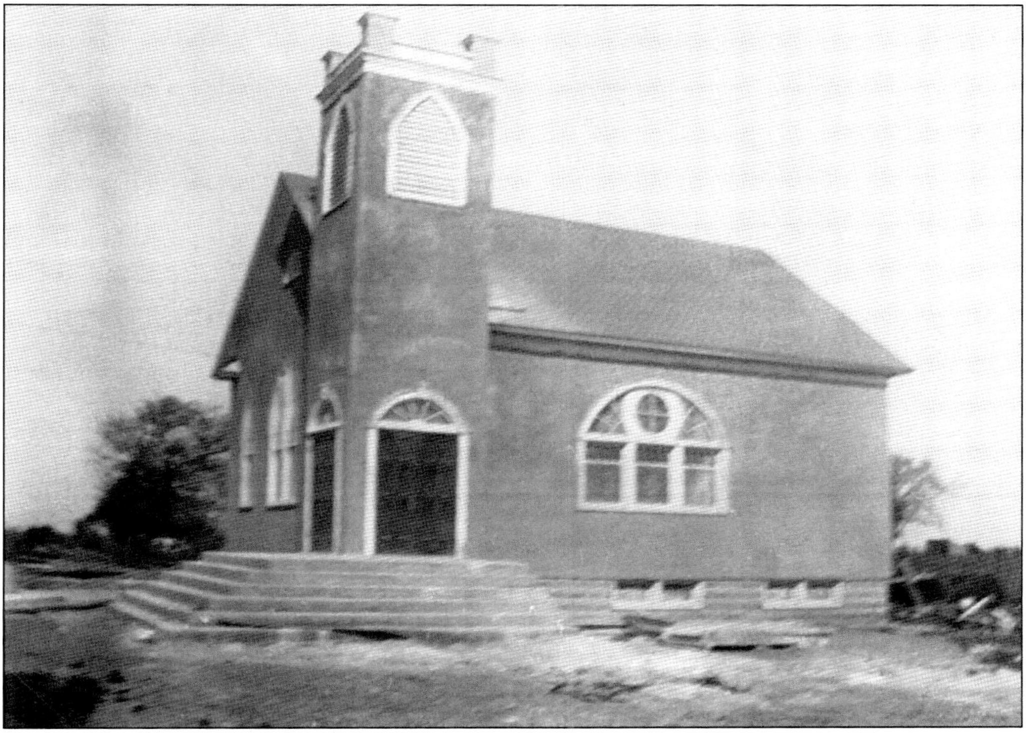

The Brushy Baptist Church was founded in 1858 and came to be known as the Baptist Church on the Chariton River. For the first five years, the congregation met in a log cabin, then built a church in the current location north of Plano. The church shown here was built in 1922.

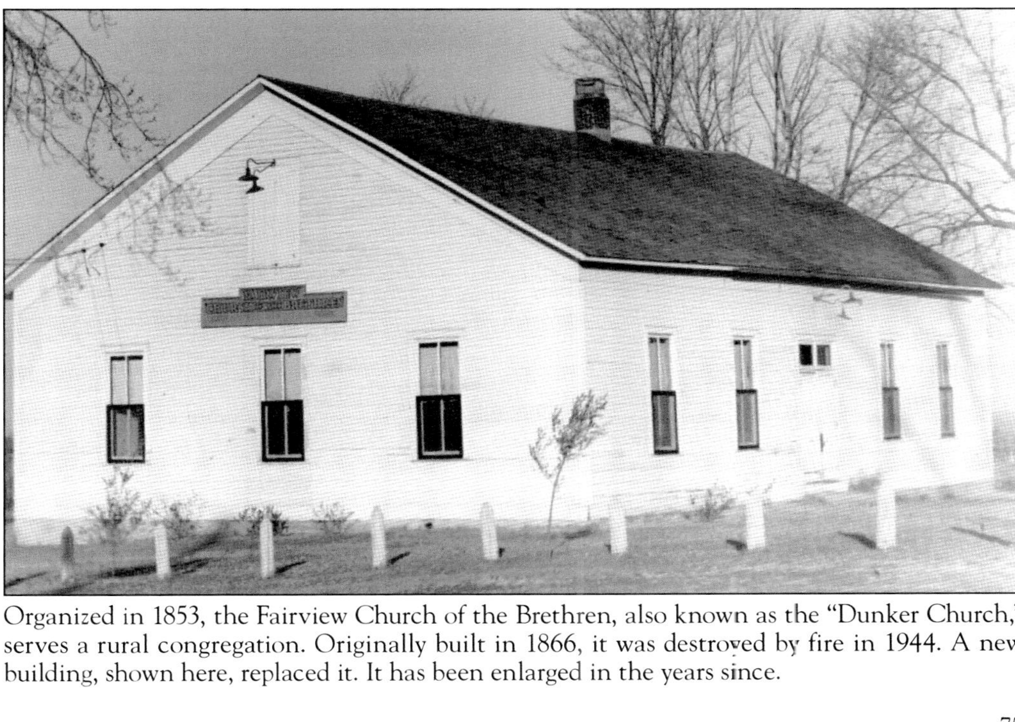

Organized in 1853, the Fairview Church of the Brethren, also known as the "Dunker Church," serves a rural congregation. Originally built in 1866, it was destroyed by fire in 1944. A new building, shown here, replaced it. It has been enlarged in the years since.

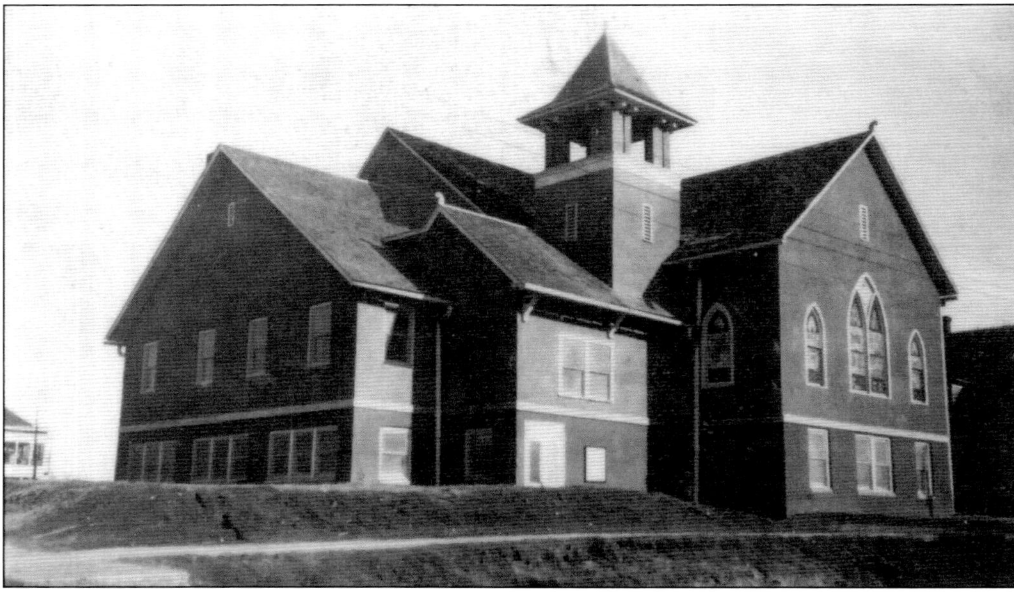

The Mystic Methodist Church closed in June 1997 after serving the town for over 100 years. Built in 1886 and rebuilt in 1907, the church had grown to 224 members by the 1930s, but by 1950 had dwindled to only 50. The congregation's decline coincided with the shrinking number of coal miners living in the area.

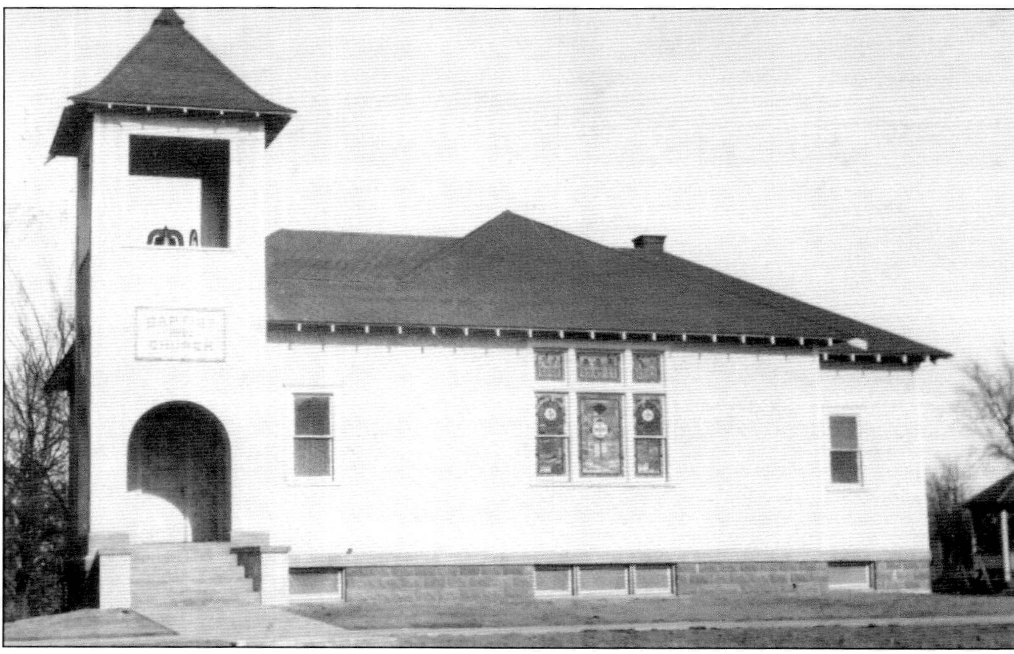

The Unionville Baptist Church was built in 1922 on the north side of the main intersection in Unionville, Iowa. The lot upon which it was built included an old church that was shared by the Baptists and Presbyterians. After the purchase of the land, the older church was moved a little to the west, renovated, and used for the American Legion Hall. Later, it served as the community center until 1938.

Five

At Your Service

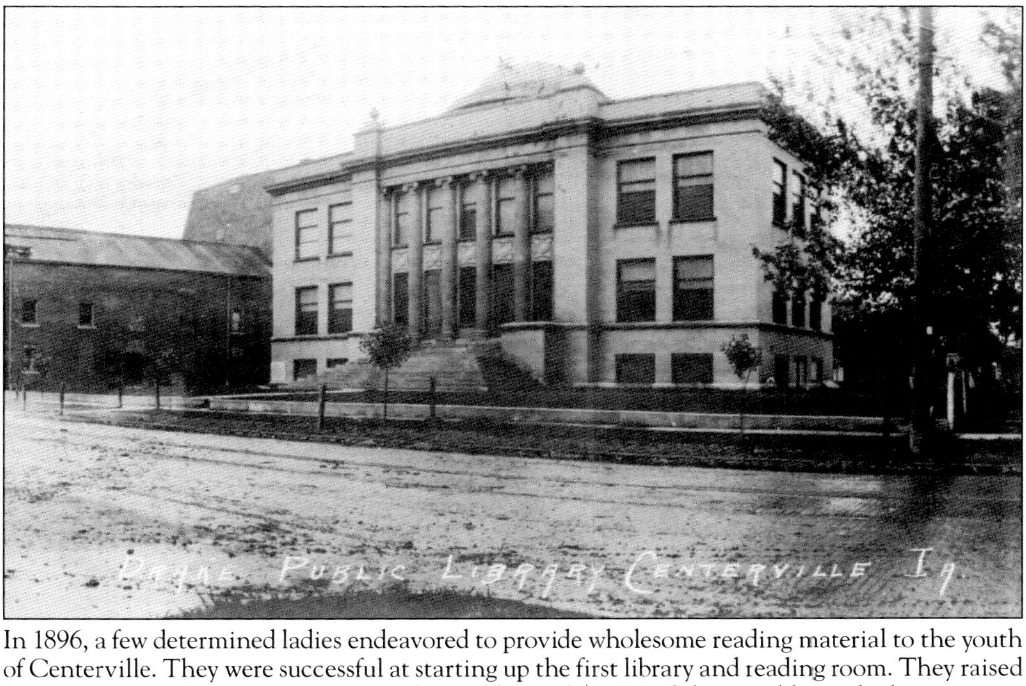

In 1896, a few determined ladies endeavored to provide wholesome reading material to the youth of Centerville. They were successful at starting up the first library and reading room. They raised funds to buy books and were promised an additional $1,000 if they could match that amount. Governor Drake saw the need for a library on a larger scale. He offered to build for the City of Centerville a new $25,000 library, provided that it would be maintained by the taxpayers. The vote occurred on May 6, 1901, and passed with an enthusiastic 1,438 "yes" votes to 65 votes against. The cornerstone was laid in November 1902, and the library was dedicated on January 16, 1903. The ladies of the reading room donated its 2,630 volumes to the new library, the beginning of a large collection.

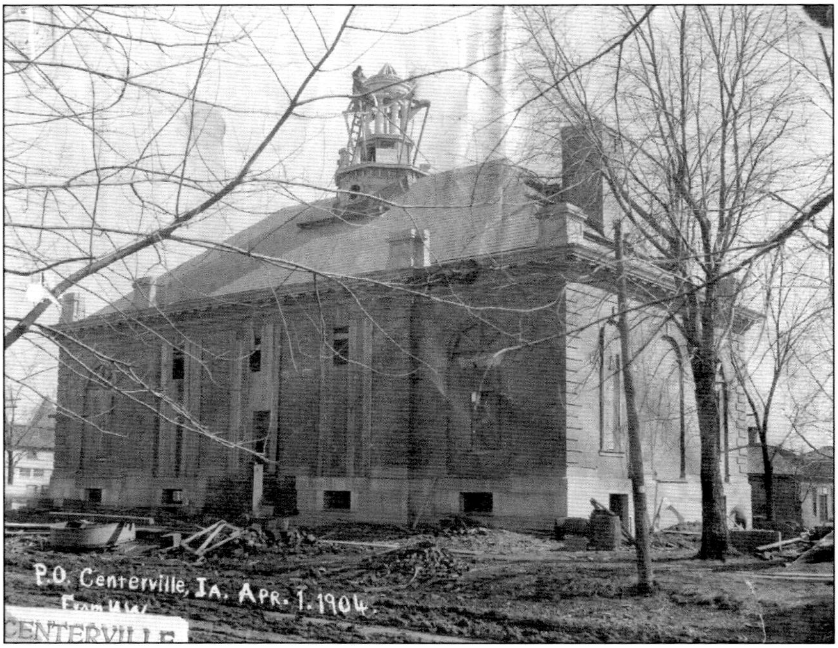

Early in 1902, it was learned that Centerville might be chosen to receive a new federal building. The town wrote letters of support, and on April 26, 1902, it was one of only 10 locations in Iowa to be awarded an appropriation. However, Centerville had to provide the lot to the federal government for $1. Immediately, officials devised a plan to run streets directly through the courtyard, dividing it into four sections. The new federal building would sit on one corner, the new courthouse on the opposite corner. The other two corners would be made into parks. This idea lost steam after a few weeks and a more appropriate location was secured on the corner of Main and Maple Streets. Shown here during construction in 1904 are the front of the building (above) and the back (below).

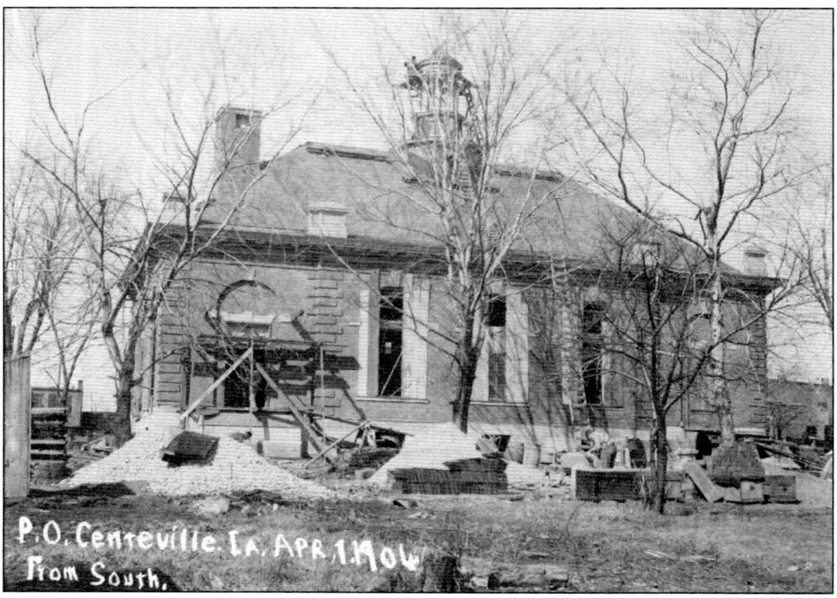

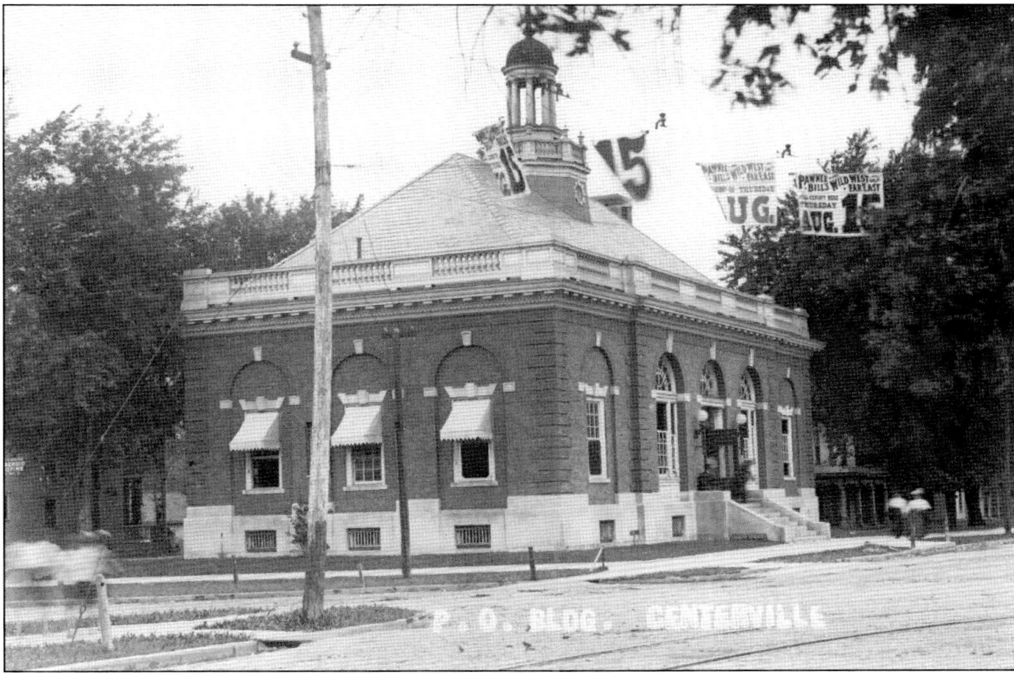

The new federal building, more commonly known as the Centerville Post Office, at 100 West Maple Street, was dedicated on August 16, 1904, just 27 days before the new Appanoose County courthouse was dedicated. Its location marked the center of all addresses in Centerville. North- and south-labeled streets begin there, as do east- and west-labeled streets. In 1931, the building received an addition to the back (below), with the architecture meticulously matched to the existing building. The cupola was removed in 1958. The Centerville Post Office on Maple Street served the community until October 1977, when the new post office on Tenth Street opened. Since 1988, the old post office building has served the community as the Appanoose County Historical and Coal Mining Museum.

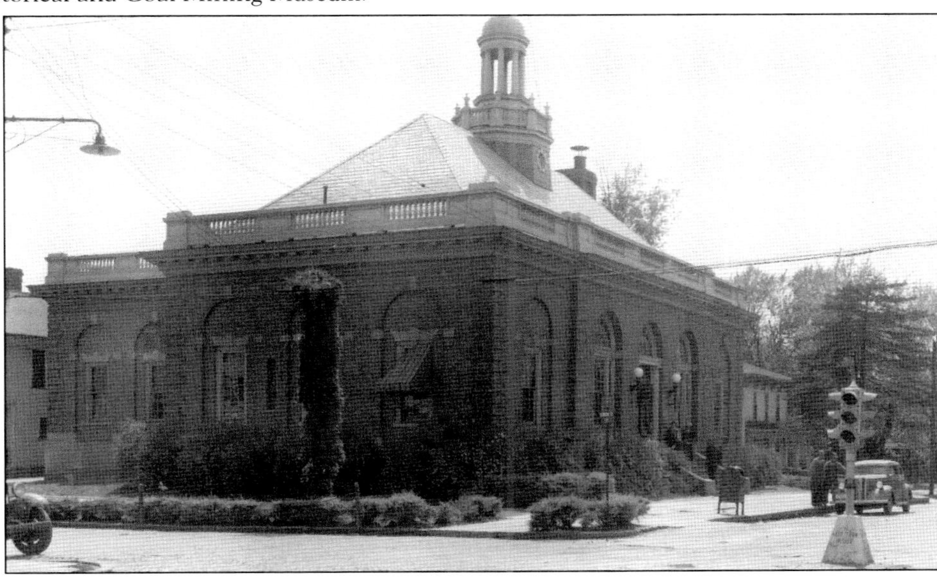

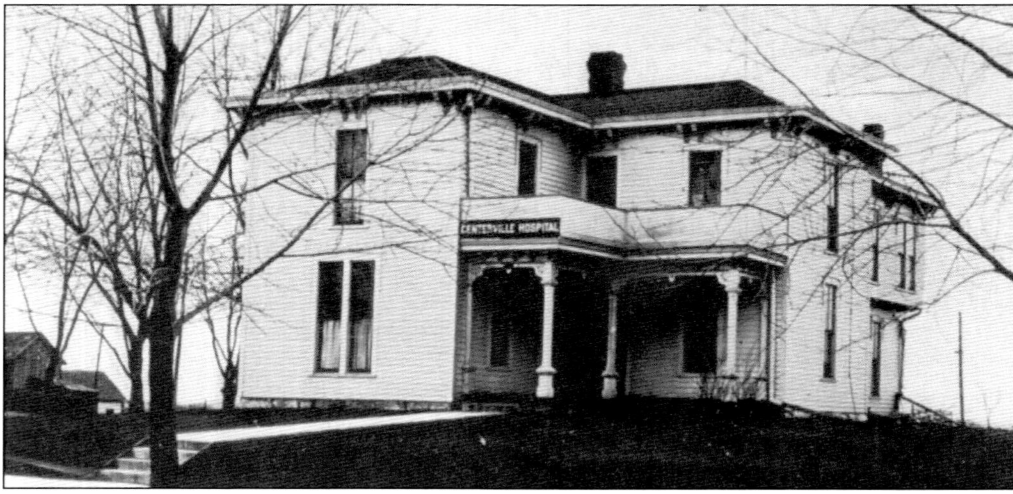

In 1902, $10,000 was raised to establish a hospital. The William Peatman home on South Main Street was purchased and renovated for this purpose (above). On November 17, 1903, the hospital was opened under the management of local physicians. In 1910, Centerville Hospital was officially renamed St. Joseph's Mercy Hospital after the Sisters of Mercy in Council Bluffs assumed all management and financial responsibilities of the hospital. This change came at the request of local businessmen and Father Loftus of St. Mary's Catholic Church. In 1911, the School of Nursing established an accredited three-year diploma program in conjunction with the hospital. In 1916, a new, 48-bed structure, shown below, was built at the same location on South Main Street to replace the old hospital. The citizens of Centerville contributed $15,000 to its construction.

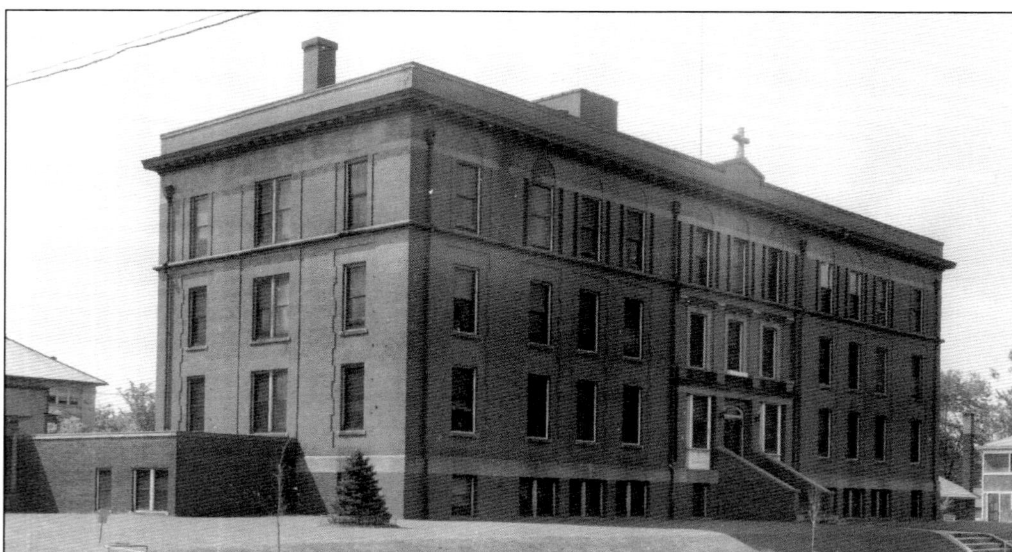

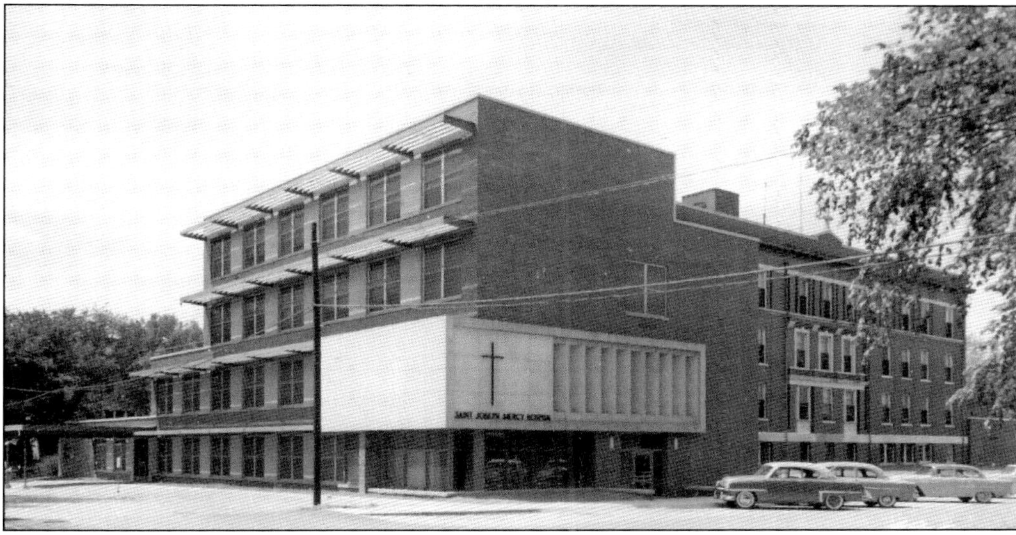

In 1953, a federal grant was approved for expansion of the hospital. The community and the Sisters of Mercy shared equally in the remainder of the cost. In 1956, the four-story addition added to the south side of the hospital was completed. By 1977, the structure was aging and obsolete. The community embarked upon a $300,000 fundraising drive to construct a new facility. The old building, shown here, was demolished in 1981.

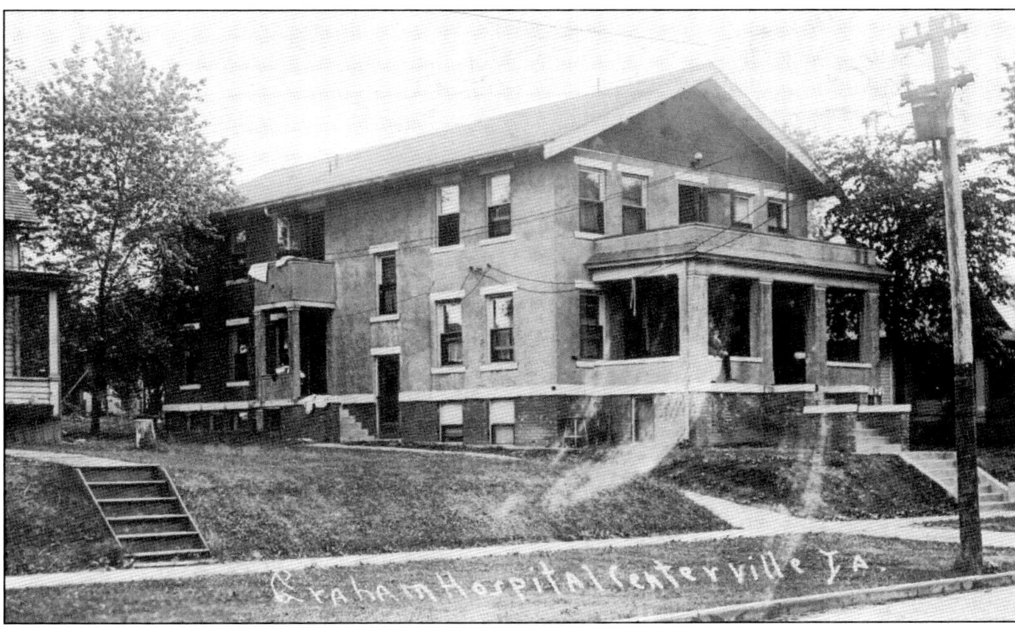

The Graham Hospital, also known as the Protestant Hospital and "coal miner's hospital," opened in 1917 as an "undenominational" alternative to St. Joseph's Mercy Hospital. Located on East State Street, it offered a subscription plan to coal miners. For 75¢ a month, the hospital would provide any treatment needed. Founder George Graham died in 1923, and the hospital was foreclosed upon in 1934. The building still stands today.

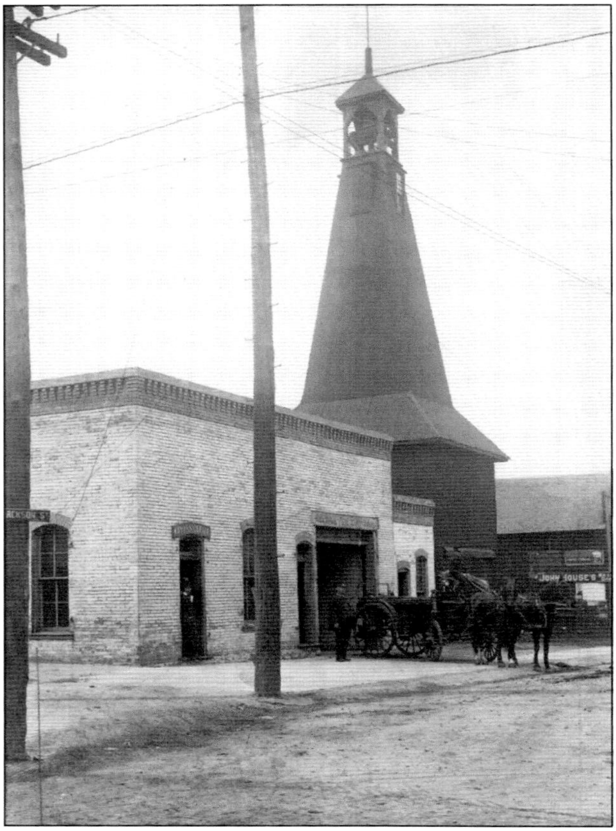

The first official firefighting group in Centerville was the Bucket Brigade in 1868. In October 1876, the Hook and Ladder Company No. 1 was organized with a hand engine, a horse cart, and a hook and ladder wagon. In 1878, a new city hall was built off the southwest corner of the Square on West Jackson Street. The west portion was dedicated to the fire department, shown in these photographs. The hose tower seen at left was used to dry the fire hoses. Below, the fire department poses with its equipment in 1909. In 1959, Centerville City Hall, the Community Center, and the Centerville Fire Department relocated to their current location on East Maple Street.

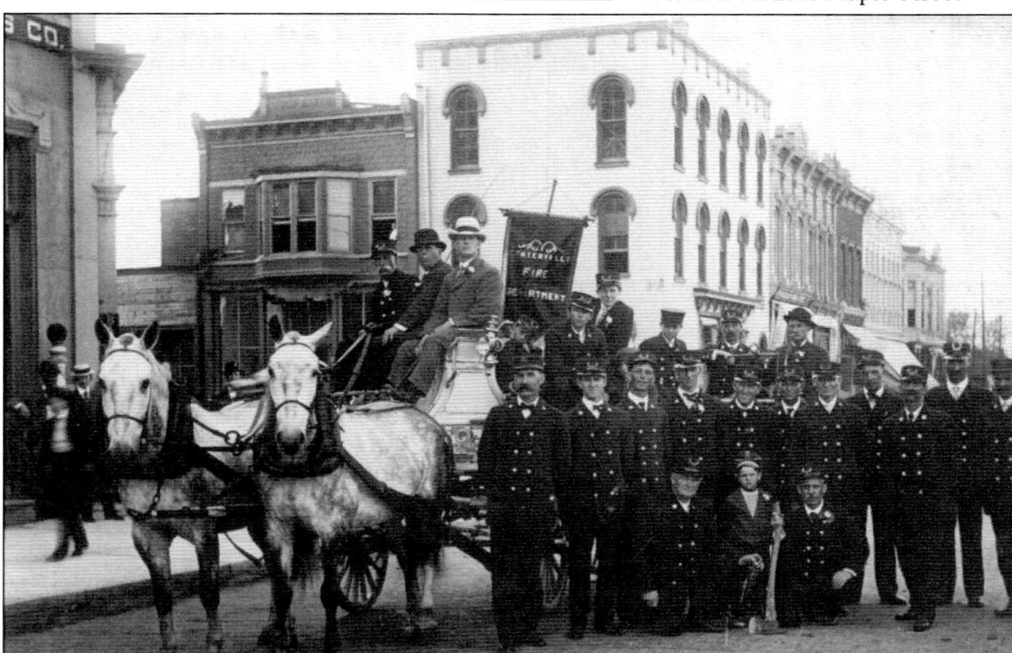

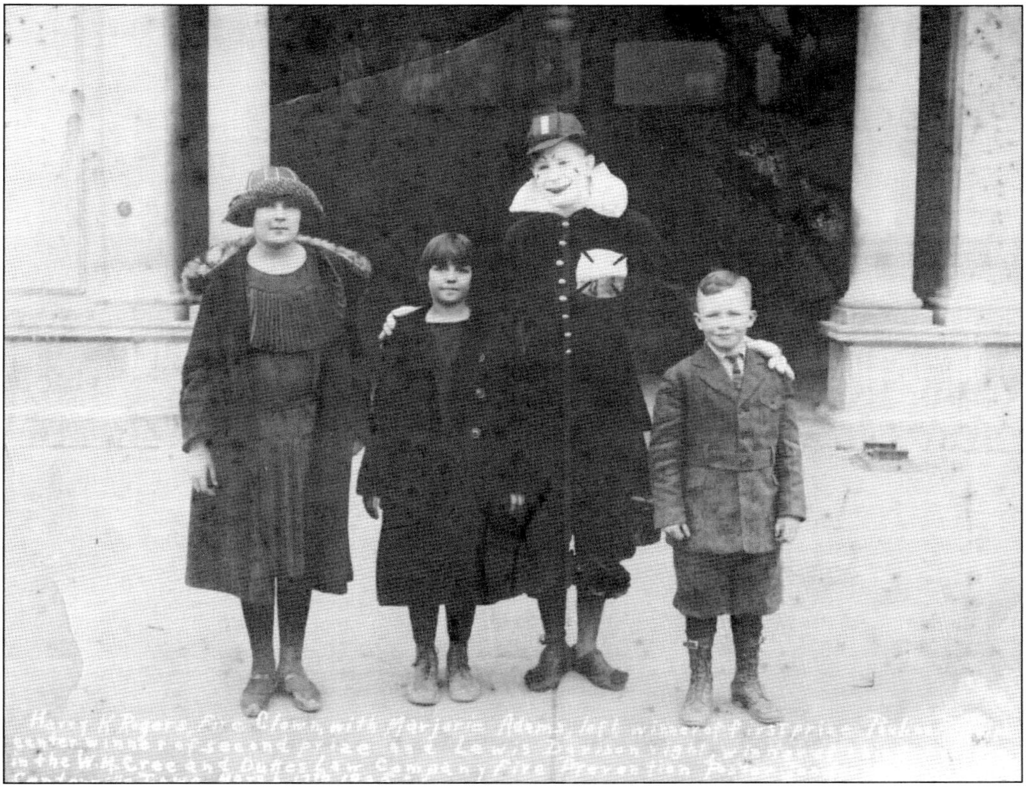

Harry Rogers, fire clown, poses with, from left to right, poster contest winners Marjorie Adams (first place), Pauline Randolph (second place), and Lewis Davison (third place). W.M Cree and Dukes Law Office sponsored the Fire Prevention Poster Contest in March 1925. Rogers and the children appear to be standing in front of Centerville High School.

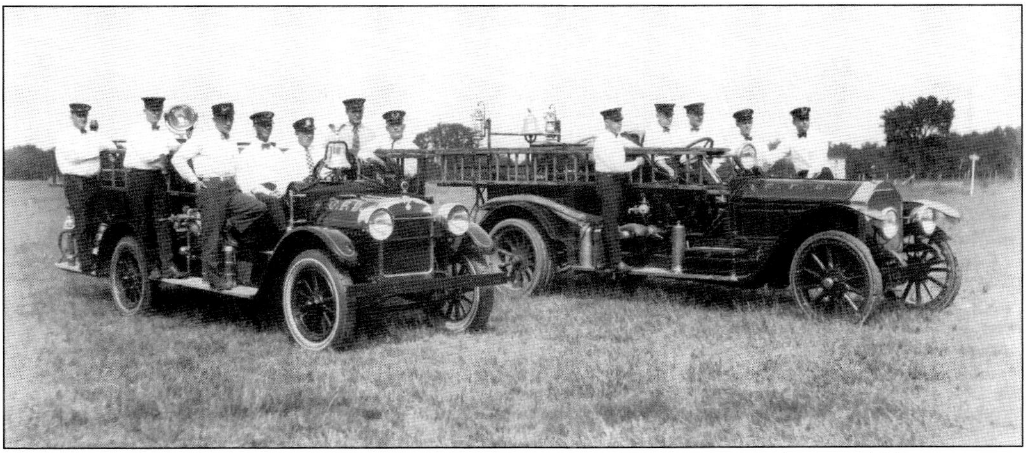

The Centerville Fire Department ordered its first fire truck in May 1918, but would have to wait until March 1919 for its arrival. It was delivered by train and was untouched until a representative from the manufacturer, American LaFrance, came to unload it and demonstrate its capabilities. It is shown here on the right. Another truck, a REO (shown on the left), was purchased in June 1925. Both trucks were in the 1925 Independence Day parade around the Square.

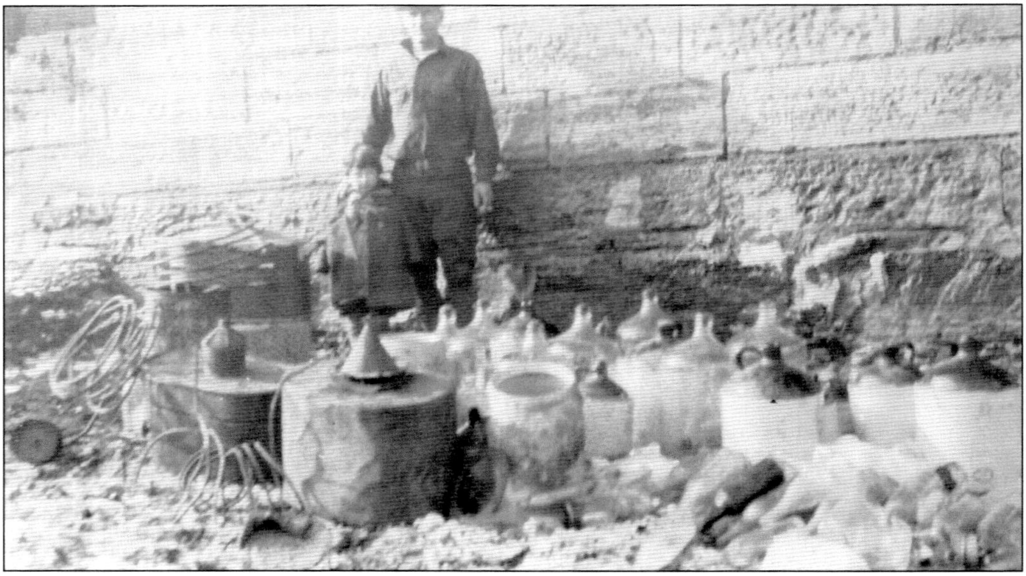

The Appanoose County Sheriff's Office was busy during the years of Prohibition. Some residents were very skillful in their manufacture of different kinds of alcohol. Grappa, wine, moonshine, hooch—whatever the name, the sheriff's department was on the case. Here, Sheriff Earl Gaughenbaugh and his daughter Earleen stand among confiscated stills and equipment outside the Appanoose County Jail on North Main Street.

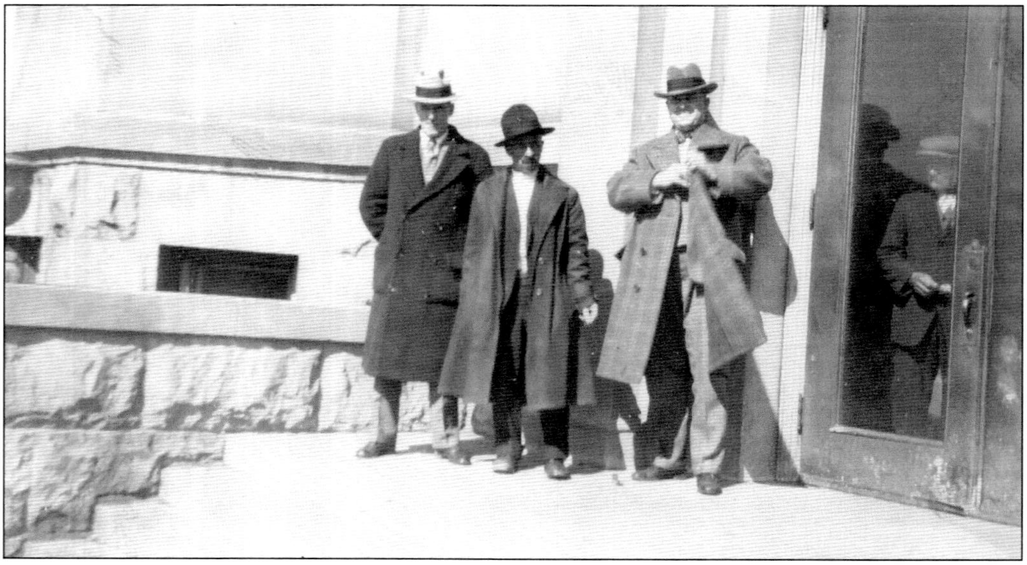

Sheriff Earl Gaughenbaugh served during Centerville's most tumultuous years. He dealt with the Ku Klux Klan, miners' strikes, the mafia, and several murders, including that of D. Fulton Rice in 1929. Rice was a local attorney representing a coal miner, George Damyanich. Impatient with Rice's speed in the case, Damyanich shot him on the south walk of the courthouse. Pictured here on the courthouse steps are, from left to right, Gaughenbaugh, Damyanich, and an unidentified official.

Chief of Police Bob Curtis poses with the city's newest parking meters in October 1965. These replaced two previous sets of meters, the first in 1946 and another in 1952. Income from the meters was used to pay for municipal projects. On the front page of the *Daily Iowegian* on April 9, 1974, ironically, one headline read "Free Parking on the Square," and another read "Lake Center Mall Groundbreaking."

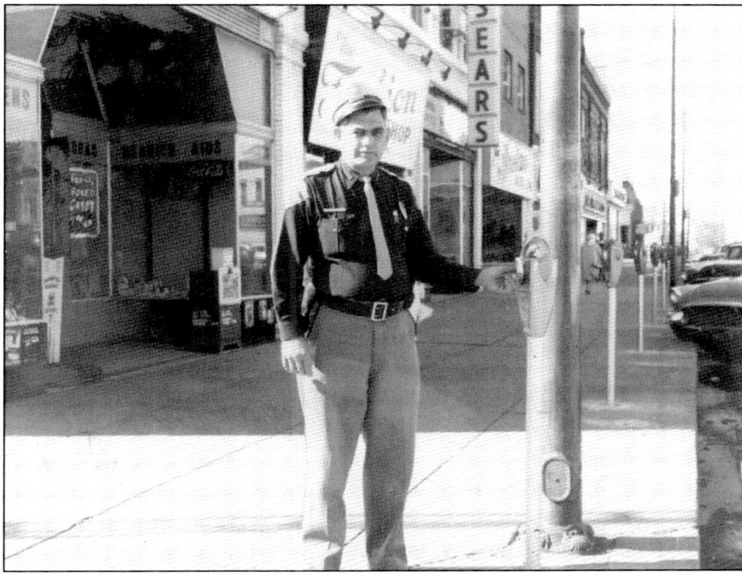

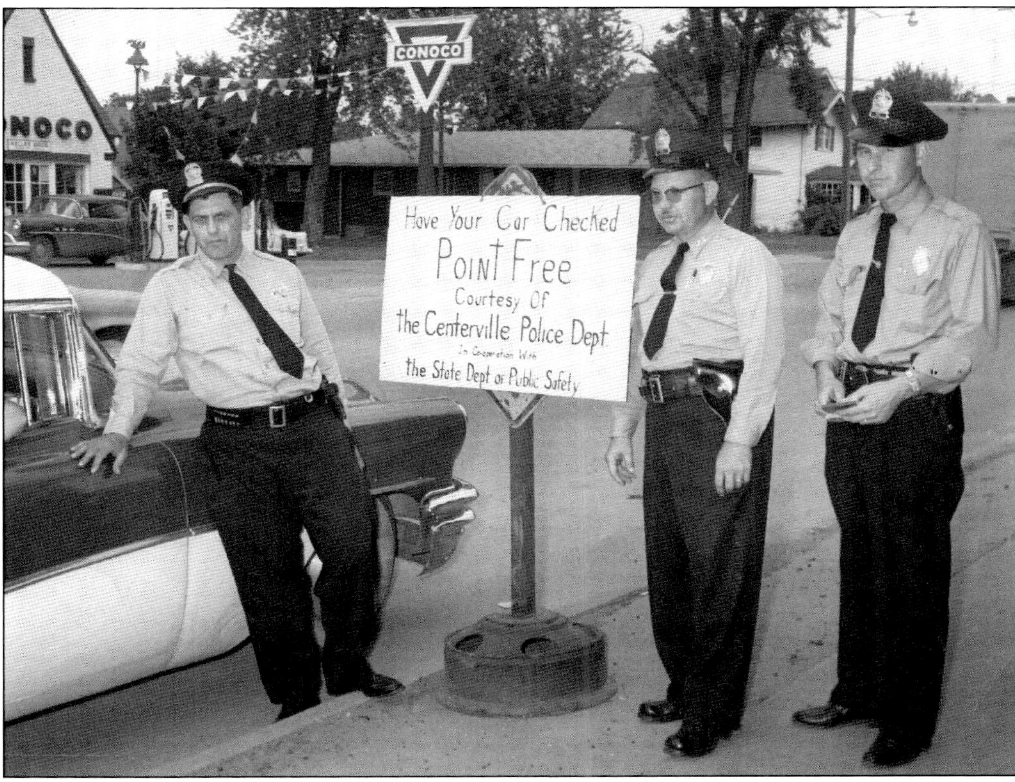

Pictured here in 1958 after moving into their new headquarters at 310 East Maple Street are, from left to right, Chief Bob Curtis, Patrolman Richard Smith, and Patrolman Al Clark. They are offering a free car safety check, "point free." The points system was instituted by the State Safety Commissioner on April 1, 1958. If a driver accumulated 10 points, his license would be suspended. Faulty equipment garnered a two-point penalty, and moving violations incurred more.

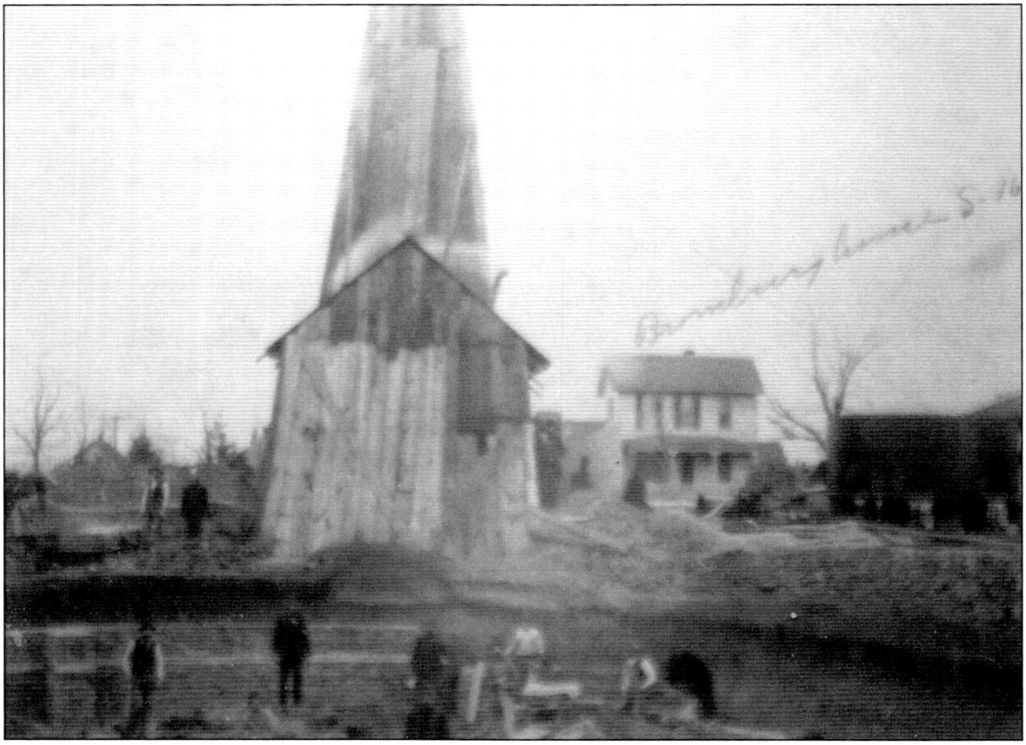

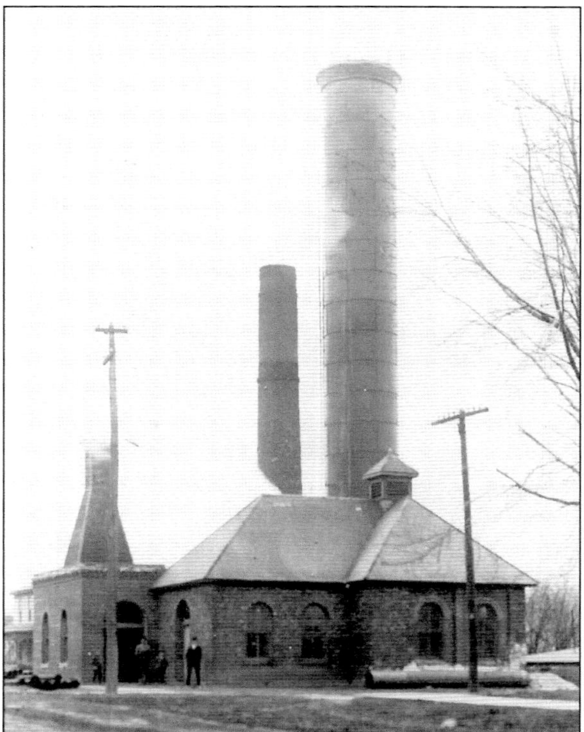

The Centerville Waterworks facility (above), built in 1896, pumped the water for Centerville from a 1,500-foot well. An additional well was sunk in 1904 (left). This facility housed the wells, pumps, and the engine to operate the pumps. By 1912, Centerville was growing, increasing the demand for water. The lower reservoir was built in 1912, a water tower at the corner of Twelfth and West Cottage Streets was built in 1914, and the upper reservoir was built in 1922 to meet the ever-increasing needs.

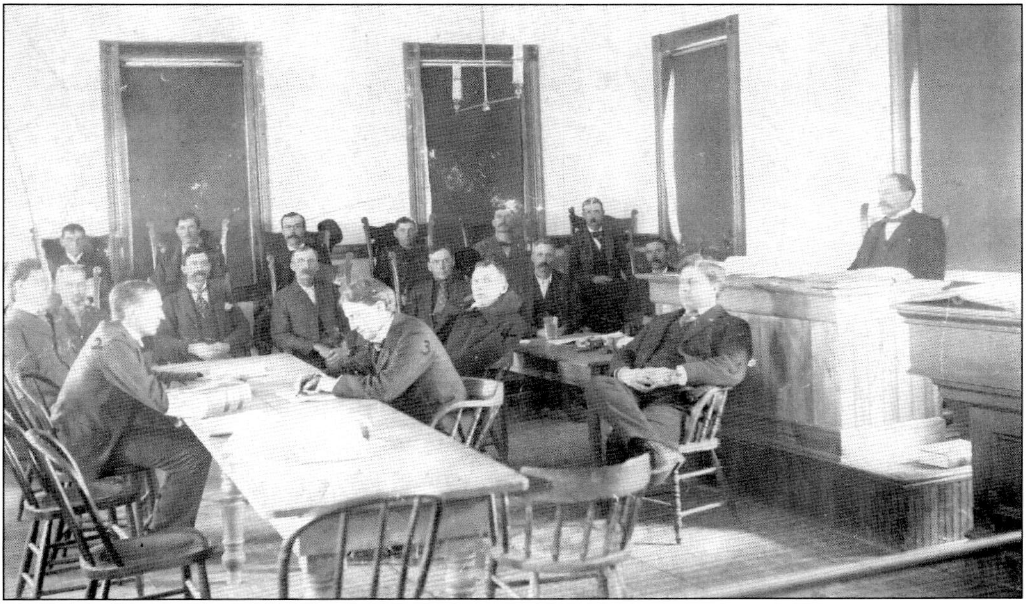

This is a view inside the Appanoose County Courthouse on December 8, 1898, during the trial of Charles Hart and Sol Davis, accused robbers of the McDonald Bank in Cincinnati. This photograph of the lawyers, judge, and jury was taken on December 8, 1898, at their request. The jury included Powell, Waters, Besse, Broshar, Carter, Cross, Laughlin, McConnell, Mishler, Silknitter, Chambers, and McGrew. The lawyers were Wilson, Mabry, Payne, Howell, and Smith. The judge was Roberts.

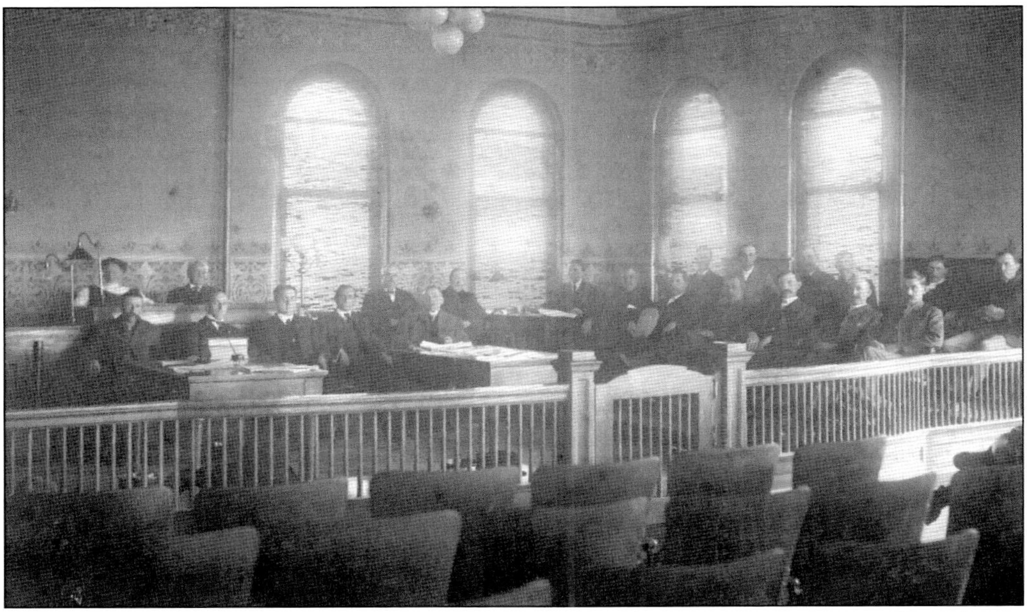

This photograph shows the inside of the courtroom in the Appanoose County Courthouse that still stands today. Text written on the back indicates that it was taken in 1907, though the nature of the proceedings is uncertain. The courthouse was only three years old at the time of this photograph, so the decor and fixtures are the originals.

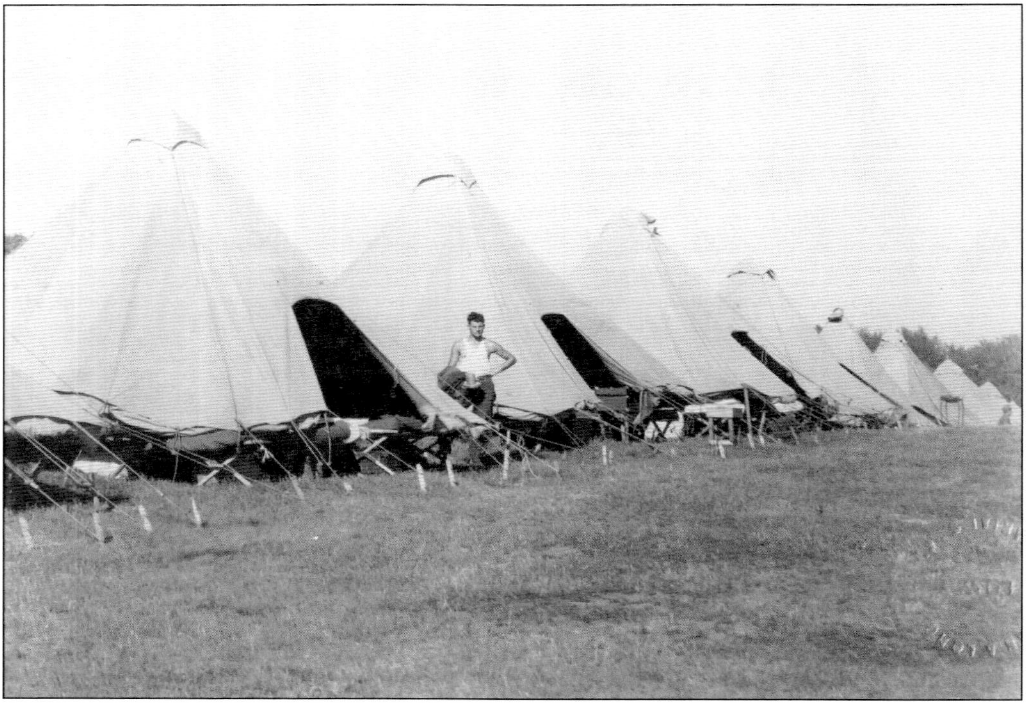

The Civilian Conservation Corps (CCC) moved into Centerville in May 1934 and set up camp at the north end of Seventh Street. Its main purpose was to implement soil conservation measures. The CCC also worked extensively creating Sharon Bluffs State Park, installing six walking bridges (the largest measuring 57 feet across), creating trails, installing natural steps along the bluff, building picnic areas with fireplaces, and constructing the shelter house. The workers of the Centerville camp, who had proven themselves outstanding in soil conservation work, were pulled away to focus on that exclusively before the park was completed. The Albia CCC camp stepped in to finish the state park, and it was opened to the public before July 4, 1935. Permanent buildings replaced the tents, as the camp stayed in Centerville for five years. The camp moved to Corydon in late 1939.

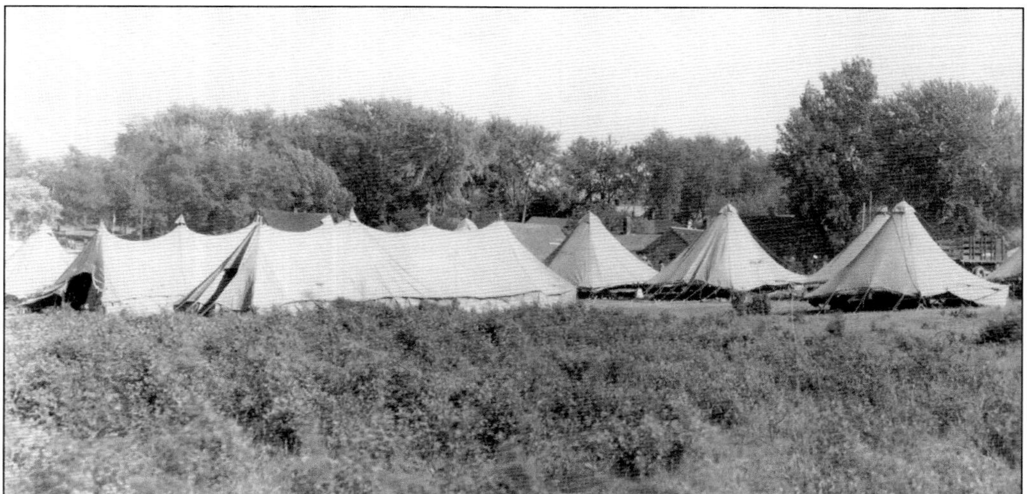

Six

Black Diamonds

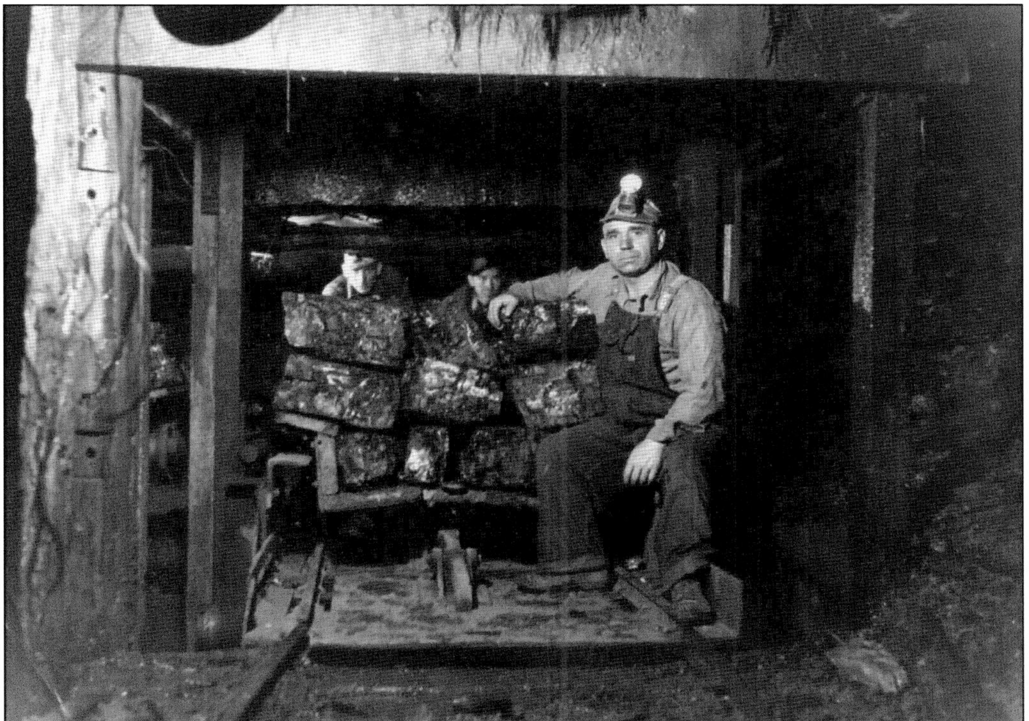

Coal, more than any other pursuit, has established the complexion of Appanoose County and its people. Almost as soon as the region was open for settlement in 1843, outcroppings on creek banks were dug out and used by the pioneer families. When the railroads arrived in 1871, coal mining became an industry. So many mines opened that it was difficult to find enough people to operate them. To fill the need for workers, European immigrants were encouraged to come to Appanoose County. By 1920, the county's population included immigrants from over 40 countries. Those immigrants, coupled with the original settlers to the county, created a dynamic melting pot.

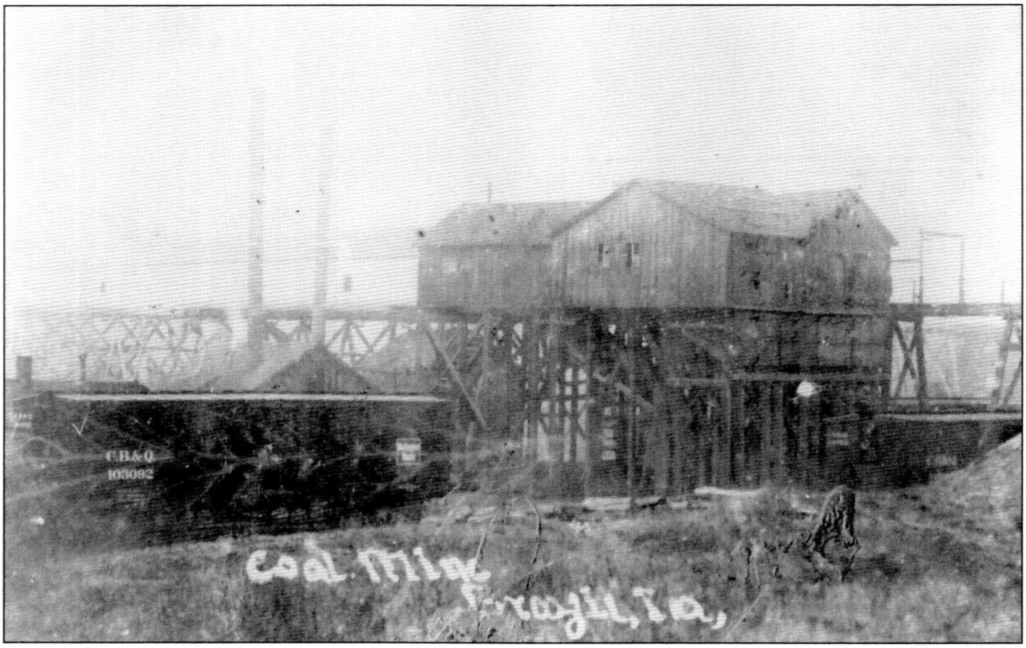

The Phoenix Mine in Brazil was in business from 1882 through the early 1920s. Originally the Tipton Coal Company, it was the third coal mine in Brazil, located in the southern part of town, east of the tracks. It was a slope mine that did a $40,000 business in 1917, the peak coal production year in Appanoose County.

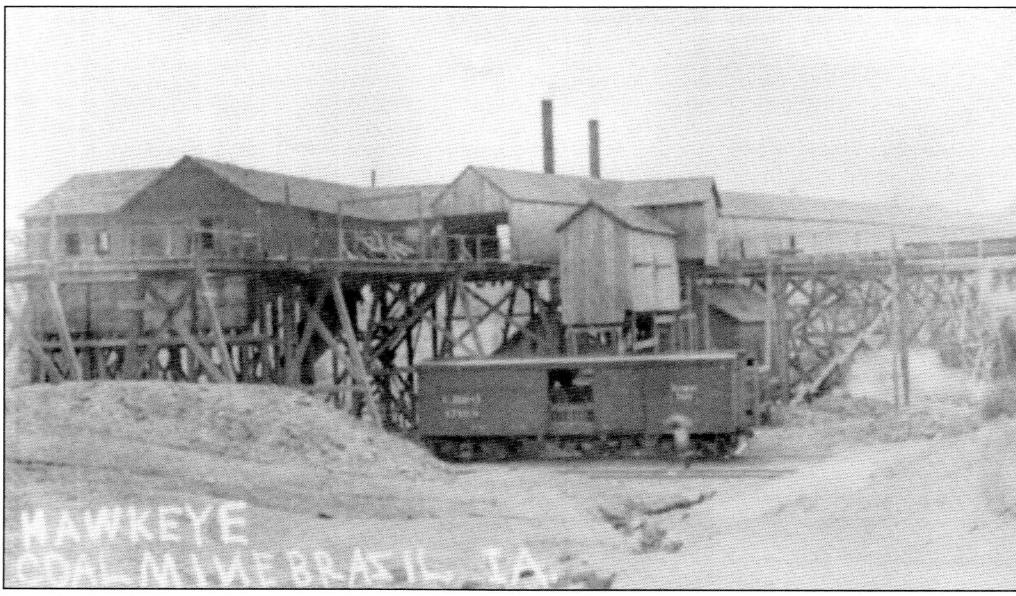

Brazil's Hawkeye Mine opened in 1882 and later became the Walnut Mine, then the Centerville Block Coal Company Mine No. 5. The mine employed over 100 men. In 1918, it was electrified and adapted to mining machines. The miners' strike in 1927 closed the mine for the summer. When the strike was settled, the boss told workers to show up Monday morning. On Sunday night, however, the mine was destroyed by arsonists.

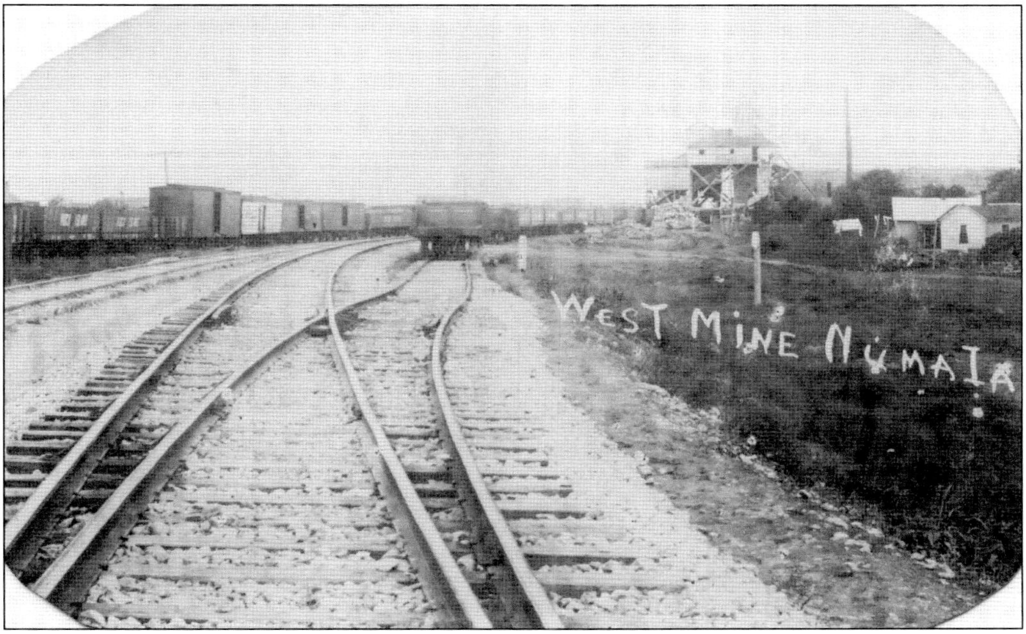

The West Mine sat just west of the town of Numa. By 1883, it was known as Diamond Mine No. 2, and later, Centerville Block Coal Company. This large shaft mine employed 160 men. The mine produced 250 tons of coal per day, but was closed in 1928 after having mined over 300 acres.

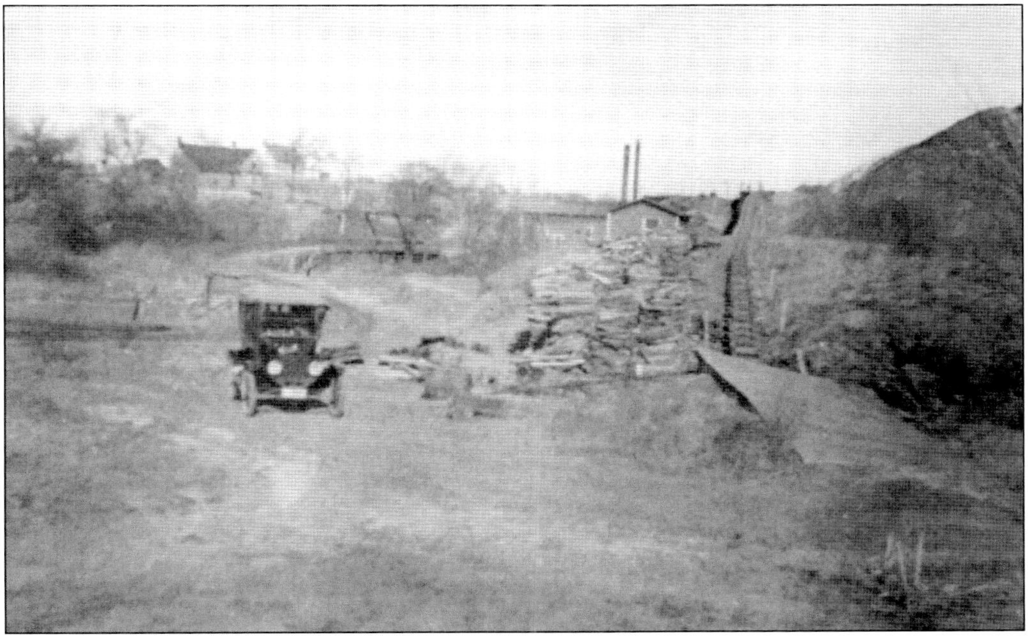

The Egypt Mine, located northeast of Brazil, operated from 1901 until 1926. A mining camp named the Harmon Subdivision was created for housing the miners and their families. It also had its own school. What made the Egypt Mine unique was its long, elaborate trestle that spanned 600 feet over Walnut Creek to connect the mouth of the slope mine to the tipple.

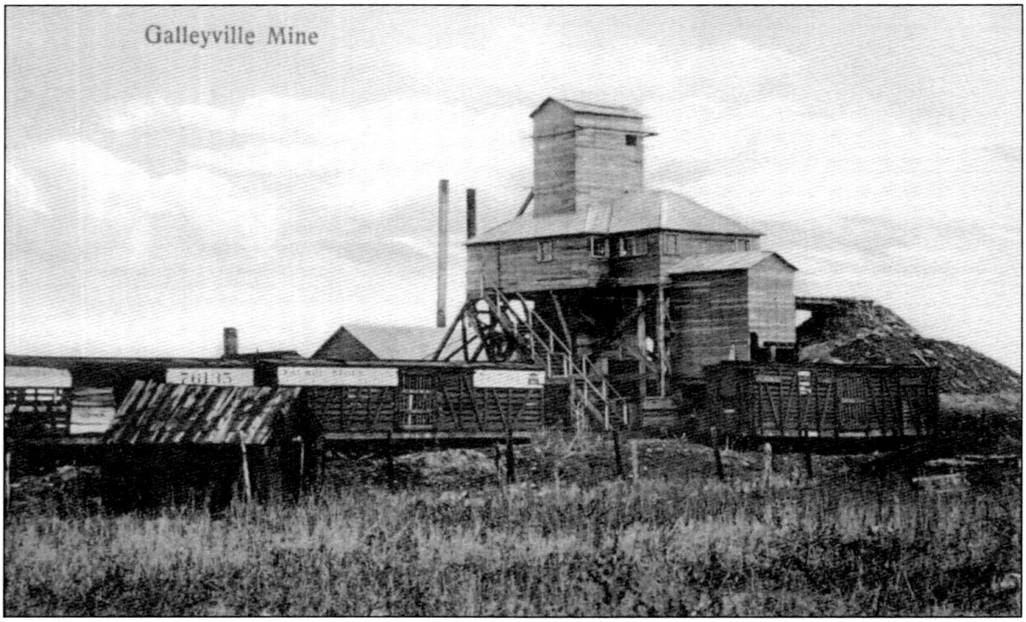

The Galleyville Mine was located just south of Centerville, where Drake Avenue meets the Numa Highway, on the north side. It was operated by the Anchor Coal Company and the National Coal Company and existed from 1892 to 1924. Many of the mine's 200 workers lived in the mining camp that developed along the Numa road.

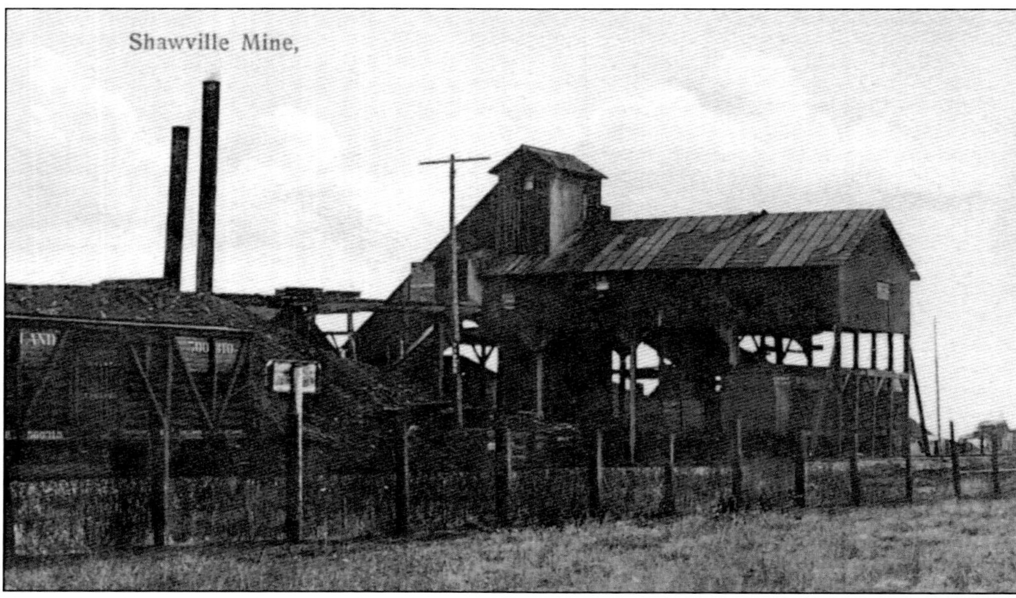

Near the Galleyville Mine was the Shawville Mine. Its camp was established on what is now 210th Avenue. This mine, too, was operated by the Anchor Coal Company. The underground tunnels in the mine met up with those of the Galleyville Mine, creating many places to hide and escape from either. In 1924, Sheriff Earl Gaughenbaugh uncovered a subterranean bootlegging operation in the Shawville Mine.

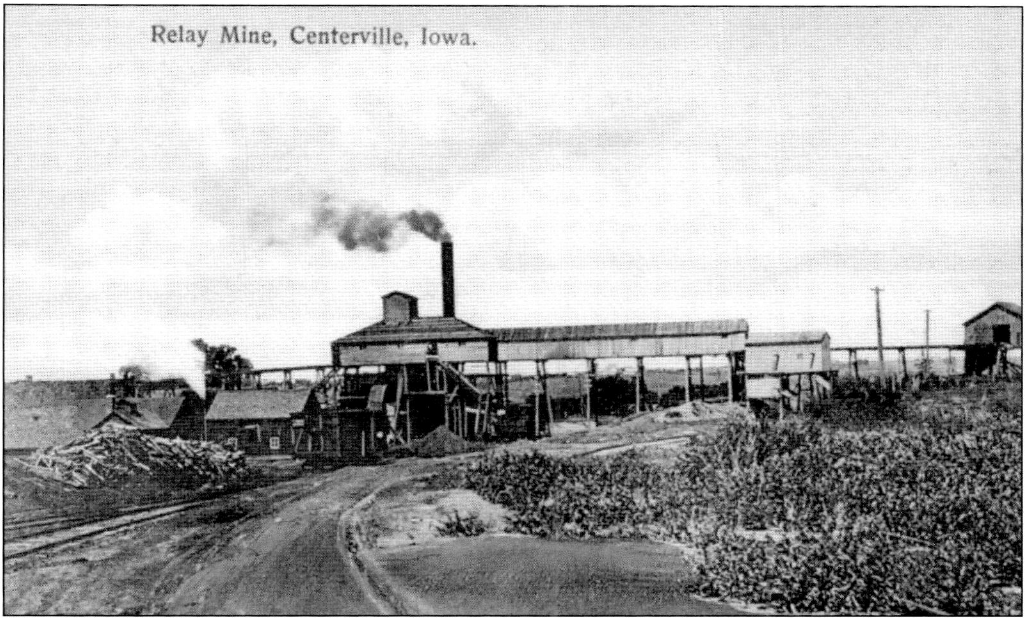

The site of Relay Mine was just west of Centerville along what is now Highway 2, on the south side of the road. It operated from 1878 until 1926. It suffered major fires in 1905 and 1907, but bounced back to become a very large and efficient mine. Its official name was Centerville Block Coal Company No. 3.

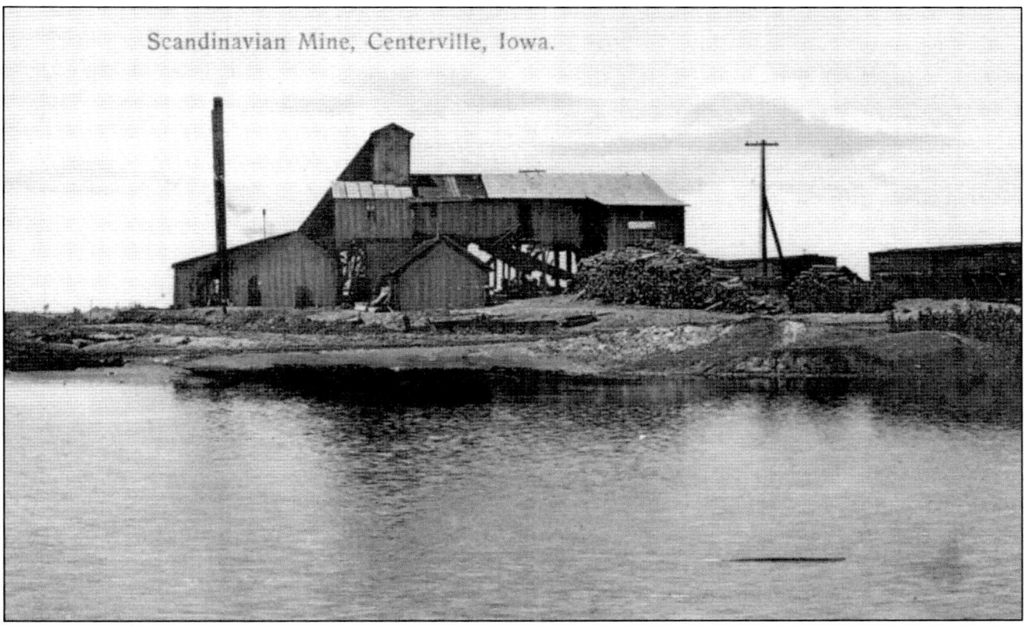

The Scandinavian Coal Mine was very large. Its mining area extended to most of the southwest quadrant of Centerville, west of Main Street and south of Maple Street, including Lakeview, Howar Junior High, and the High School. The tipple was located just north of Cottage Street. Many of the residents of "Swedetown" on South Fifteenth and Sixteenth Streets worked at the mine.

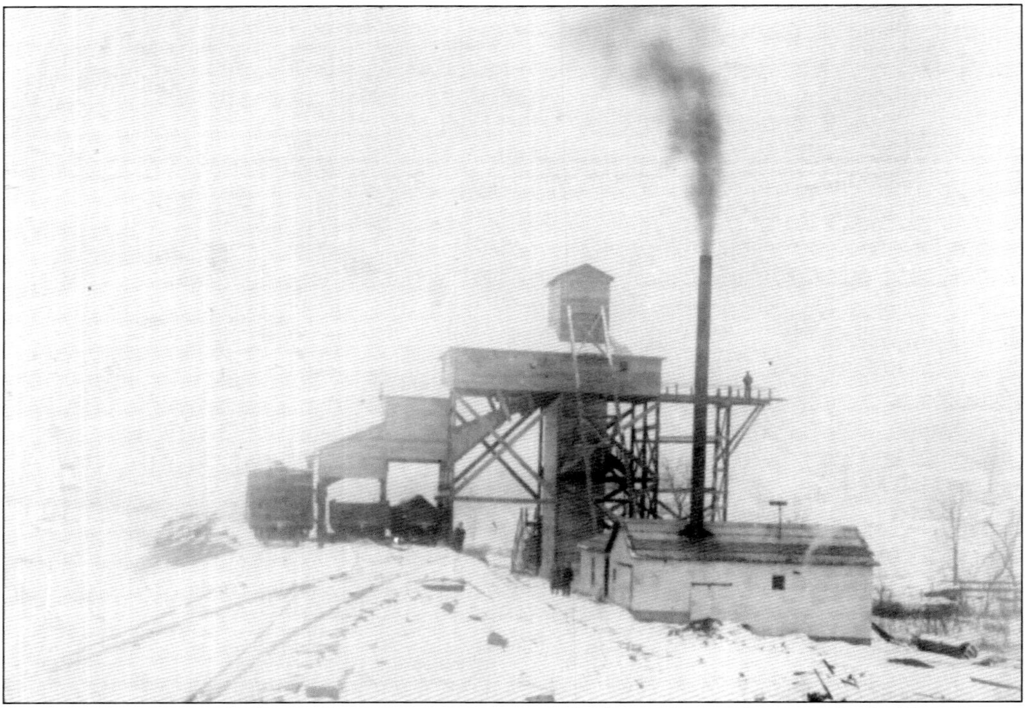

This 1895 photograph shows the Green Top Mine, which was located one and a half miles east of Numa. One historical account says it was abandoned and that the tipple had fallen into the shaft. But later, new life was breathed into the mine when it became the Martin Block Coal Company in 1911. In 1923, it became the Numa Coal Company.

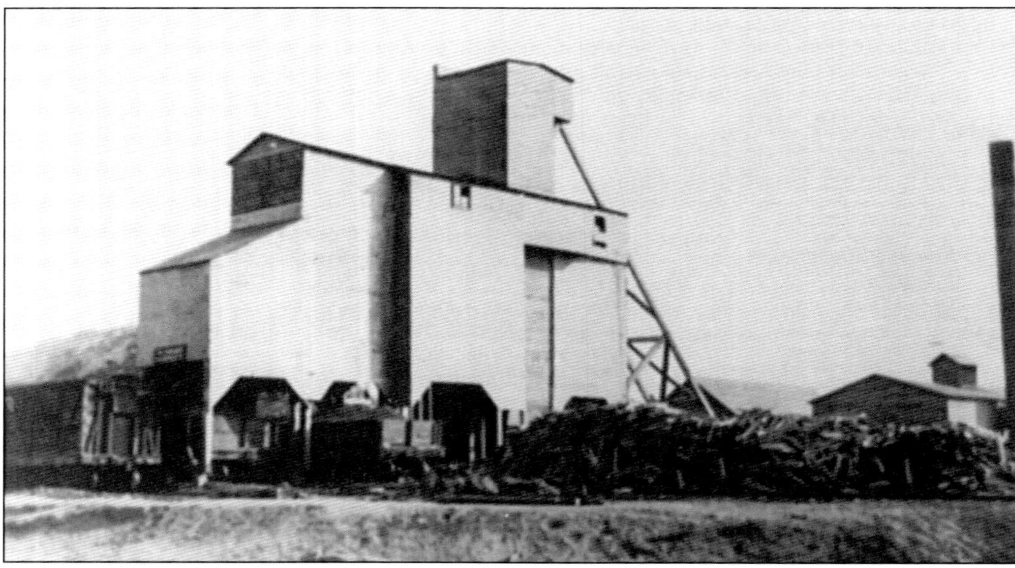

This photograph of the Martin Block Coal Company was taken between 1911 and 1923. The mine was owned by Archie F. Martin. In 1913, the village named after him, Martinstown, was officially platted. There were about 50 houses in Martinstown, mostly occupied by Italian and Croatian immigrants. Martinstown was also known as Shantytown.

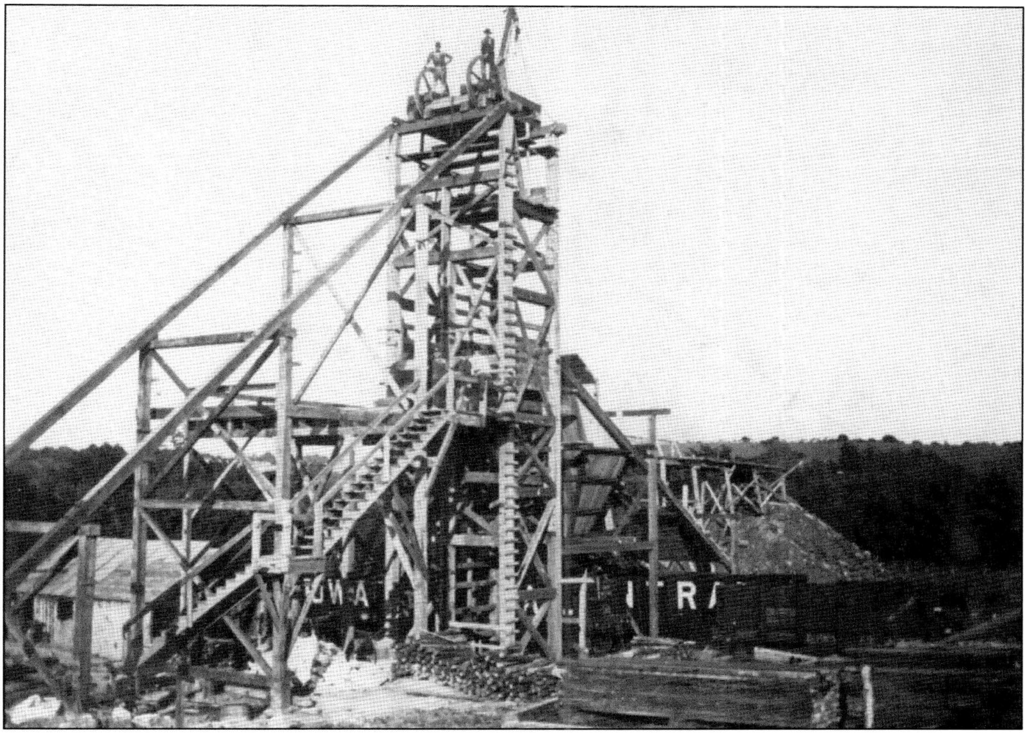

The Darbyville, or "Darby," Mine operated from 1891 until 1901. The mine covered about 12 acres in the small town of Darby. It struggled during the miners' strikes in 1897 and only operated at 40 to 60 percent of capacity at other times. The end came when, during a heavy rain, the drainage tube under the railroad was plugged with a barrel, and water poured into the Darbyville Mine, flooding it.

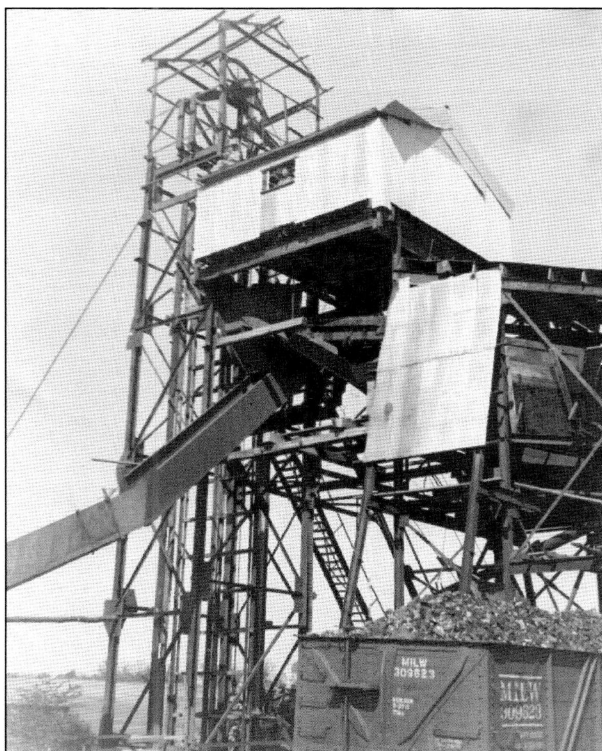

The New Block Coal Mine was located west of Streepyville. It operated from 1929 until 1967, becoming one of the longest-running mines in the county. The US Department of the Interior awarded the mine a "safety seal" in 1938 for its low lost-time accident rate. Only four mines in the United States received the award. New Block's safety record was second in the nation in 1938.

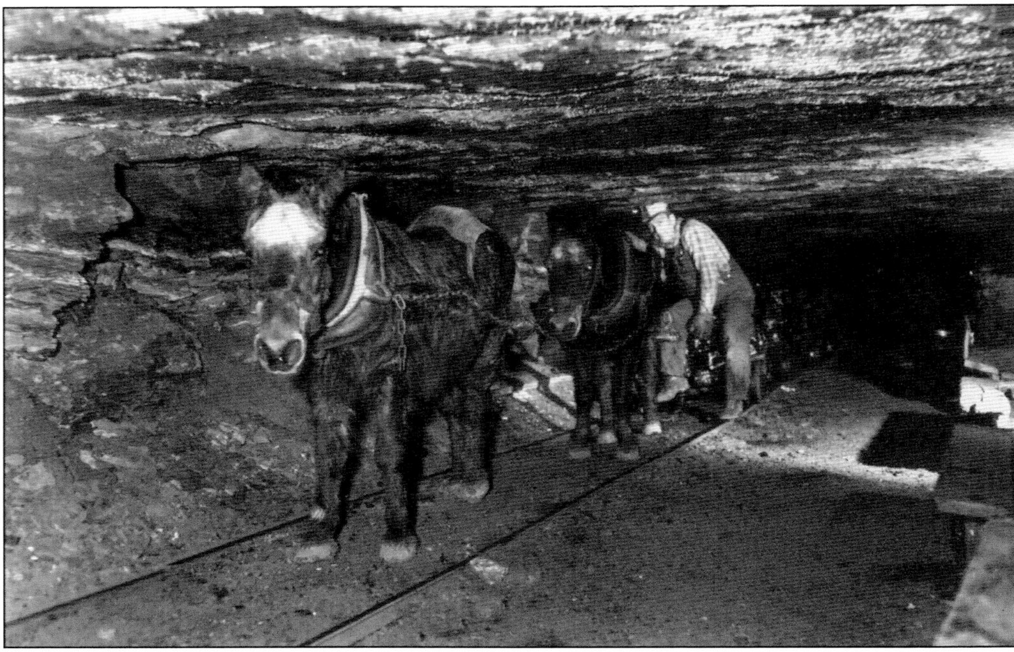

The New Gladstone Mine has earned the moniker "The Last Pony Mine in America." It closed in 1971 due to the reconstruction of Highway 2 west of Centerville. Iowa State University produced a documentary called *The Last Pony Mine*, filmed in the New Gladstone Mine. It is available for viewing at the Appanoose County Historical and Coal Mining Museum and also on the Internet.

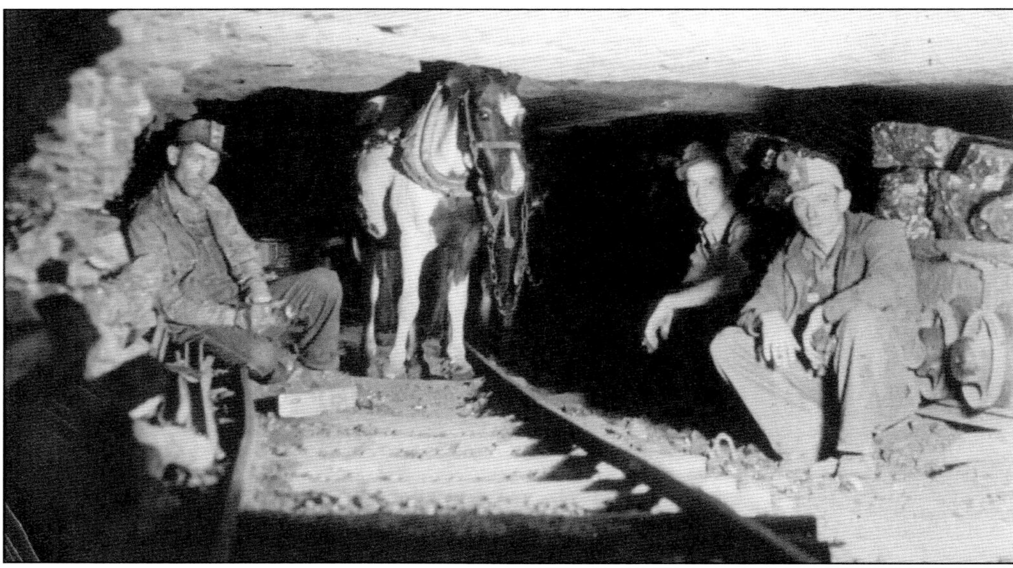

Ponies were used in many coal mines in Appanoose County. Known as "pit ponies," they were usually Shetland ponies with a good temperament. The tunnels in Appanoose County mines typically had a low clearance, but were high enough so that the ponies could maneuver. In slope mines, they hauled the loads out of the mines; in shaft mines, they sometimes rode the "cage" down the shaft and worked in the tunnels.

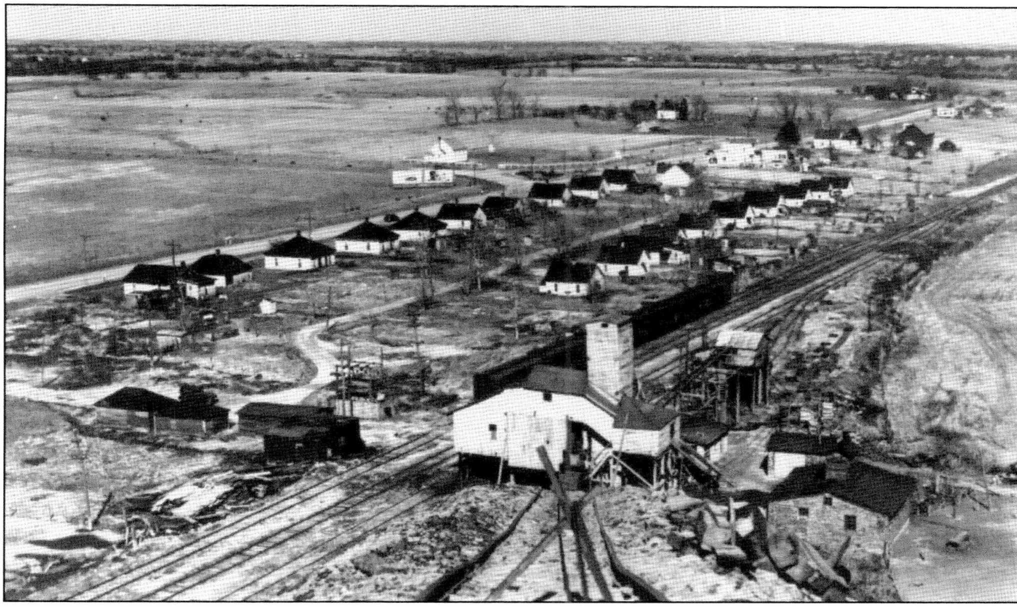

This was the town of Sunshine, just west of Centerville. Mining camps often had company stores, but Sunshine also had a gas station, a common well, a tavern, and a school. The Sunshine Coal Company was a large enterprise, with four mines that covered a total of almost 1,000 acres. This photograph was taken from atop the "slag pile." (Courtesy of Photography by the Browns.)

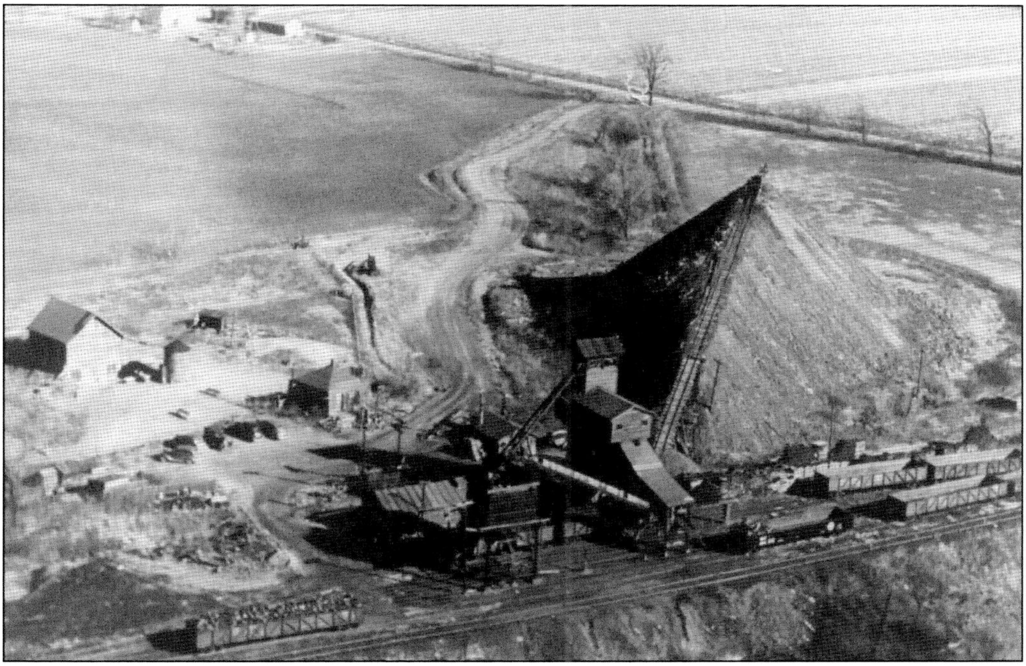

The Old King Coal Company was just west of Sunshine Mine No. 1. The slag pile is the pointed hill built of the waste products from the mining process, usually dirt and clay mixed with coal. These piles could spontaneously combust from the heat that was produced within. If the slag pile burned, it became shale, the red rock used as a cheap alternative to gravel on county roads.

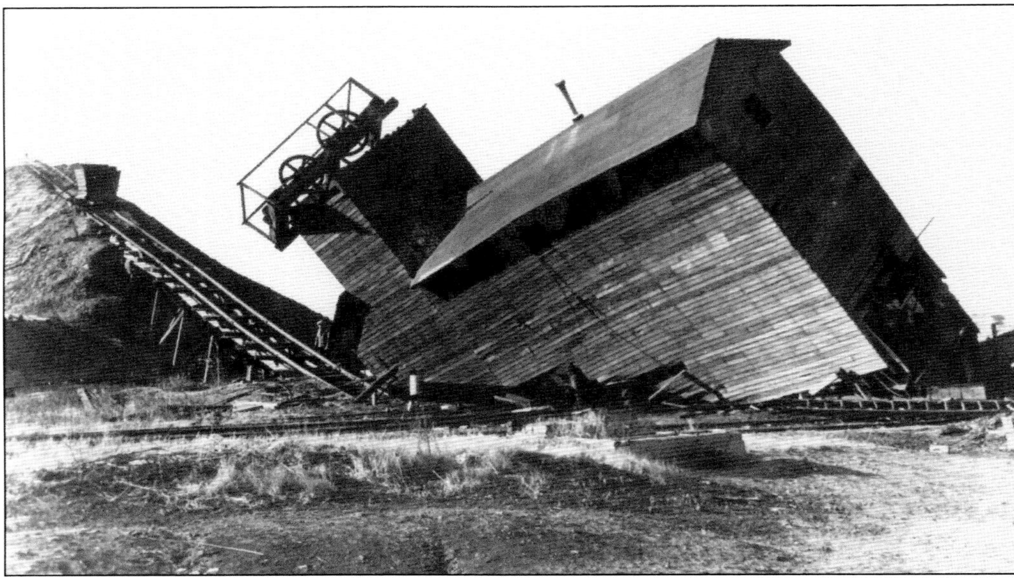

There were many mining injuries, deaths, and disasters. In the beginning, lack of union representation meant extremely unsafe conditions. Collapsing tunnels, black damps, unsafe mechanical devices, even nasty pit ponies, all caused injury and death in the coal mines. Sometimes the mine itself was destroyed by fire or collapse, as in this photograph of the Midway Mine, also known as McConville Mine No. 2, located northwest of Centerville.

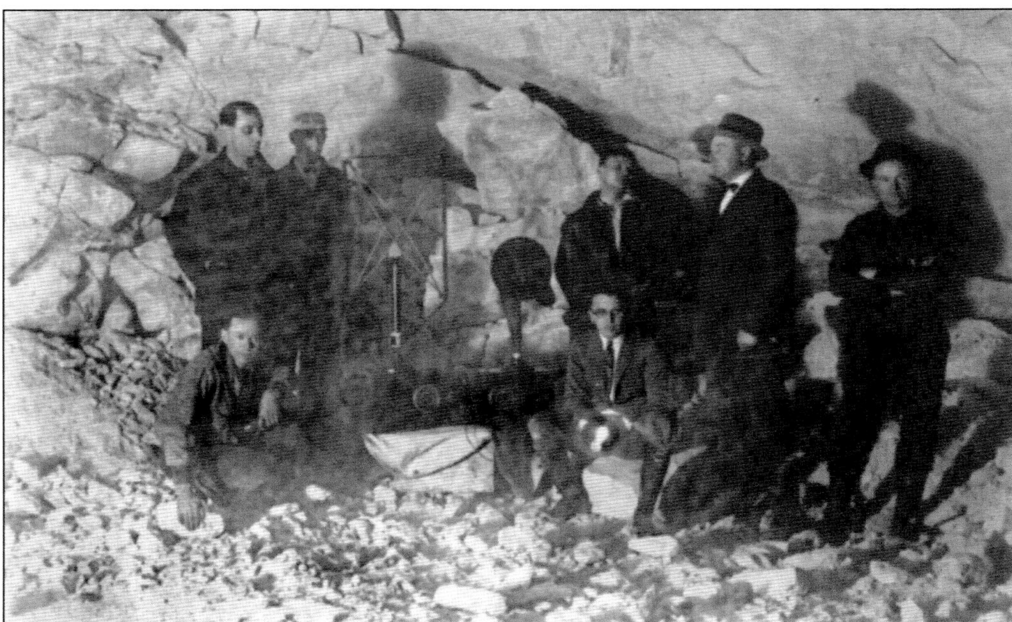

Another mining enterprise in Appanoose County was the gypsum mine that operated from 1912 until 1930. It was discovered within the same boundaries of the Scandinavian Coal Mine, just south of Garfield Street. However, the gypsum was much deeper, 550 feet down, whereas the coal was only 100 feet deep. It was closed after only 18 years due to excessive water from an underground stream.

Seven

TROLLEY TRACKS

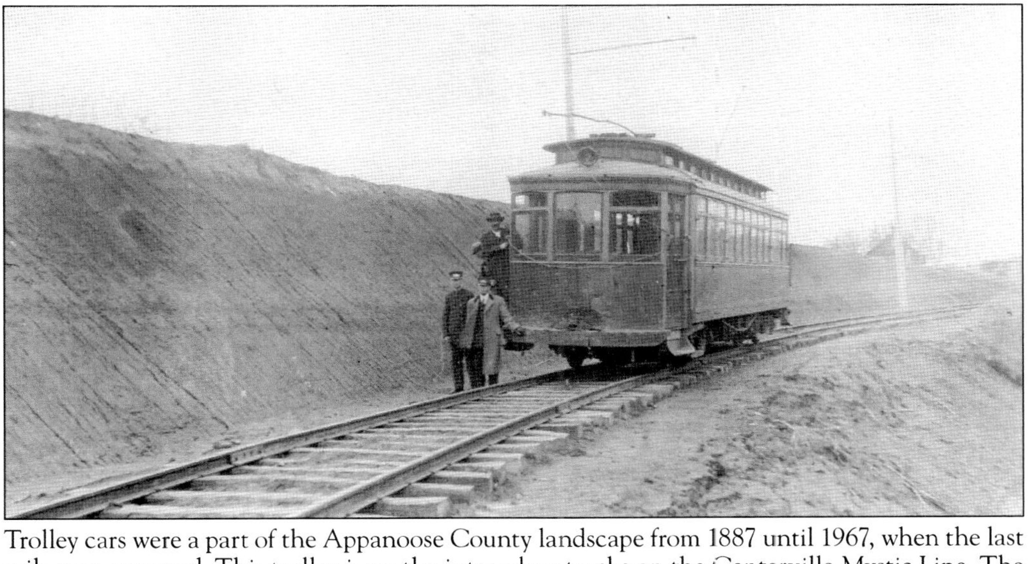

Trolley cars were a part of the Appanoose County landscape from 1887 until 1967, when the last rails were removed. This trolley is on the interurban tracks on the Centerville-Mystic Line. The freshly graded slope indicates that it was early in the life of the interurban system, around 1910.

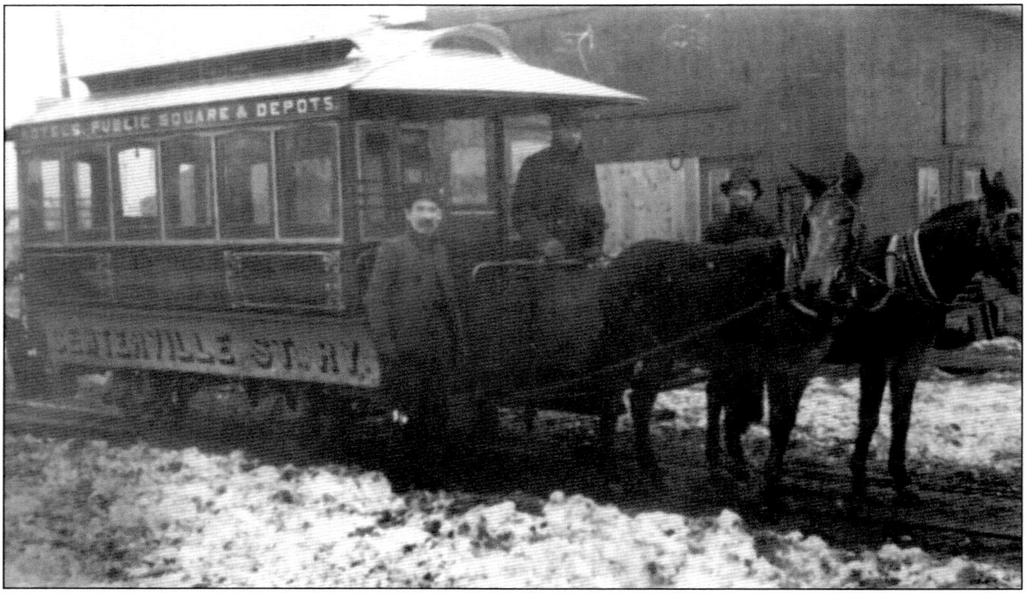

The first trolleys in Centerville were pulled by mules. This mule car system started in 1887 and carried passengers from the Square to the two train depots on the Levee. The line had two cars and 13 mules and was known as the People's Street Railway and, later, Centerville Street Railway when it changed hands in 1891. Pictured here are, from left to right, operators William Strickler, William Roby, and Charlie Cooper.

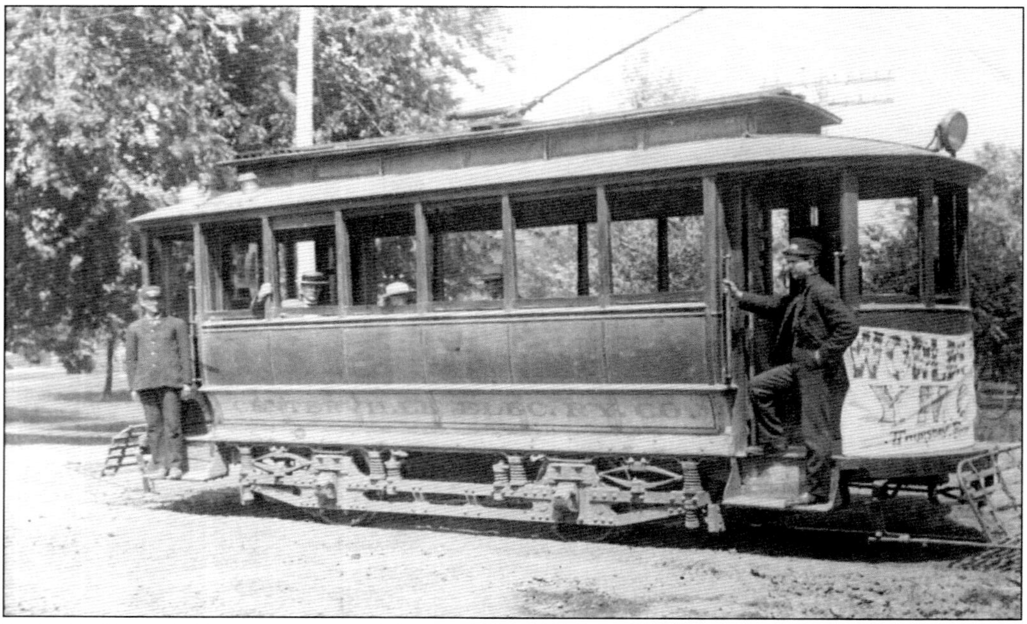

In 1902, Citizen's Electric Light and Gas purchased the mule car line and electrified it. The new line required heavier rail installed at standard gauge. An additional streetcar was added to the line. Pictured outside the trolley are operators Casey Swanson (left) and Ben Efaw. Frank Payne, president of Citizen's Electric, is seated in the trolley. The utility company would later be known as Centerville Light and Traction Company.

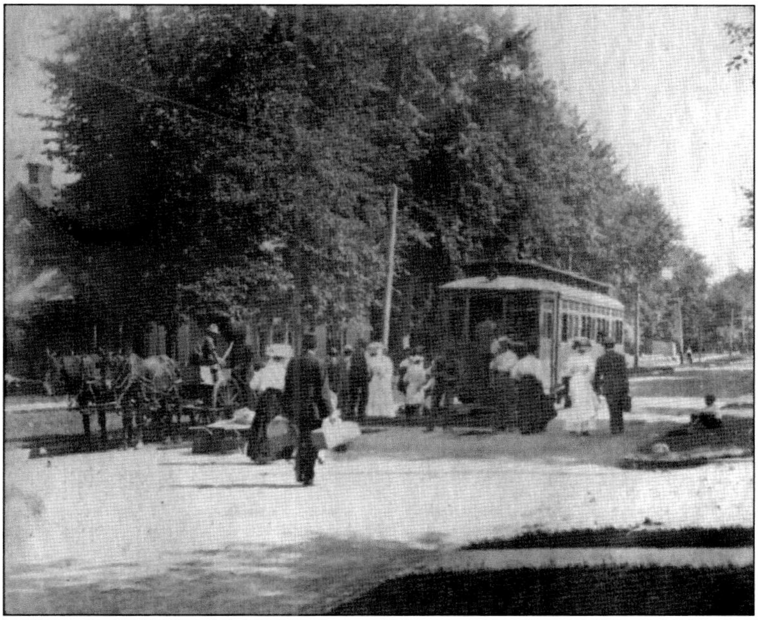

This streetcar stop on Drake Avenue is busy with commuters. The trolley route ran from the depot north to Walsh Street, where it turned west and continued to South Sixteenth Street, turning north to pass Garfield School. It then went west on Sheridan Avenue until meeting with Drake Avenue, which took it all the way to Maple Street. The trolley traveled to Main Street, then north on Main to enter the Square.

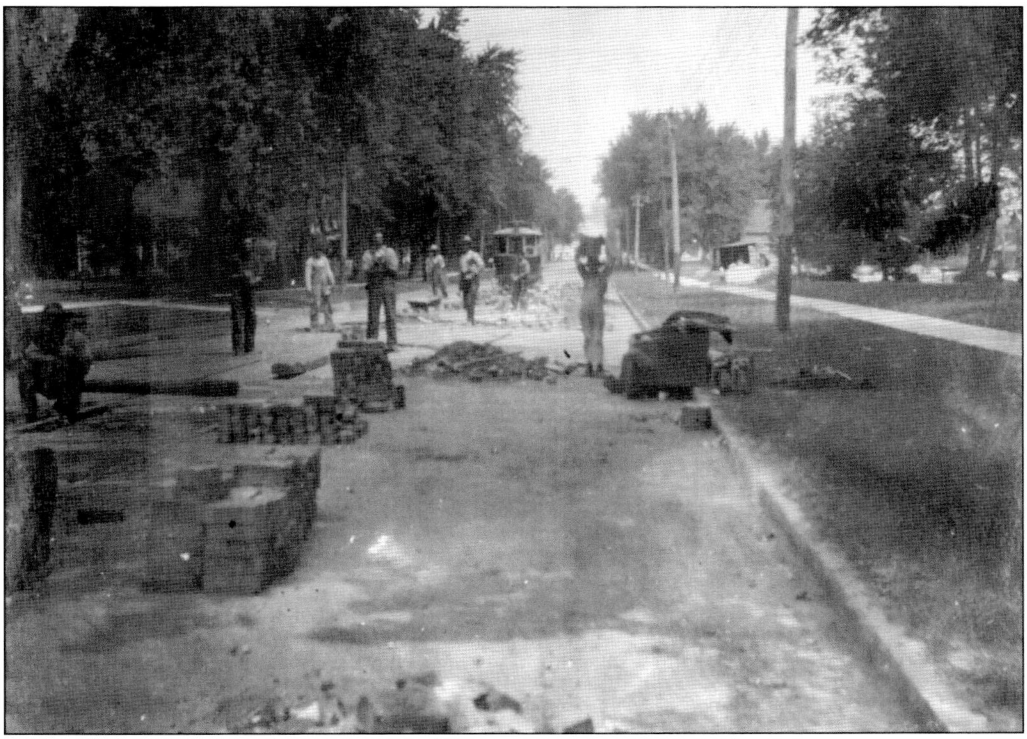

The first decade of the 20th century saw dramatic improvements in Centerville. Along with many of the architectural masterpieces that were built during this period, including the courthouse, Drake Library, and the new post office, less obvious projects were bringing Centerville into the modern era. Sewer lines were installed and streets were paved with brick. Drake Avenue, shown here with a streetcar in the background, was paved with brick in 1905.

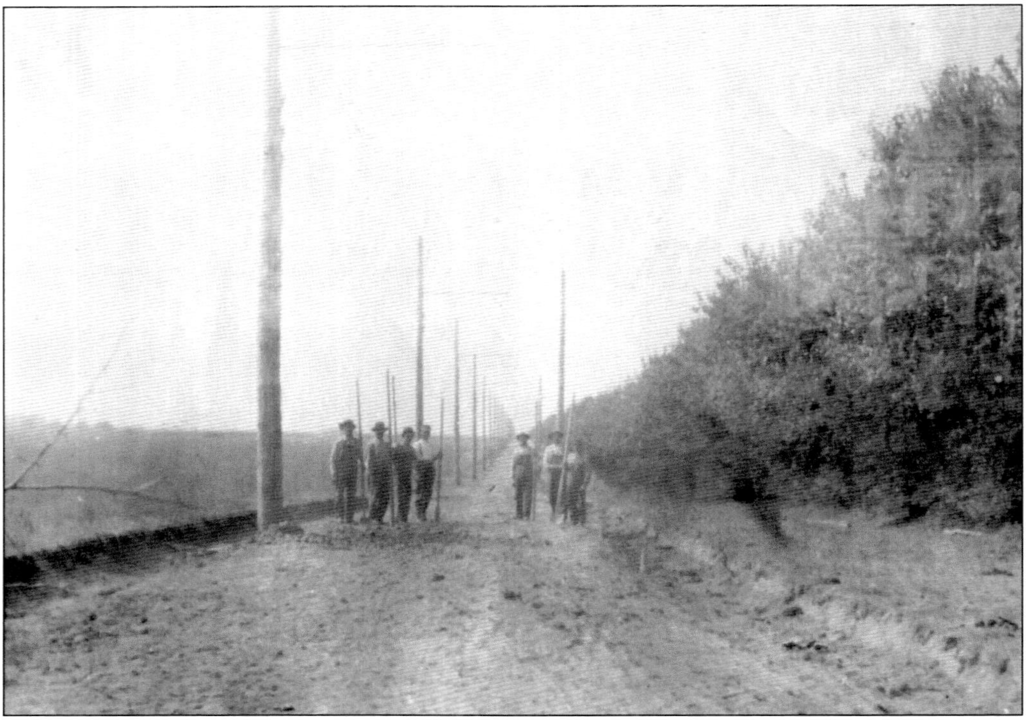

In 1909, the idea of an interurban system was put before the community, pushed with great eloquence, and successfully funded. Construction of the interurban line to Mystic began later that year. It was a major undertaking, including obtaining right-of-ways, building up the rail beds, and installing the rails and the electrical system to operate the interurban cars. Above, the poles are being set beside the track. Below, the electrical cables are being prepared.

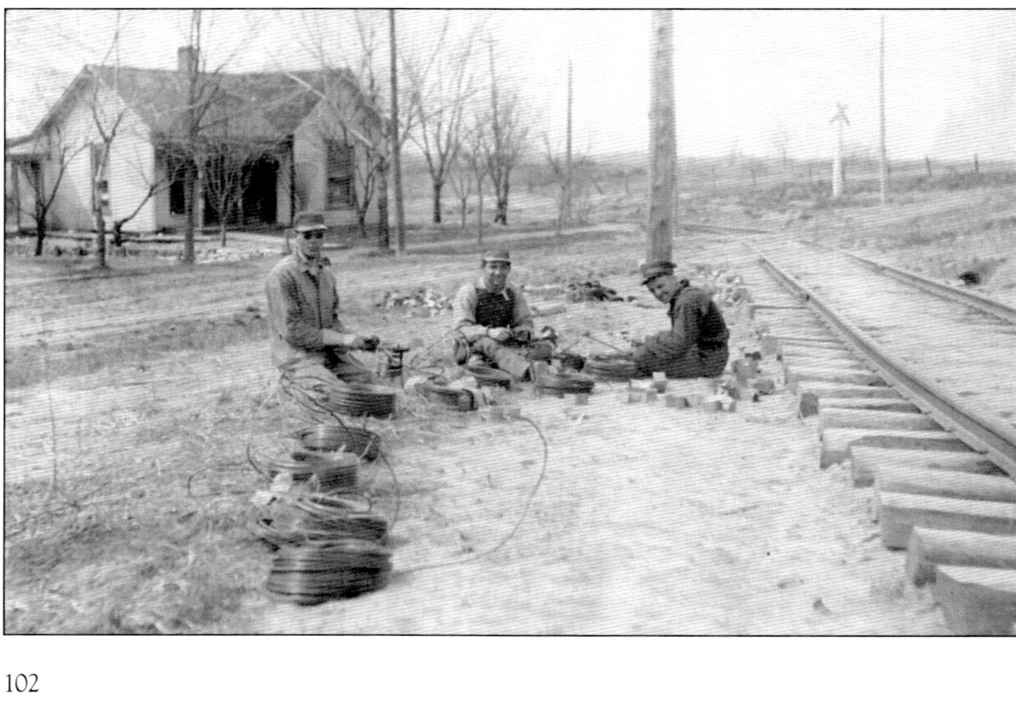

The tall ladder contraption seen here was used to install the overhead cable along the trolley system. The poles on top of the trolleys, one on each end, were spring-loaded. When released, they were guided to connect with the cable. This provided the current needed to operate the trolleys.

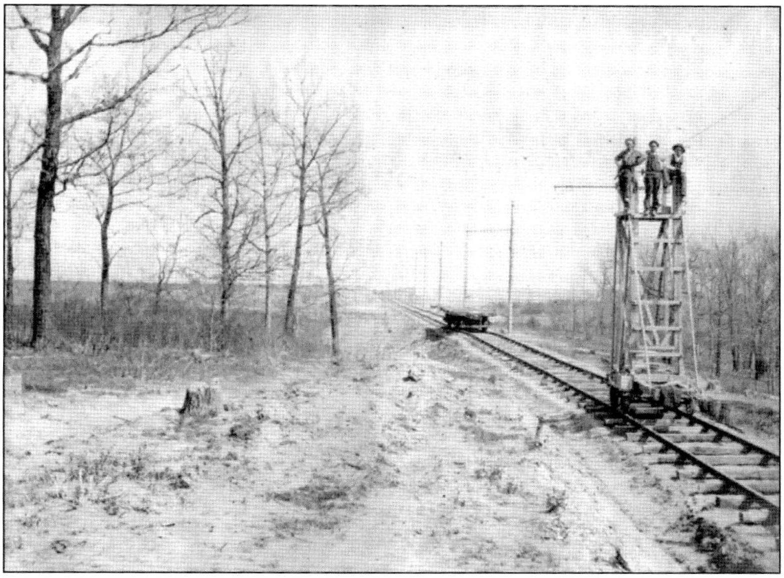

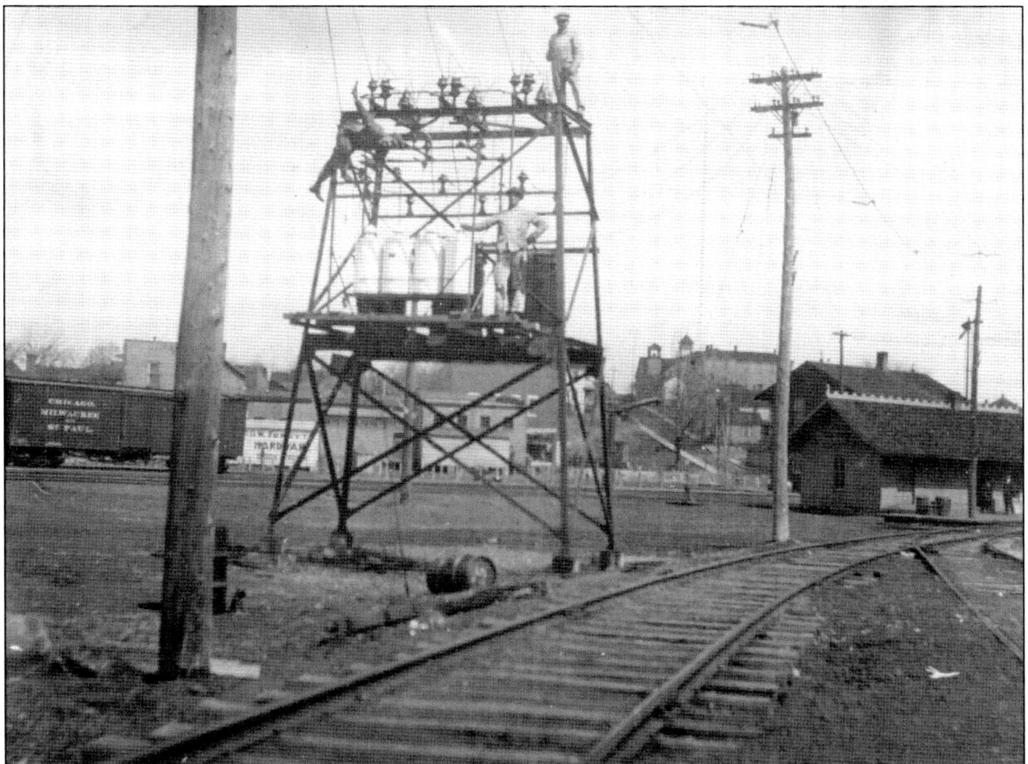

Workers in Mystic stand on a transformer that sits directly next to the interurban tracks. The Centerville to Mystic Interurban began operation in 1910. It operated from the Square northward, toward the country club. Once electricity was established to Mystic for interurban service, the power was also offered to coal mines along the line and to Mystic residents.

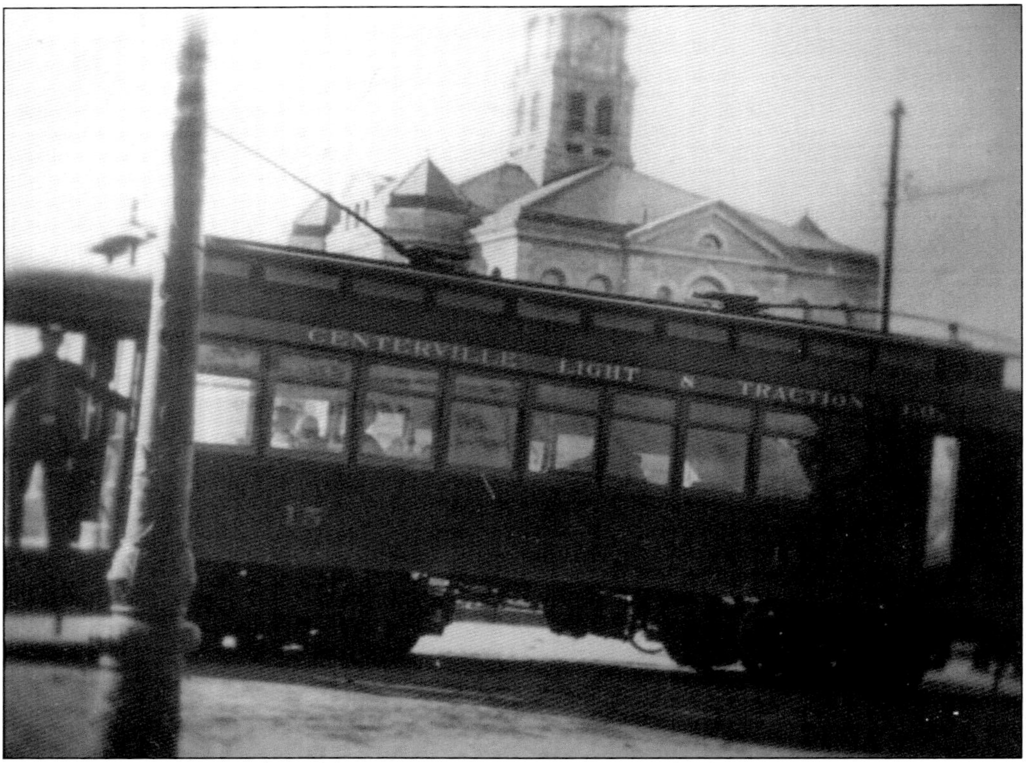

One of the first cars purchased for service to Mystic was Car 15, built by the McGuire-Cummings Company. As soon as it began operation, the Mystic Line was busy carrying shoppers to Mystic or Centerville, Mystic students to school in Centerville, and coal miners to work. A car departed hourly, and the trip would usually take 25 minutes.

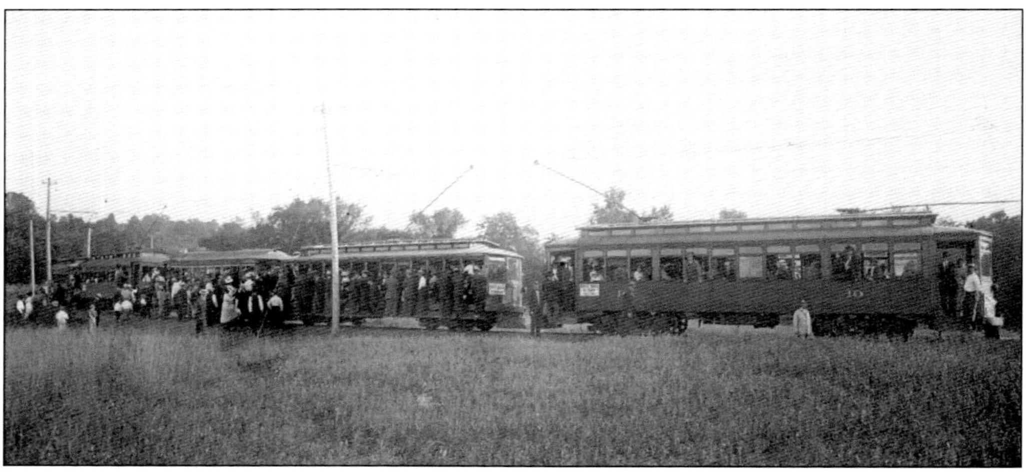

The Mystic Line was so busy that it eventually had at least five cars in service. There were stops along the line for the ballpark, the country club, and Glen Hagen Park. Here, five cars unload passengers for a ball game at the baseball field, which was located in the vicinity of the current county fairgrounds.

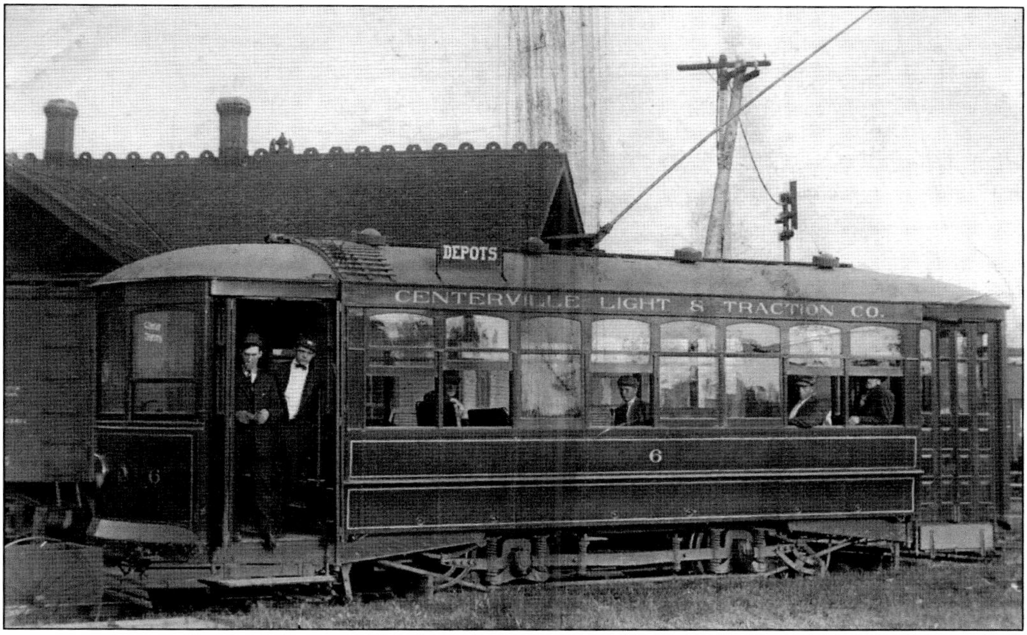

Here is Car 6 in front of the Mystic interurban depot. Along the Mystic Line, there were interurban stops at Glen Hagen Park, the Haydite Plant, the Midway Mine, Sterling Mine No. 2 and No. 3, Sunshine Mine No. 2, Masters, and Brazil. The stop for the Haydite Plant was established only in the later years, after passenger service had been discontinued. Freight, however, was still hauled over the line.

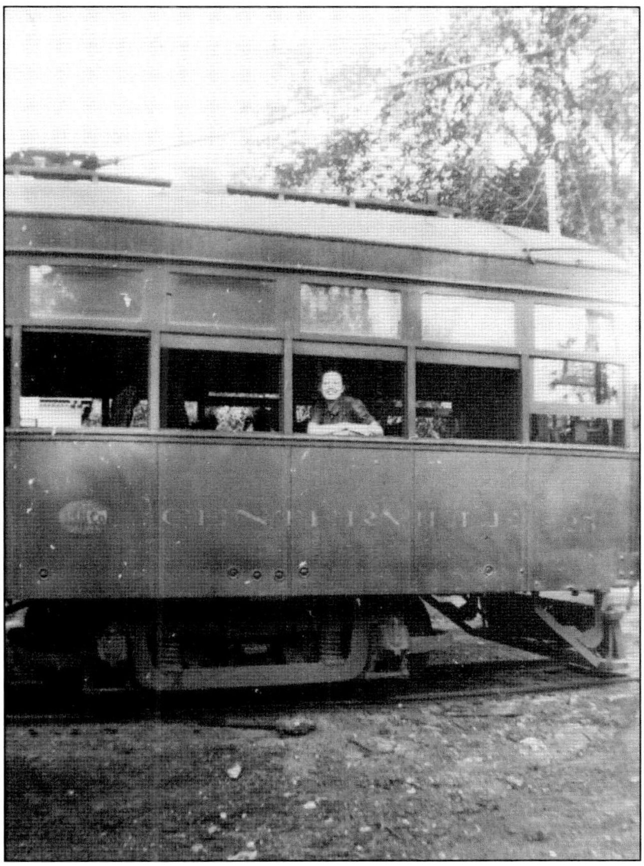

Helen Carlson sits in Car 25 prior to departure to an Iowa Southern Utilities Company picnic at Glen Hagen Park in 1937. Passenger service had been discontinued in 1933, but, being the owner of the railway and the park, ISU still used the trolley for company outings. (Courtesy of Helen Carlson.)

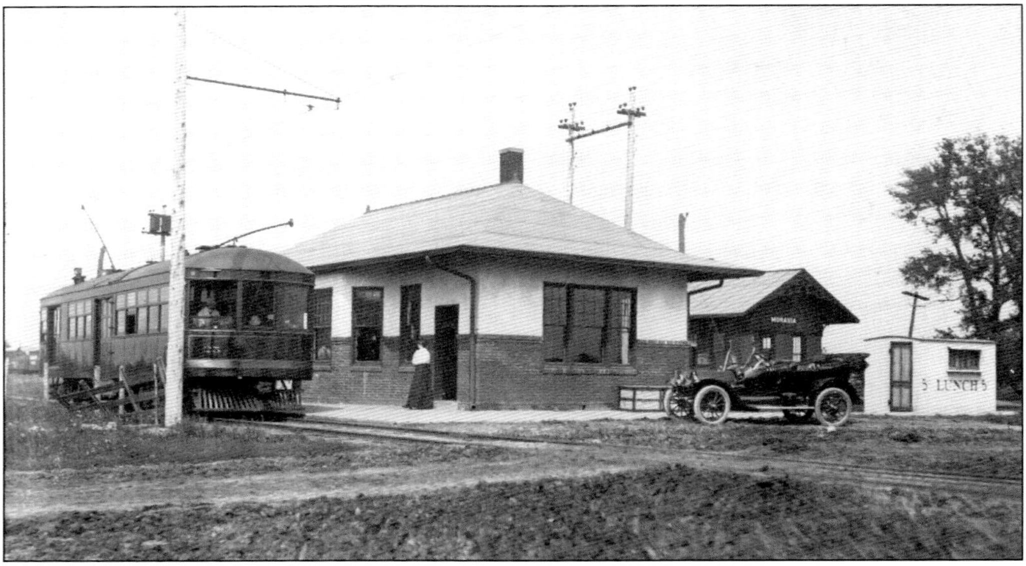

In 1914, Frank Payne and D.C. Bradley purchased the conventional rail service between Centerville and Albia, then known as the Southern Iowa Traction Company. They electrified it and connected it to the Centerville Light and Traction Company's Mystic Line just east of the Appanoose Country Club and called it the Centerville Albia & Southern Railway. The interurban depot in Moravia is shown here.

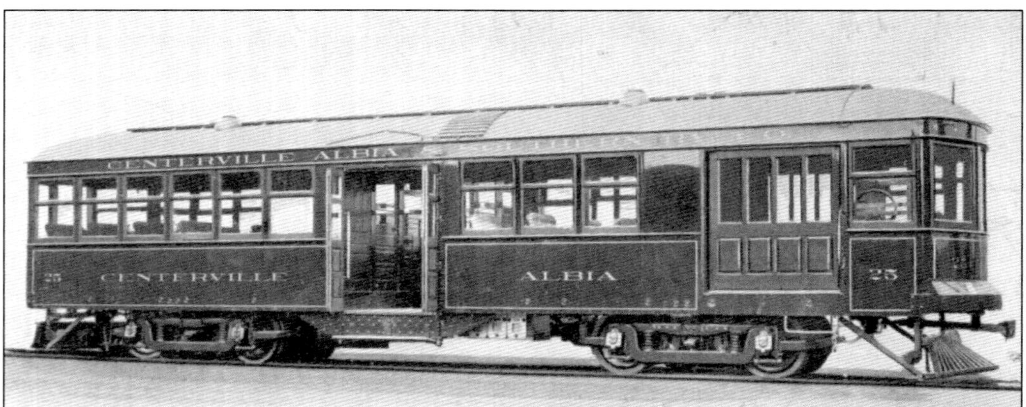

For the new line, the Centerville Albia & Southern purchased two cars. Made by the American Car Company, these cars were much faster, running up to 50 miles per hour. They had three separate compartments: one for nonsmokers, or a "ladies" compartment; a smoking compartment; and a baggage compartment.

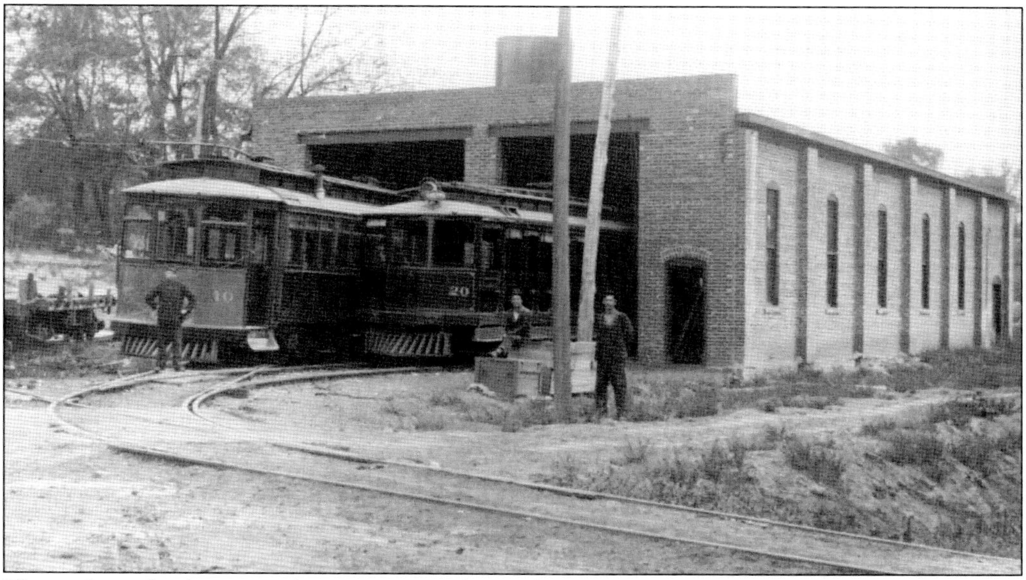

The carbarn for the interurban system was located on Madison Street, north of the power plant. The city streetcars were stored in a different carbarn, on South Sixteenth Street. The streetcar system was a separate entity from the interurban system. Streetcars ran in the city streets, connecting points within the city. The interurban connected towns using larger, faster cars and depots at points in between.

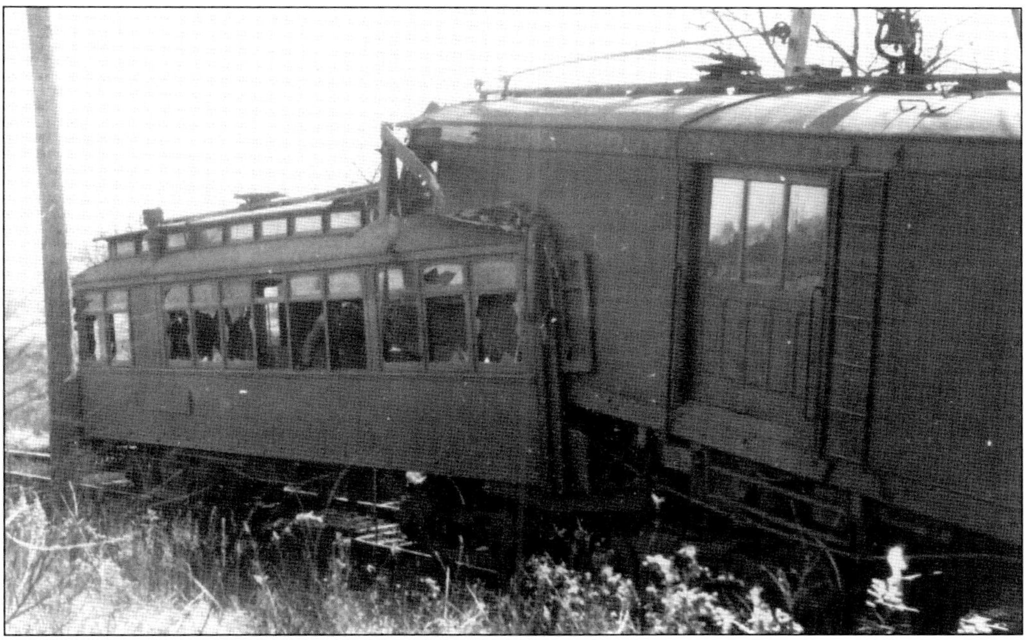

The trolleys, both city streetcars and interurbans, had their share of trouble. This collision occurred on November 18, 1932, when a freight car going toward Centerville collided with a westbound interurban passenger car. Four people were injured. During this time, passenger service had been declining steadily as more automobiles hit the road. Interurban passenger service to both Mystic and Albia was discontinued on July 1, 1933.

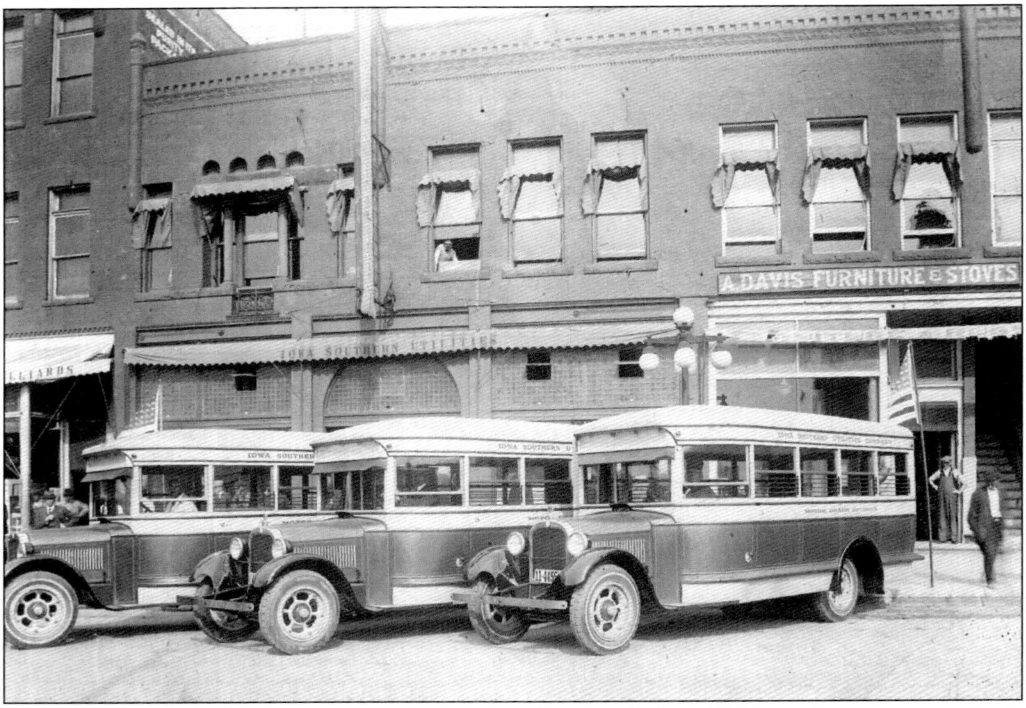

Centerville's city streetcar service was discontinued on April 25, 1925. The utility company, which by this time had become the Iowa Southern Utilities Company, replaced the streetcar line with three buses, shown above. The buses were never a profitable venture, however, and ridership declined steadily. The Great Depression made it even worse. Bus service ended on May 31, 1931. Pictured below is the maintenance facility for the bus line.

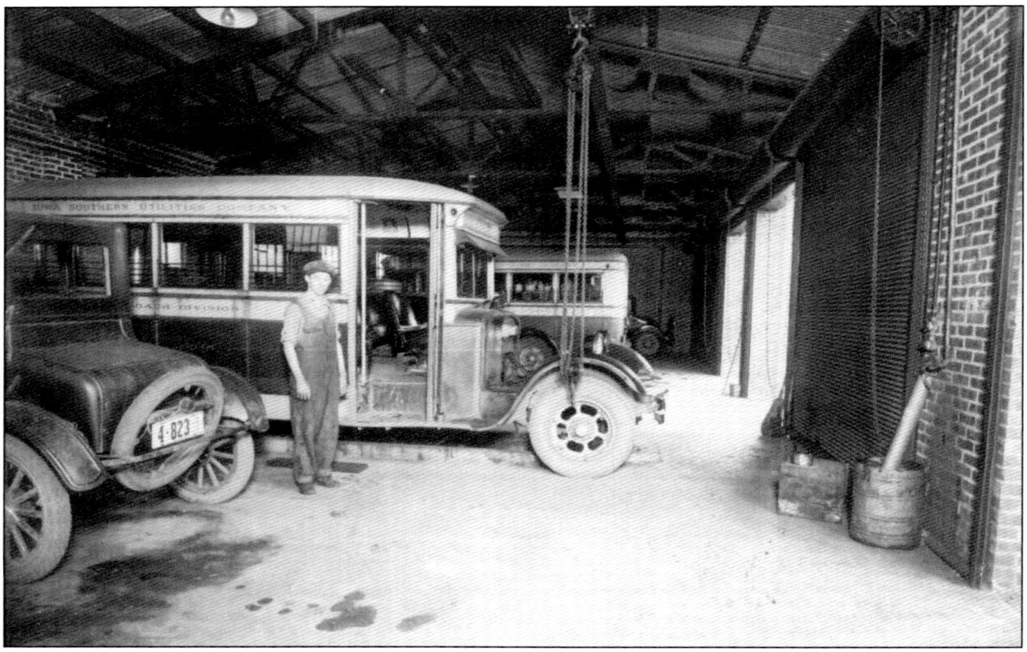

Freight service continued on the interurban line to service the businesses along the route, mostly coal mines. As the tracks wore down, part of the Mystic Line was abandoned in 1944. In 1948, the line from Moravia to Albia was also abandoned. As coal mines along the Mystic line closed, so did the rail service. The line ran to the Haydite plant until the 1960s. About that same time, a feeling of nostalgia for the old electric railways was blossoming. From 1955 until 1966, the rail fan group, the Iowa Railway Historical Museum, held excursions known as "fan trips" on what was left of the railway. One of the flyers for a fan trip is shown at right. The photograph below shows Car 9 on the tracks near a coal mine.

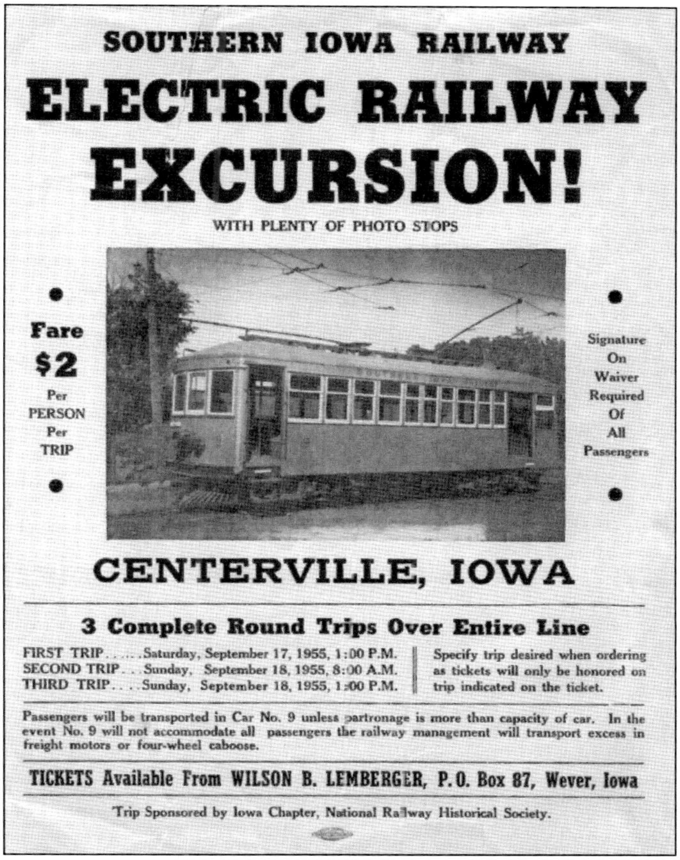

SOUTHERN IOWA RAILWAY

ELECTRIC RAILWAY EXCURSION!

WITH PLENTY OF PHOTO STOPS

Fare $2 Per PERSON Per TRIP

Signature On Waiver Required Of All Passengers

CENTERVILLE, IOWA

3 Complete Round Trips Over Entire Line

FIRST TRIP. . . . . Saturday, September 17, 1955, 1:00 P.M.
SECOND TRIP. . . Sunday, September 18, 1955, 8:00 A.M.
THIRD TRIP. . . . Sunday, September 18, 1955, 1:00 P.M.

Specify trip desired when ordering as tickets will only be honored on trip indicated on the ticket.

Passengers will be transported in Car No. 9 unless partronage is more than capacity of car. In the event No. 9 will not accommodate all passengers the railway management will transport excess in freight motors or four-wheel caboose.

TICKETS Available From WILSON B. LEMBERGER, P. O. Box 87, Wever, Iowa

Trip Sponsored by Iowa Chapter, National Railway Historical Society.

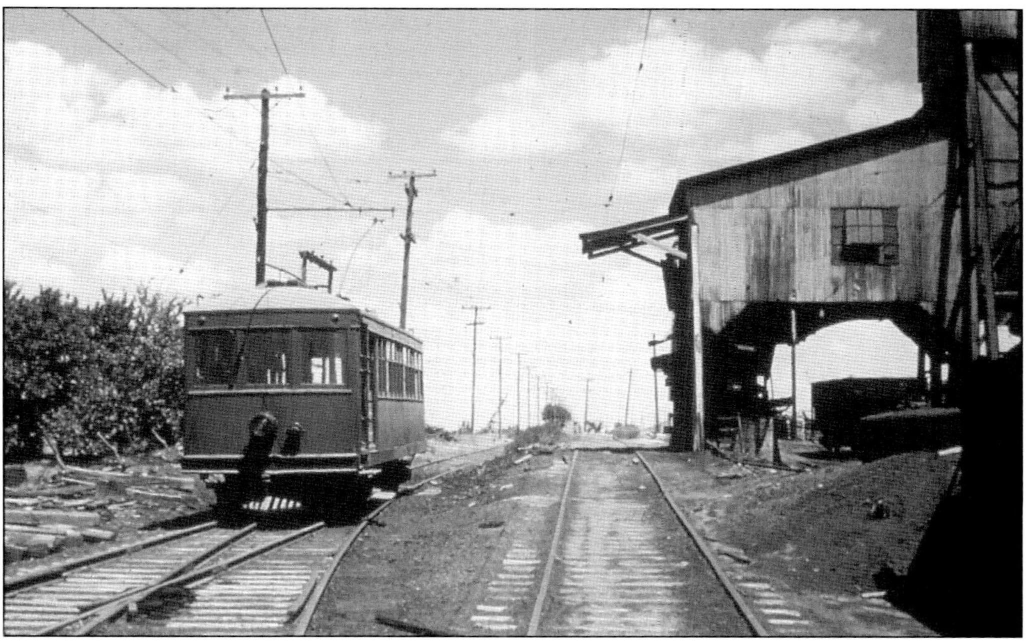

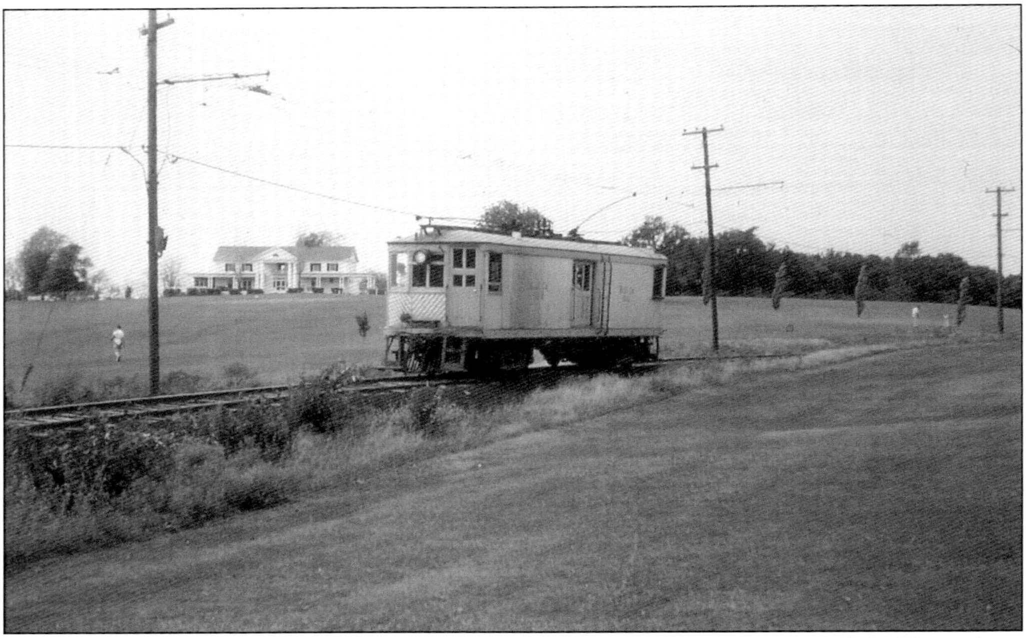

Here, the interurban line crosses the golf course at the Appanoose Country Club. The railway was established in this area before the golf course was laid out. This photograph was taken during one of the railway museum's excursions.

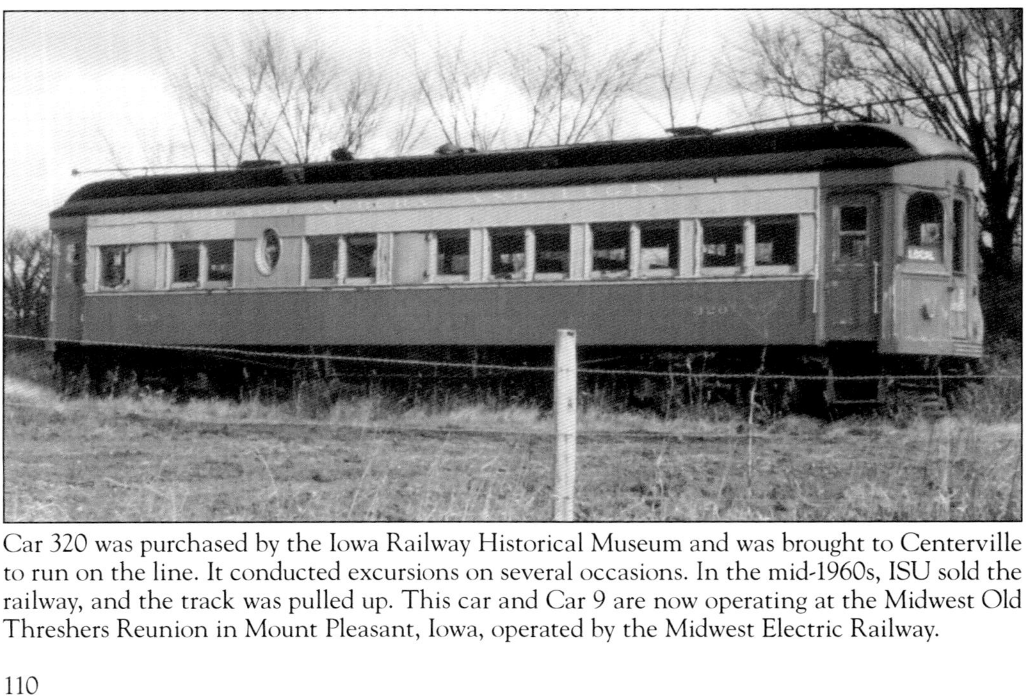

Car 320 was purchased by the Iowa Railway Historical Museum and was brought to Centerville to run on the line. It conducted excursions on several occasions. In the mid-1960s, ISU sold the railway, and the track was pulled up. This car and Car 9 are now operating at the Midwest Old Threshers Reunion in Mount Pleasant, Iowa, operated by the Midwest Electric Railway.

Eight

Coming Together

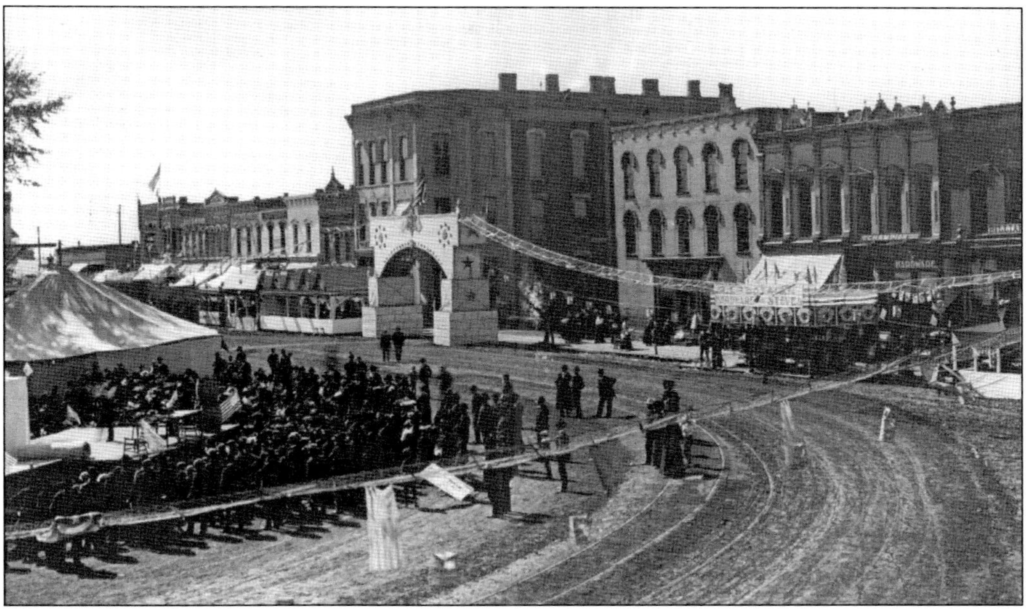

In September 1899, Centerville's weeklong street fair was an extravaganza like no other before it. Banners connected arches, built on each side of the Square, to obelisks at each corner. Merchants showcased their wares in booths in front of their businesses. Stages on every corner of the courtyard presented speakers, musicians, and vaudeville acts. Parades were held each day and special events each night. William Jennings Bryan and Buffalo Bill were highlights of the fair.

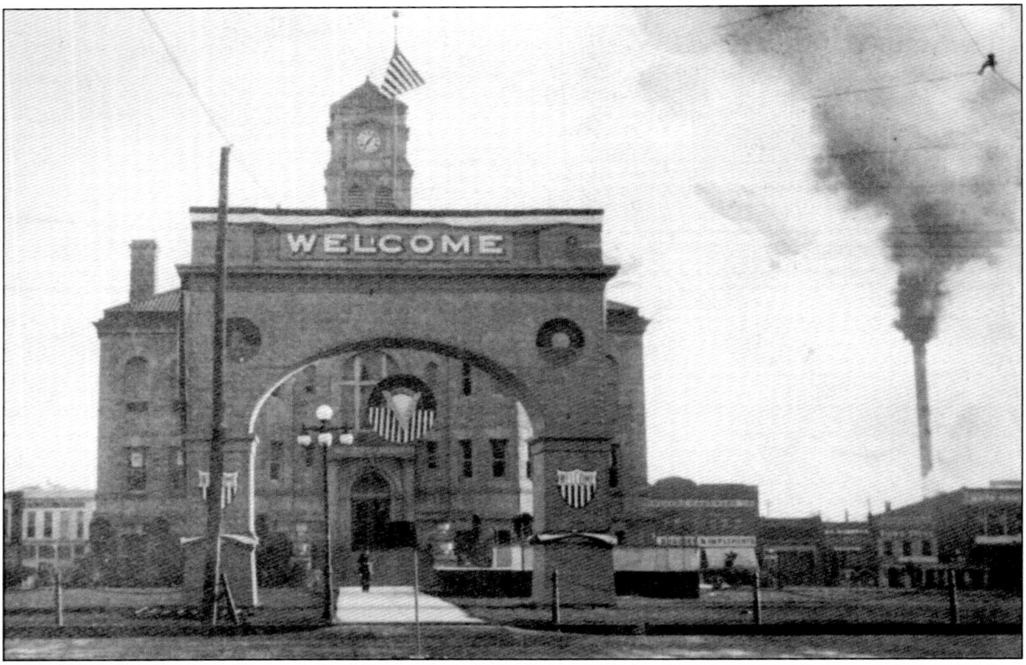

In May 1919, this Victory Arch, also called the Liberty Arch, was constructed to welcome home Appanoose County's Company D, 168th Regiment, Rainbow Division from World War I. Built over the south walk of the courthouse lawn, the arch was composed of a wooden frame covered with canvas and weighted with sand. It measured 34 feet high and 38 feet wide. After eight months of community use, the arch was sold for $50 and was removed in January 1920.

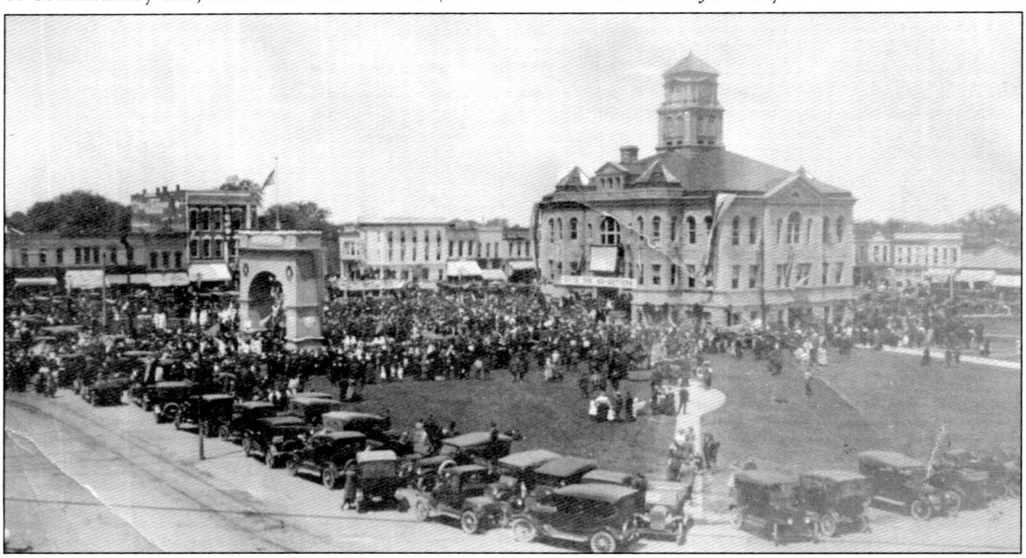

Thousands of people celebrated the homecoming of Company D on May 17, 1919. When the boys arrived, the city was filled with the roar of anvils, firecrackers, the fire whistle, and the ringing of bells. The courthouse and the Victory Arch were draped with hundreds of yards of bunting, myriad lights, and rainbow colors. Store windows featured rainbows and posters of Company D's commander, Maj. Glenn C. Haynes.

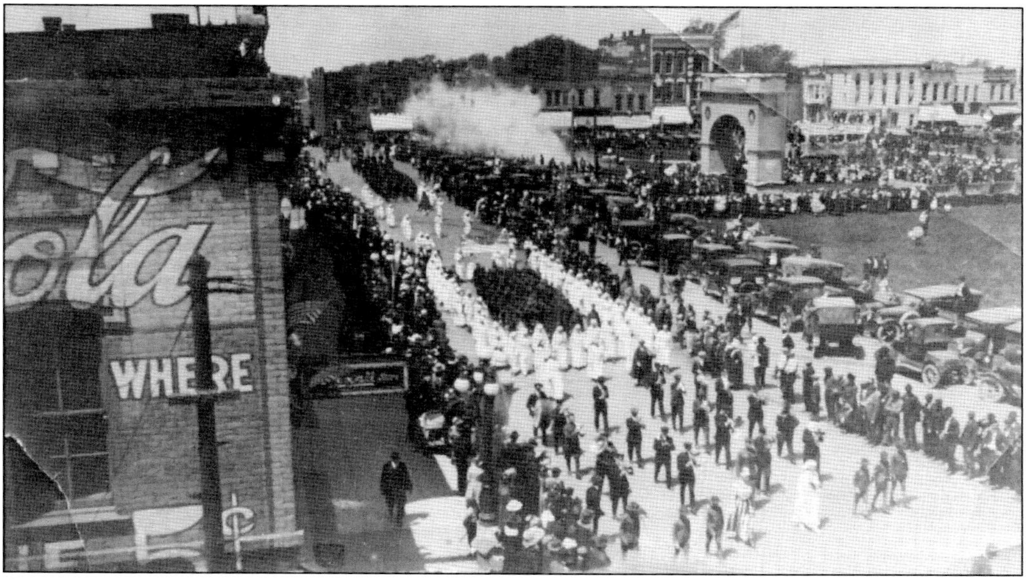

Company D's homecoming parade in May 1919 started with a police unit, followed by Miss Liberty and Miss Peace escorted by Boy Scouts. A Centerville band marched, followed by Red Cross ladies forming a large rectangle around the boys of Company D. Red Cross officers followed the rectangle, and a formation of uniformed soldiers in other World War I companies came next.

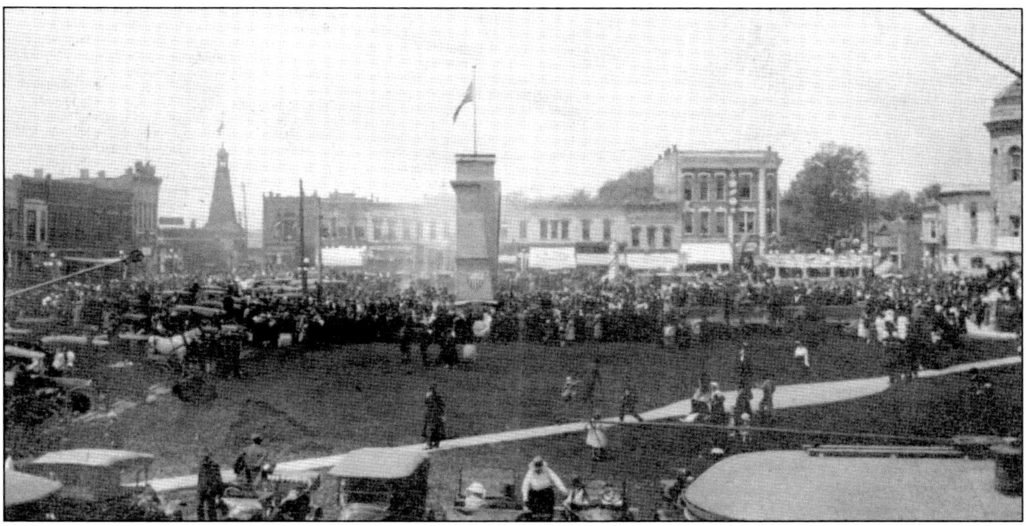

Although the enthusiasm of the crowd for the 1919 homecoming of Company D was overwhelming, many onlookers were in tears. Within Company D, 21 men had died in the fighting, and many were still recovering from wounds. After parading around the Square, the battle-hardened remnant of Company D ended at the reviewing stand north of the Victory Arch. Here, many soldiers reunited with relatives after a separation of almost two years.

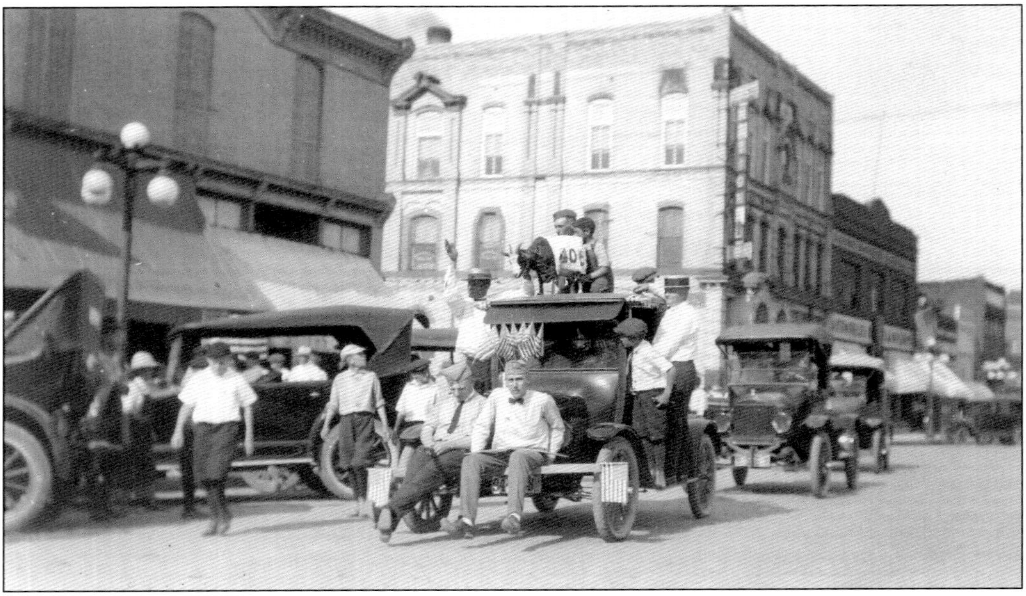

The 40 & 8 Parade on June 14, 1922, entertained the city while it celebrated the initiation of 53 members into a local charter *voiture* ("boxcar" in French). The event, a combination of slapstick comedy and patriotism, reminded the veterans of traveling in boxcars in France. The boxcars, labeled "40 Hommes et 8 Chevaux," could carry 40 men or 8 horses, thus the name of the organization, La Société Des Quarante Hommes et Huit Chevaux. The initiates, World War I veterans and members of the American Legion, were hustled around the Square by 40 & 8 members from other cities who tossed torpedoes at their feet. Men clad in barrels, BVD's, and women's clothing marched around the Square. Other men, with their shirttails hanging out, went around on all fours, tied together with ropes.

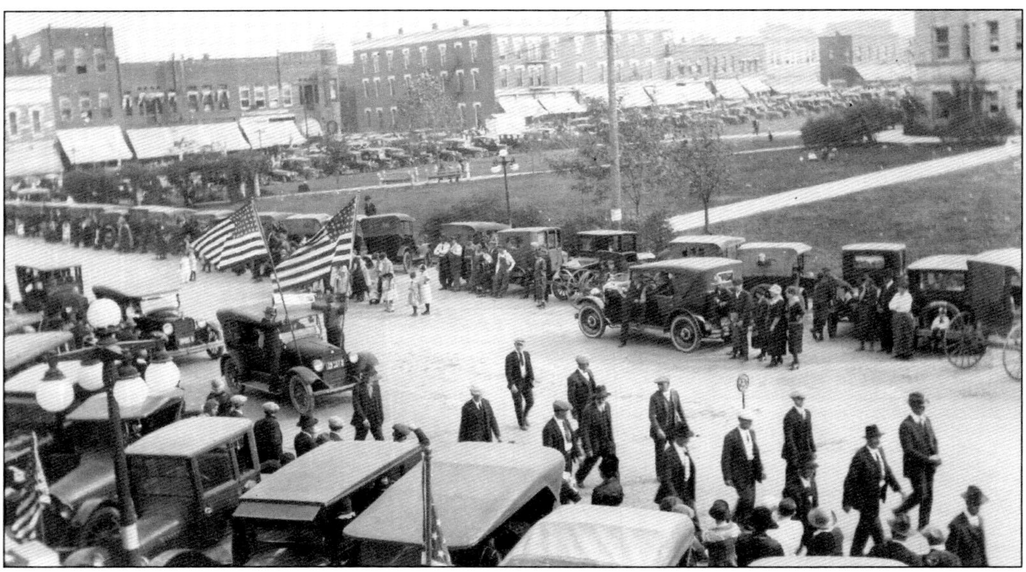

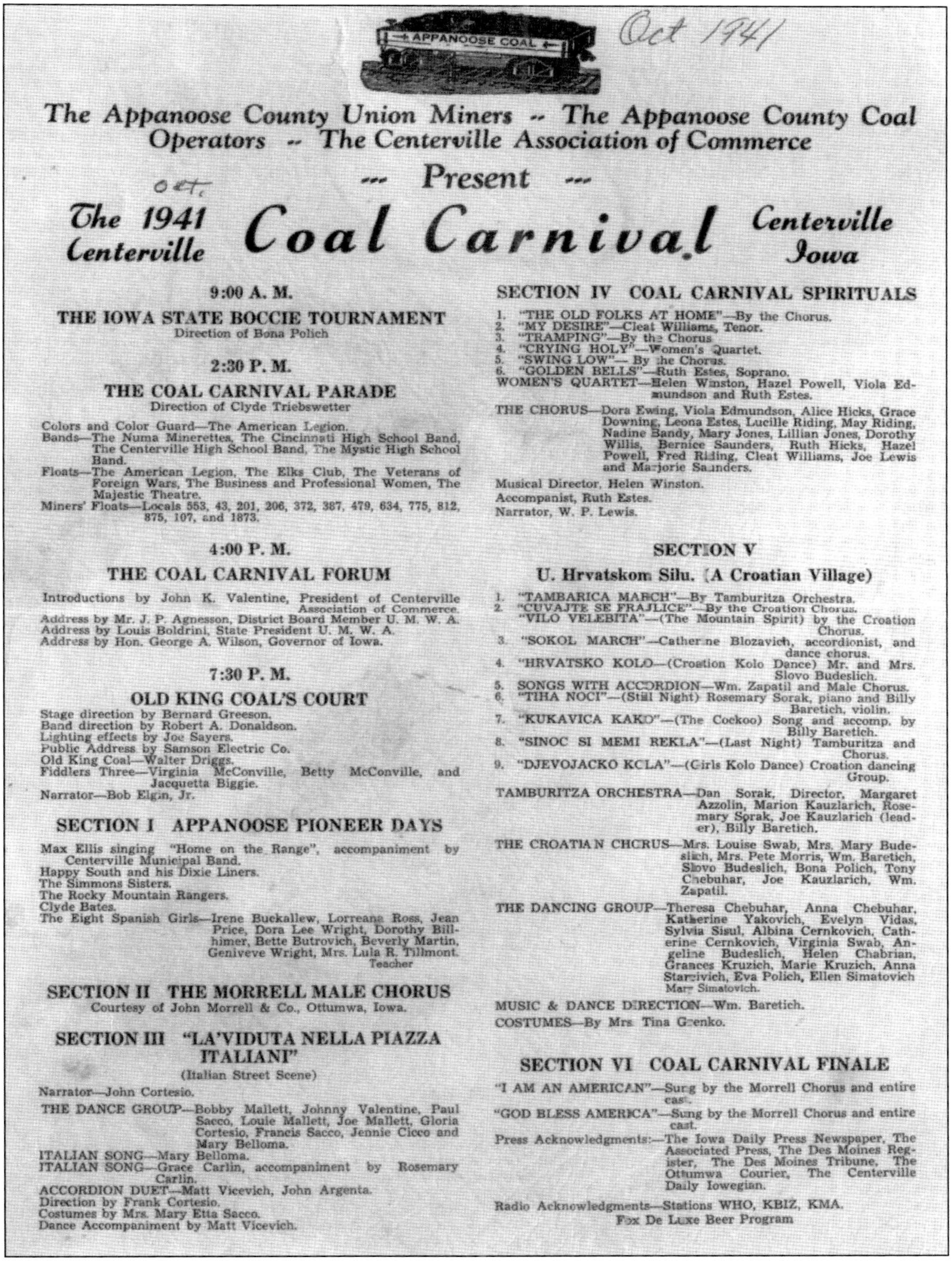

APPANOOSE COAL

Oct 1941

The Appanoose County Union Miners -- The Appanoose County Coal Operators -- The Centerville Association of Commerce

--- Present ---

The 1941 Centerville **Coal Carnival** Centerville Iowa

9:00 A. M.

THE IOWA STATE BOCCIE TOURNAMENT
Direction of Bona Polich

2:30 P. M.

THE COAL CARNIVAL PARADE
Direction of Clyde Triebswetter

Colors and Color Guard—The American Legion.
Bands—The Numa Minerettes, The Cincinnati High School Band, The Centerville High School Band, The Mystic High School Band.
Floats—The American Legion, The Elks Club, The Veterans of Foreign Wars, The Business and Professional Women, The Majestic Theatre.
Miners' Floats—Locals 553, 43, 201, 206, 372, 387, 479, 634, 775, 812, 875, 107, and 1873.

4:00 P. M.

THE COAL CARNIVAL FORUM

Introductions by John K. Valentine, President of Centerville Association of Commerce.
Address by Mr. J. P. Agnesson, District Board Member U. M. W. A.
Address by Louis Boldrini, State President U. M. W. A.
Address by Hon. George A. Wilson, Governor of Iowa.

7:30 P. M.

OLD KING COAL'S COURT
Stage direction by Bernard Greeson.
Band direction by Robert A. Donaldson.
Lighting effects by Joe Sayers.
Public Address by Samson Electric Co.
Old King Coal—Walter Driggs.
Fiddlers Three—Virginia McConville, Betty McConville, and Jacquetta Biggie.
Narrator—Bob Elgin, Jr.

SECTION I APPANOOSE PIONEER DAYS

Max Ellis singing "Home on the Range", accompaniment by Centerville Municipal Band.
Happy South and his Dixie Liners.
The Simmons Sisters.
The Rocky Mountain Rangers.
Clyde Bates.
The Eight Spanish Girls—Irene Buckallew, Lorreana Ross, Jean Price, Dora Lee Wright, Dorothy Billhimer, Bette Butrovich, Beverly Martin, Geniveve Wright, Mrs. Lula R. Tillmont, Teacher

SECTION II THE MORRELL MALE CHORUS
Courtesy of John Morrell & Co., Ottumwa, Iowa.

SECTION III "LA'VIDUTA NELLA PIAZZA ITALIANI"
(Italian Street Scene)

Narrator—John Cortesio.
THE DANCE GROUP—Bobby Mallett, Johnny Valentine, Paul Sacco, Louie Mallett, Joe Mallett, Gloria Cortesio, Francis Sacco, Jennie Cicco and Mary Belloma.
ITALIAN SONG—Mary Belloma.
ITALIAN SONG—Grace Carlin, accompaniment by Rosemary Carlin.
ACCORDION DUET—Matt Vicevich, John Argenta.
Direction by Frank Cortesio.
Costumes by Mrs. Mary Etta Sacco.
Dance Accompaniment by Matt Vicevich.

SECTION IV COAL CARNIVAL SPIRITUALS

1. "THE OLD FOLKS AT HOME"—By the Chorus.
2. "MY DESIRE"—Cleat Williams, Tenor.
3. "TRAMPING"—By the Chorus
4. "CRYING HOLY"—Women's Quartet.
5. "SWING LOW"— By the Chorus.
6. "GOLDEN BELLS"—Ruth Estes, Soprano.

WOMEN'S QUARTET—Helen Winston, Hazel Powell, Viola Edmundson and Ruth Estes.

THE CHORUS—Dora Ewing, Viola Edmundson, Alice Hicks, Grace Downing, Leona Estes, Lucille Riding, May Riding, Nadine Bandy, Mary Jones, Lillian Jones, Dorothy Willis, Bernice Saunders, Ruth Hicks, Hazel Powell, Fred Riding, Cleat Williams, Joe Lewis and Marjorie Saunders.

Musical Director, Helen Winston.
Accompanist, Ruth Estes.
Narrator, W. P. Lewis.

SECTION V

U. Hrvatskom Silu. (A Croatian Village)

1. "TAMBARICA MARCH"—By Tamburitza Orchestra.
2. "CUVAJTE SE FRAJLICE"—By the Croation Chorus.
   "VILO VELEBITA"—(The Mountain Spirit) by the Croation Chorus.
3. "SOKOL MARCH"—Catherine Blozavich, accordionist, and dance chorus.
4. "HRVATSKO KOLO—(Croation Kolo Dance) Mr. and Mrs. Slovo Budeslich.
5. SONGS WITH ACCORDION—Wm. Zapatil and Male Chorus.
6. "TIHA NOCI"—(Still Night) Rosemary Sorak, piano and Billy Baretich, violin.
7. "KUKAVICA KAKO"—(The Cockoo) Song and accomp. by Billy Baretich.
8. "SINOC SI MEMI REKLA"—(Last Night) Tamburitza and Chorus.
9. "DJEVOJACKO KOLA"—(Girls Kolo Dance) Croation dancing Group.

TAMBURITZA ORCHESTRA—Dan Sorak, Director, Margaret Azzolin, Marion Kauzlarich, Rosemary Sorak, Joe Kauzlarich (leader), Billy Baretich.

THE CROATIAN CHORUS—Mrs. Louise Swab, Mrs. Mary Budeslich, Mrs. Pete Morris, Wm. Baretich, Slovo Budeslich, Bona Polich, Tony Chebuhar, Joe Kauzlarich, Wm. Zapatil.

THE DANCING GROUP—Theresa Chebuhar, Anna Chebuhar, Katherine Yakovich, Evelyn Vidas, Sylvia Sisul, Albina Cernkovich, Catherine Cernkovich, Virginia Swab, Angeline Budeslich, Helen Chabrian, Grances Kruzich, Marie Kruzich, Anna Starcivich, Eva Polich, Ellen Simatovich Mary Simatovich.

MUSIC & DANCE DIRECTION—Wm. Baretich.
COSTUMES—By Mrs. Tina Grenko.

SECTION VI COAL CARNIVAL FINALE

"I AM AN AMERICAN"—Sung by the Morrell Chorus and entire cast.
"GOD BLESS AMERICA"—Sung by the Morrell Chorus and entire cast.
Press Acknowledgments:—The Iowa Daily Press Newspaper, The Associated Press, The Des Moines Register, The Des Moines Tribune, The Ottumwa Courier, The Centerville Daily Iowegian.

Radio Acknowledgments—Stations WHO, KBIZ, KMA.
Fox De Luxe Beer Program

The Coal Carnival was a huge celebration held for only two years, 1940 and 1941, mainly to promote the sale of Iowa coal. The festival was a grand affair with parades, notable speakers, including the governor, and a Native American portraying Chief Appanoose. The Iowa Bocce Ball Tournament was held, and the many types of entertainment highlighted the cultural diversity of coal-mining families.

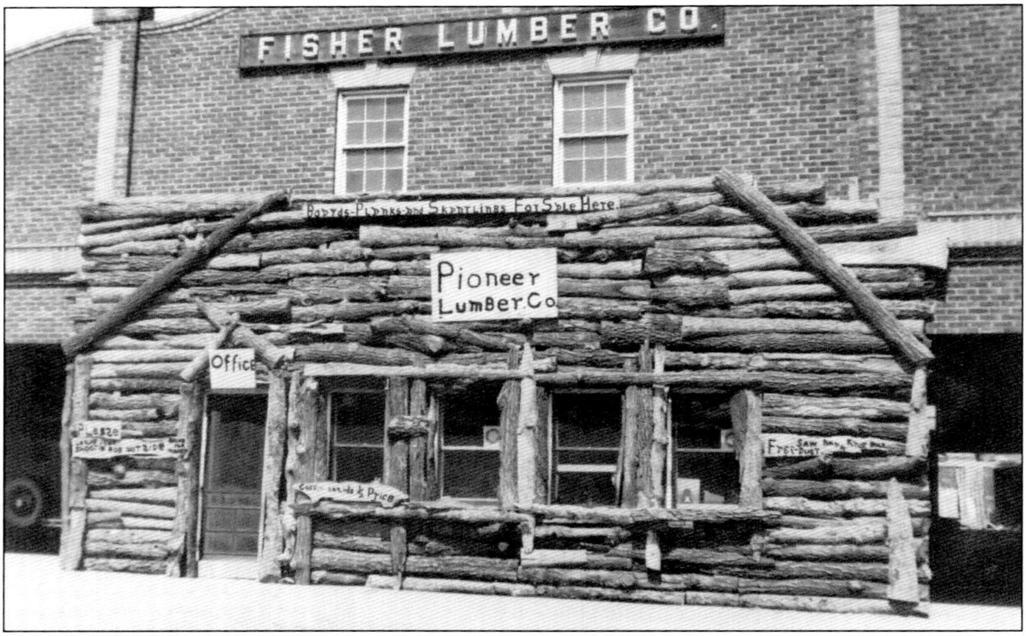

In 1938, the state Territorial Centennial Committee requested that every town have a celebration that would lead up to the state celebration, The Iowa Territorial Centennial State Fair. Appanoose County obliged, with a three-day festival that highlighted the county's history. In this throwback to pioneer days, businesses placed log facades on their storefronts, as seen above. Men grew beards; women wore long dresses and bonnets. A huge historical pageant was held at the high school stadium every night of the event, which lasted from August 24 to 26. The pageant included skits portraying the coming of the Moravians, an old-fashioned wedding, an Indian village, the Underground Railroad, soldiers, dancers, singers, musicians, and much more. The first day of the celebration incorporated the annual Children's Day parade, and the huge Centennial Parade was held on Friday.

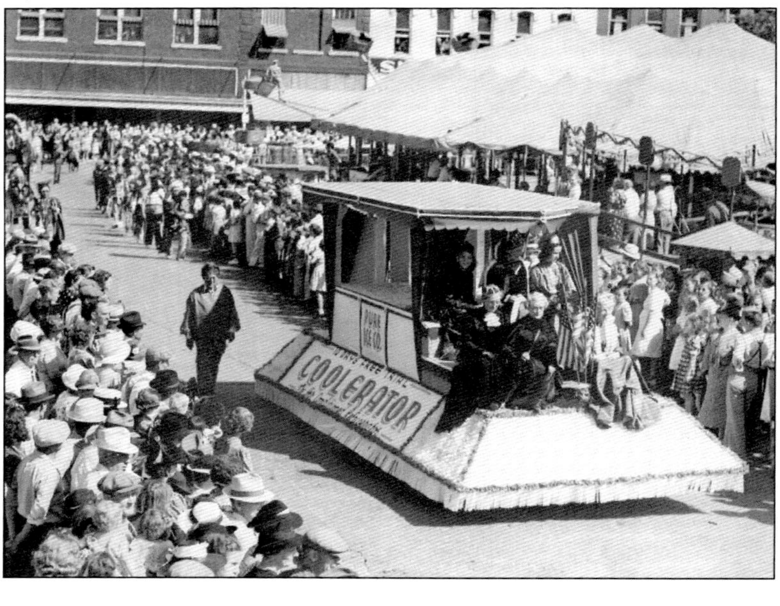

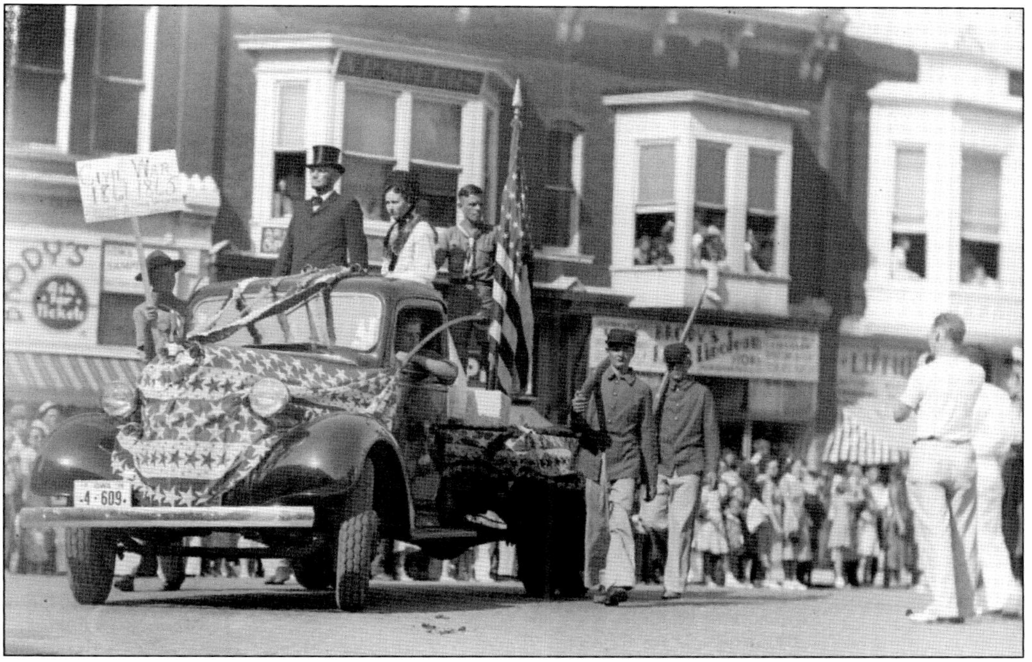

Sherman West, one of the county supervisors, was tall and lanky; with a beard and top hat, he was a dead ringer for Abraham Lincoln. He became Lincoln for the entire celebration, and was photographed often during the festivities. In the above photograph, he rides the Civil War remembrance entry in the parade. Maxine Miller was crowned Centennial Queen, her coronation being held on the first night of the pageant at the high school. Bicycle races were held on Thursday on the Square, though the bicyclist seen below was only part of the parade. This is the longtime owner of Beer's Drug Store, Paul Beer, riding an antique bicycle owned by Harry Luther. It was the first pneumatic-wheeled bicycle in southern Iowa. Given to him as a gift, the bicycle came from England. The rims were inside the tires.

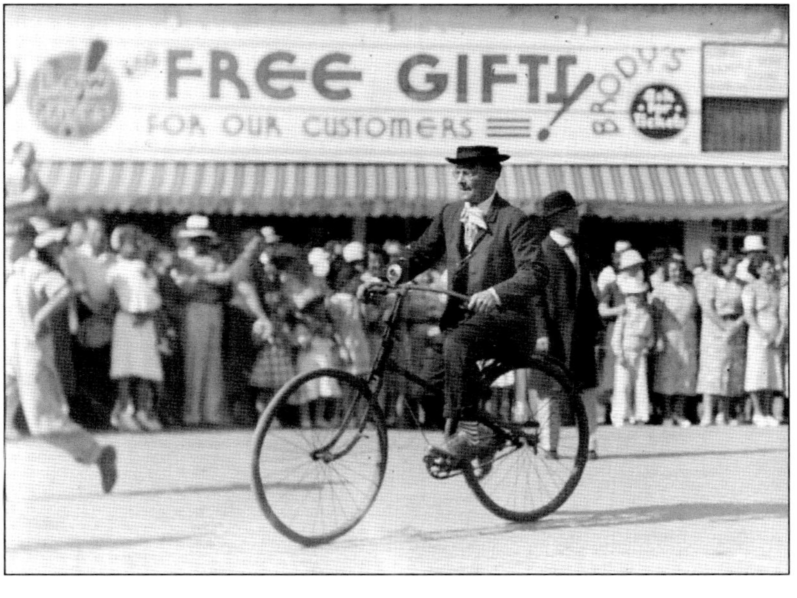

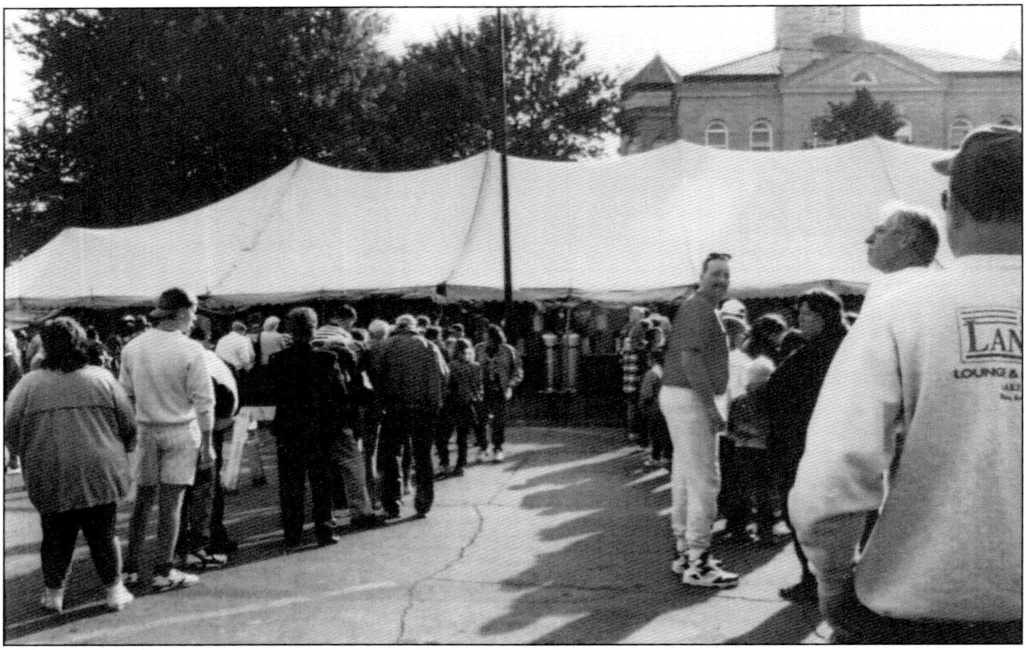

Pancake Day is the longest-running annual celebration in Centerville. It began in 1949 on a Thursday in October as a way for the businesses of Centerville to thank local patrons. Pancake flour was donated by local Pillsbury Mills, the coffee by Tones, and the butter and cream by multiple local dairies. The first Pancake Day did not have a parade, but it did have pancakes, a beauty pageant, and lots of fun activities. The parade was added the next year. Eventually, Pancake Day was moved to the last Saturday in September. Famous names like Barbara Mandrell, Minnie Pearl, Rocky Marciano, and J.C. Penney have attended Pancake Day. Above, the familiar line of hungry attendees forms outside the pancake tent. Below, a Pancake Day parade from the 1950s features several bands and floats. (Below, courtesy Royal Simmons.)

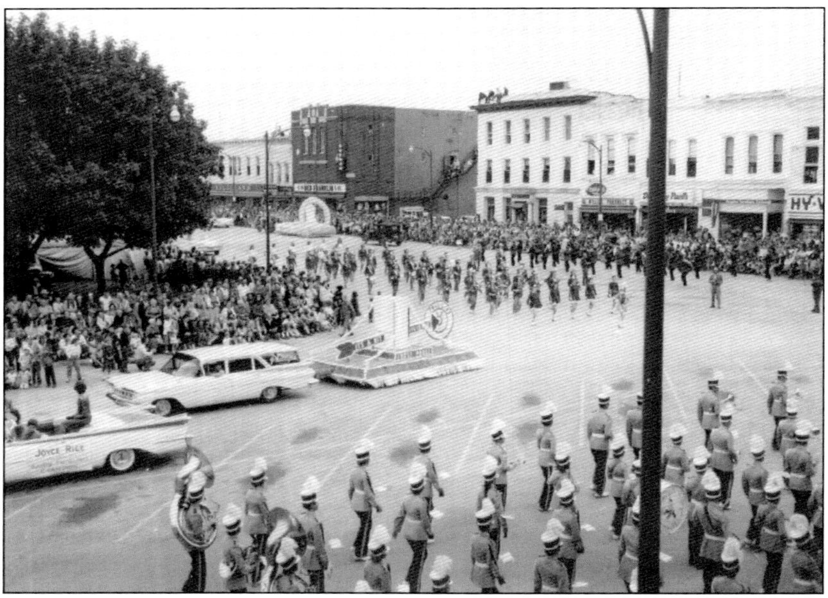

Nine

FAVORITE PASTIMES

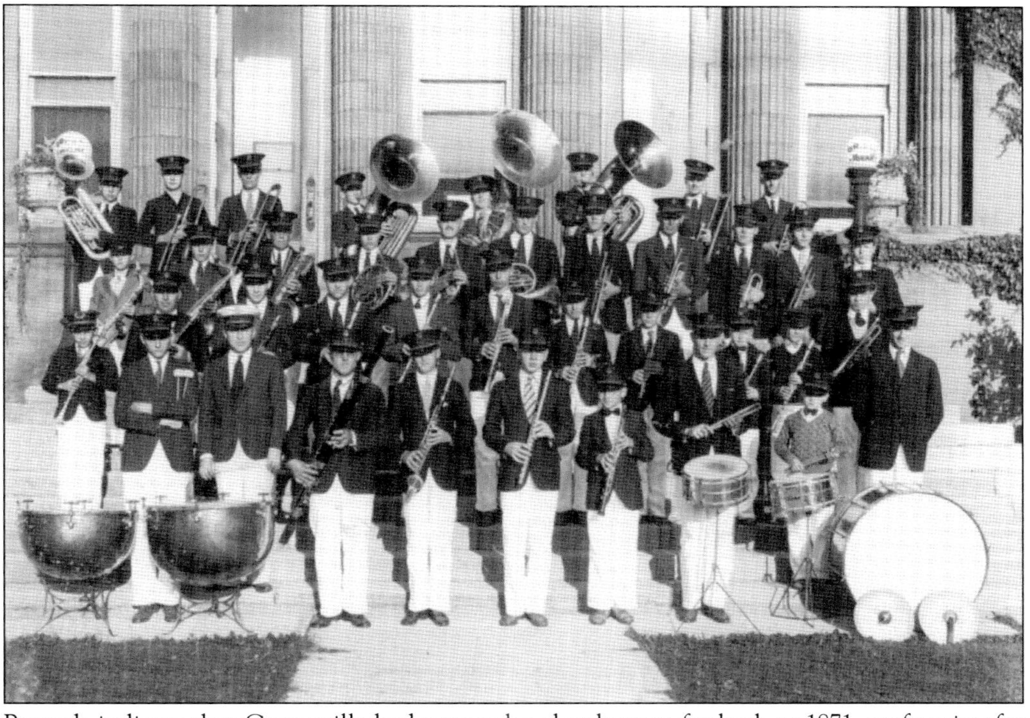

Records indicate that Centerville had a town band at least as far back as 1871, performing for many community functions and festivals. This 1932 photograph of the Centerville Municipal Band includes many talented musicians who went on to careers in instrumental music, including Frank Minkler (orchestra director at CHS), Roy Houser (Culver Stockton College), and William Gower and Himie Voxman (both at the University of Iowa).

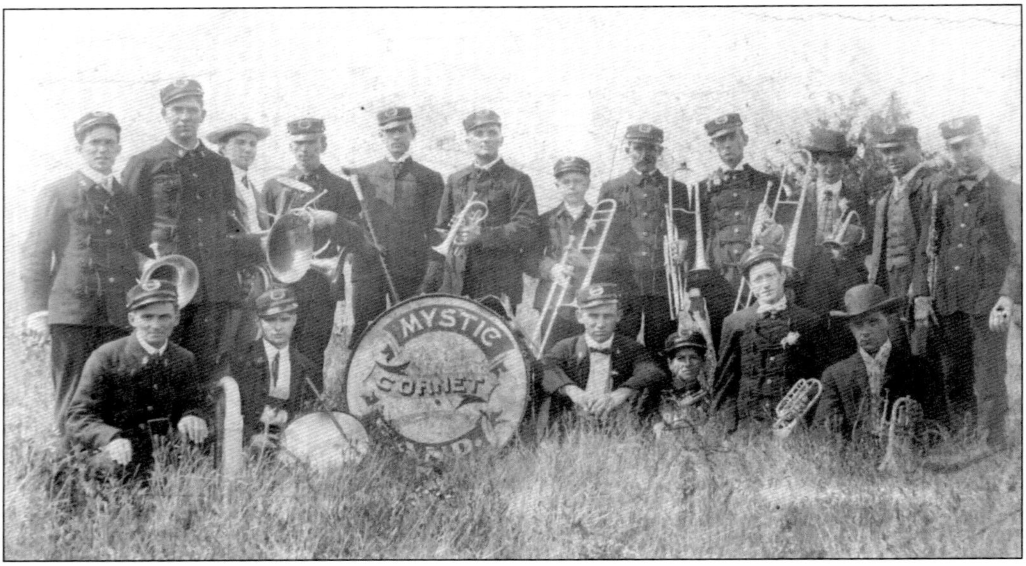

Talented musicians could be found all over the county. Numerous towns in Appanoose County had bands, often calling themselves a "cornet band." Exline, Cincinnati, Brazil, Unionville, and Mystic, pictured here, had outstanding bands that performed all over the county and sometimes for other counties.

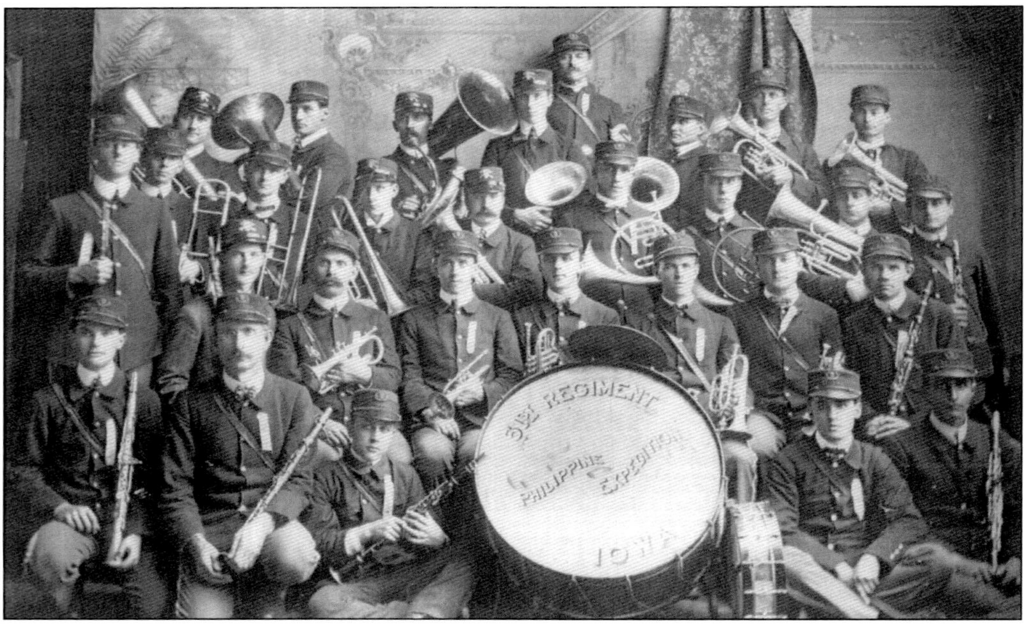

The most notable band in Appanoose County history was the 51st Regiment Band, under the direction of George Landers. The military band was first organized in 1888 as the 3rd Regimental Band. It was called to active duty for the Spanish-American War and was stationed in the Philippines. Upon arrival home, it toured for several months and earned numerous accolades.

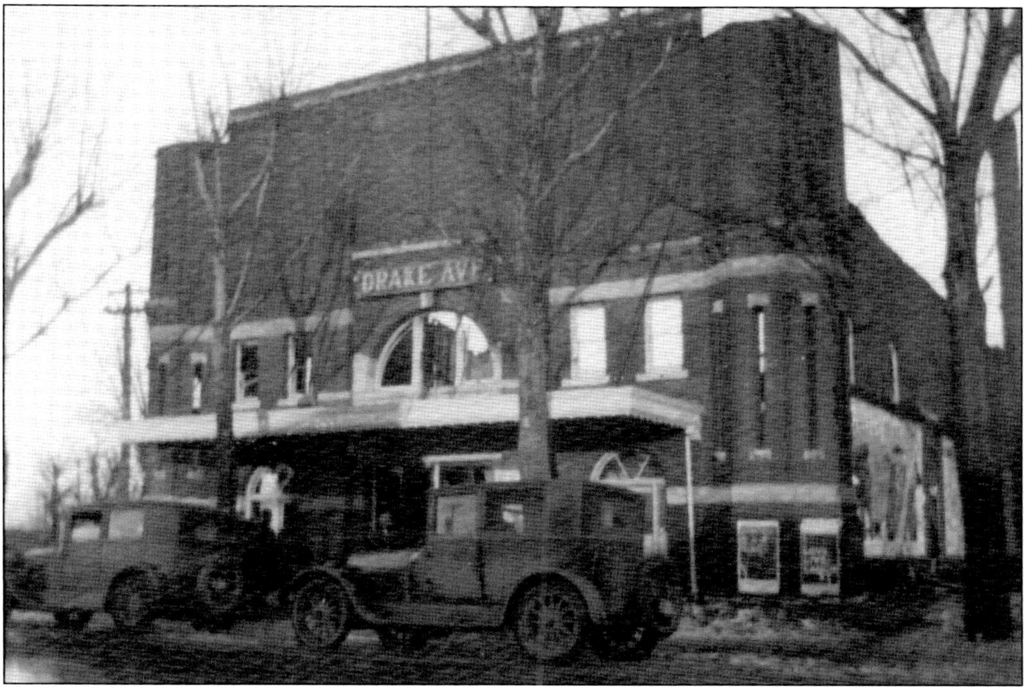

The Armory Opera House, located immediately north of Drake Library, was built in 1897, with the impetus provided by band director Maj. George Landers, H.C. Haynes, and local boy and famous actor Corse Payton. Payton wanted the opera house to be first-class. He furnished $5,000 of the required $9,000 to start the project. On Thursday, January 27, 1899, the Armory Opera House formally opened to the public.

In 1912, a new armory was built, and Armory Opera House became the Drake Avenue Theatre. A variety of events were showcased during the theater's three decades, including boxing exhibitions, masquerade balls, a mock trial, concerts, school events, graduations, and traveling stock company plays. It became a movie theater in 1929. Due to a fire in the projection room, it burned to the ground on February 2, 1930.

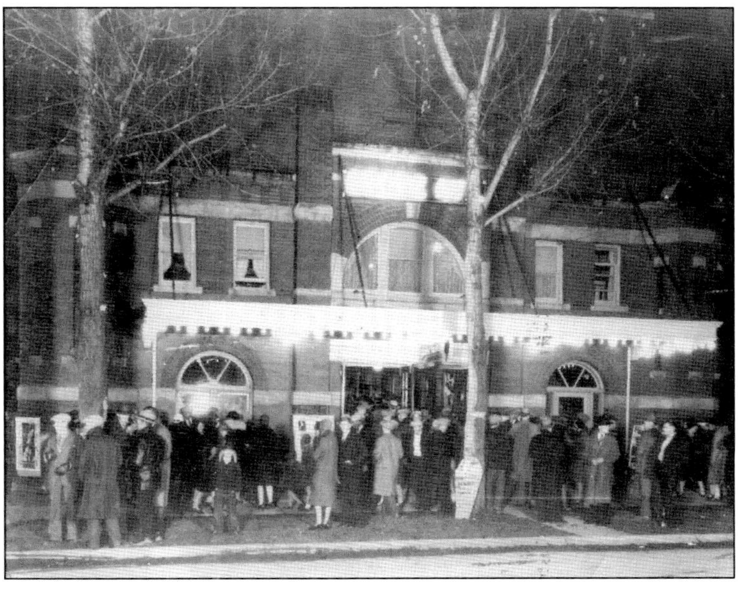

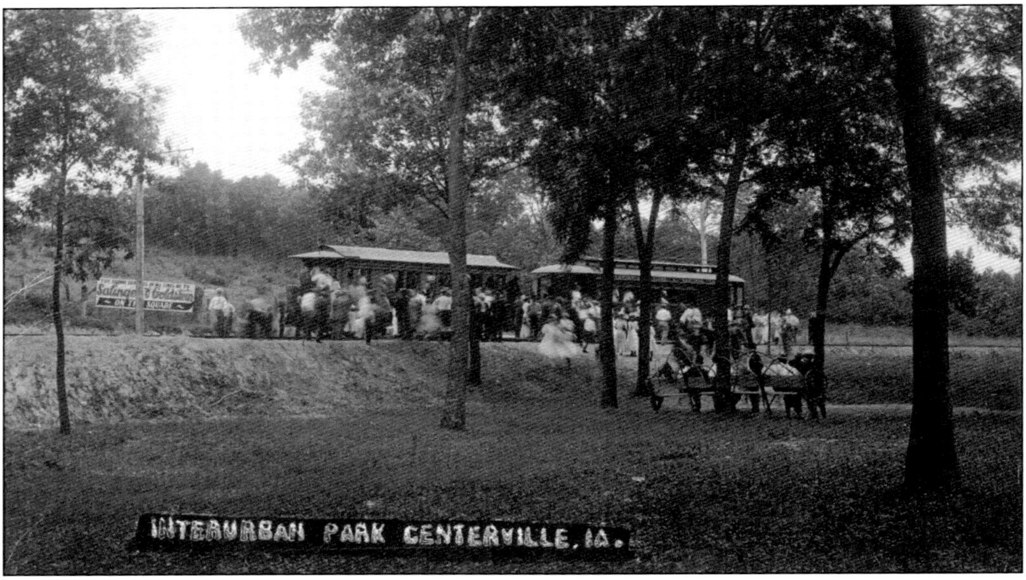

Glen Hagen Park, originally known as the Interurban Park, was created by Centerville Light and Traction along the interurban line to Mystic in the valley north of the country club in 1910. It was common for owners of interurban systems, usually utility companies, to open a park accessible only by trolley to generate revenue. Glen Hagen Park had a skating pavilion, playground, band shell, and numerous concession booths.

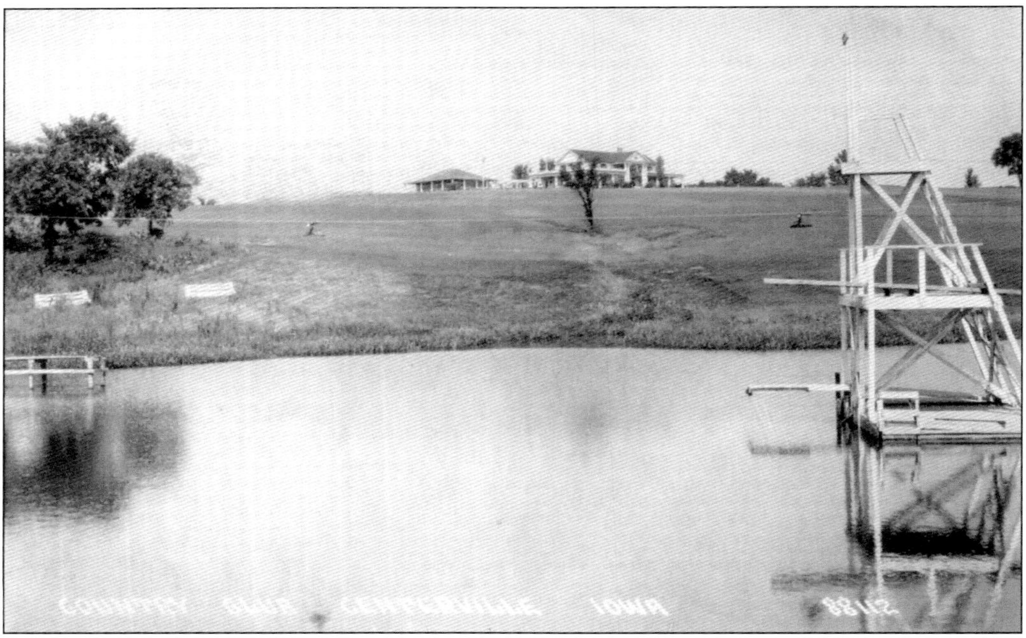

The pond by the third green of the Appanoose Country Club was the site of many water activities in the club's early years. Two clubhouses can be seen here. The smaller clubhouse had been built in 1912 near Glen Hagen Park and was moved to this location prior to the construction of the larger clubhouse in 1923, which is still in use today. This golf course was built over the existing interurban line.

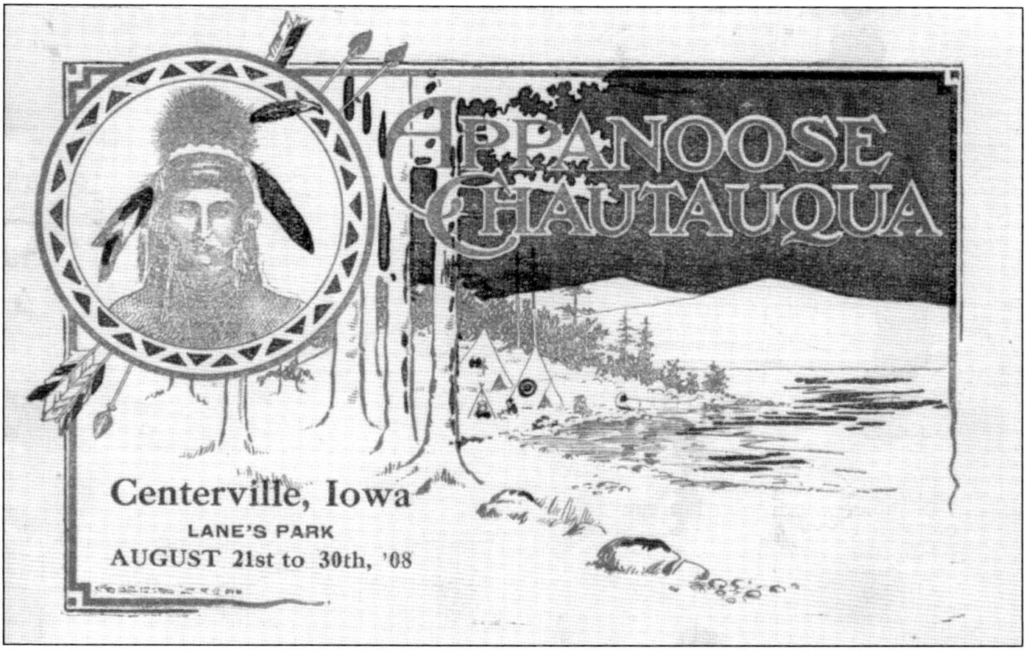

A Chautauqua was an early form of workshop that was educational, entertaining, and cultural. Appanoose County held many Chautauquas in various locations, including Lane's Park, as shown here. This Chautauqua included musicians, humorists, impersonators, moving pictures, singers, orators, a talk on tuberculosis, Bible study, orator William Jennings Bryan, and the local 51st Regiment Band. It lasted for 10 days, from early mornings until late in the evenings.

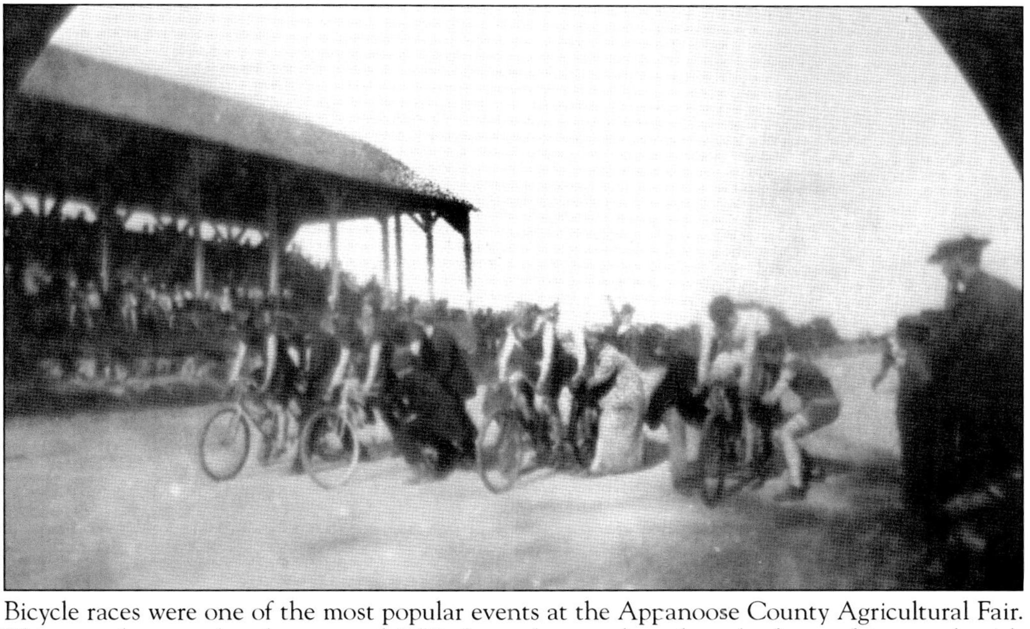

Bicycle races were one of the most popular events at the Appanoose County Agricultural Fair. This rare photograph, taken around 1895, shows the grandstands at the former fairgrounds with a lineup of bicycle racers ready to race. The fairgrounds were located on the "north hill," in the vicinity of Haynes Avenue, north of its curve to the east. This fairground was sold in 1906.

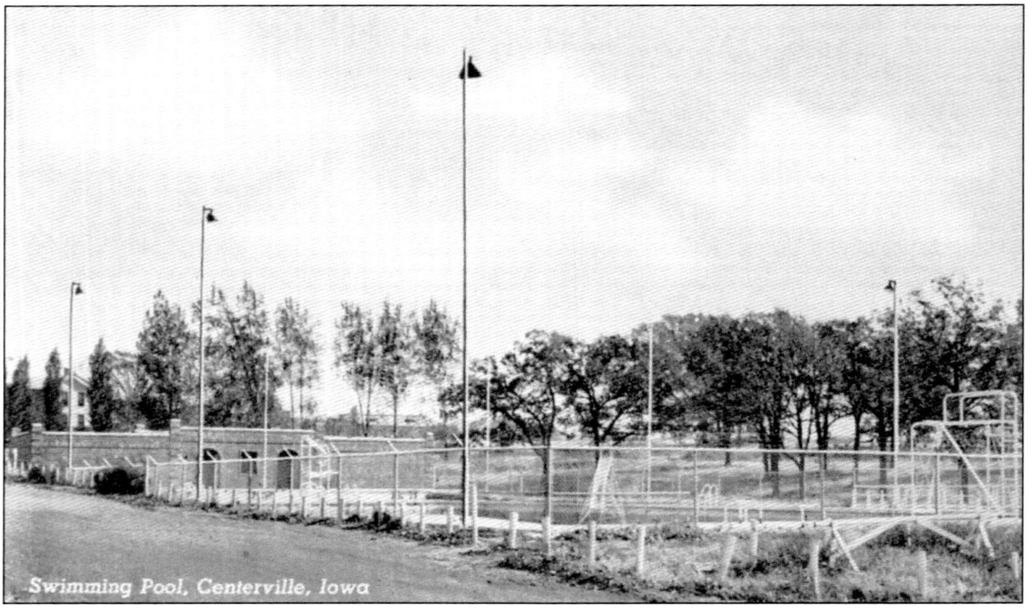

In December 1937, Centerville approved a $10,000 bond to be used to build a new $55,000 swimming pool in City Park. The new pool would be a WPA project, with the government paying for 75 percent of the cost and the city paying 25 percent. The new pool measured 75 by 150 feet, and the depth ran from 18 inches to nine and a half feet. The pool opened on Sunday, June 4, 1939.

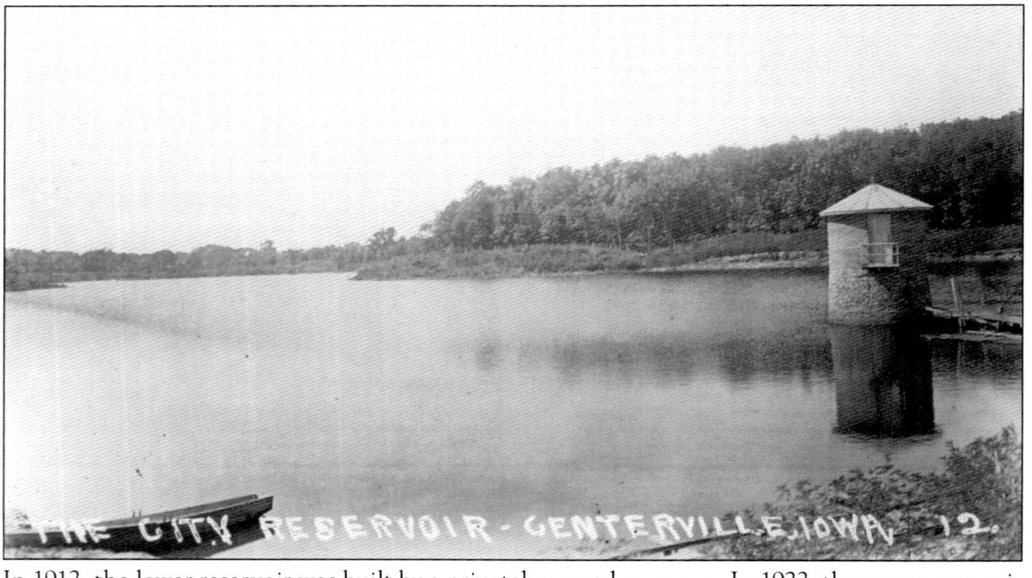

In 1912, the lower reservoir was built by a privately owned company. In 1922, the upper reservoir was constructed. It was not until June 1948 that the City of Centerville purchased the property and chose the name Centerville Municipal Waterworks. After the city's 2007 decision to obtain water from the Rathbun Regional Water Association, the two reservoirs now serve as attractive recreational sites.

Ten

When the Going Gets Tough . . .

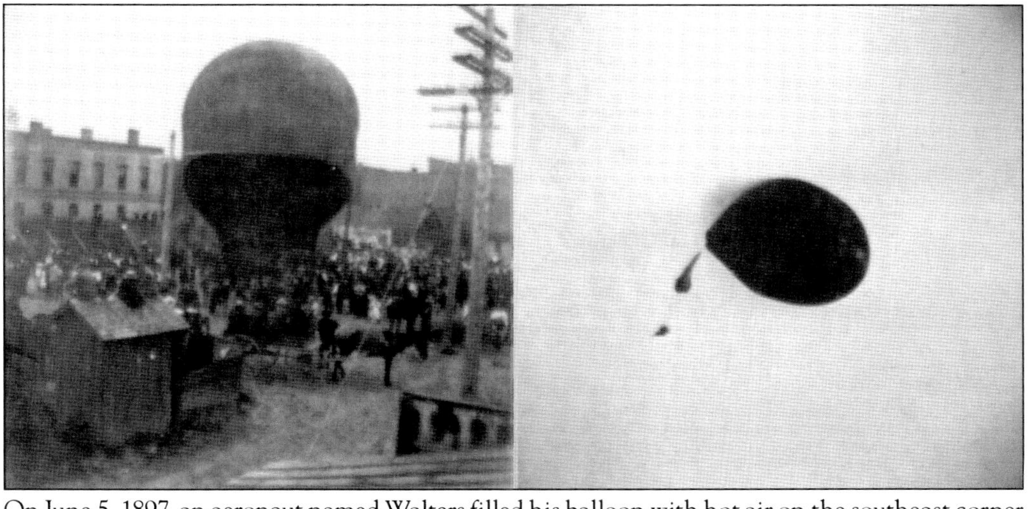

On June 5, 1897, an aeronaut named Walters filled his balloon with hot air on the southeast corner of the Square, drawing a crowd of onlookers. The balloon shot upward, but a gust came from the southwest and the balloon careened downward and caught telegraph wires. The aeronaut fell, head first, onto a shed. He was taken to a nearby doctor's office, but he did not survive.

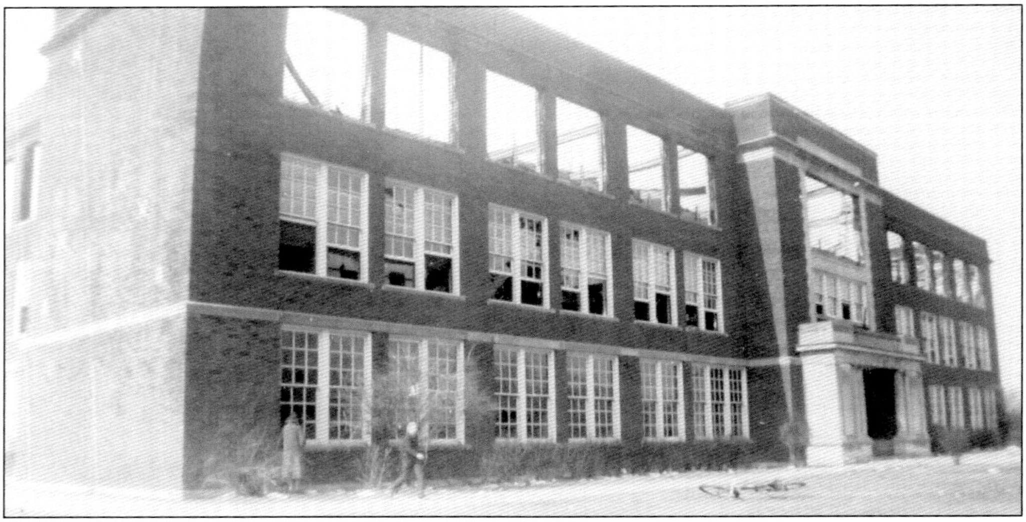

This photograph by Helen Carlson shows the gutted remains of Centerville High School. On March 7, 1938, this building was destroyed by fire. School superintendent E.W. Fannon reported that the blaze was discovered to have started in a small closet, just off the boys' restroom near the auditorium stage on the second floor. The fire spread rapidly to the third floor of the building.

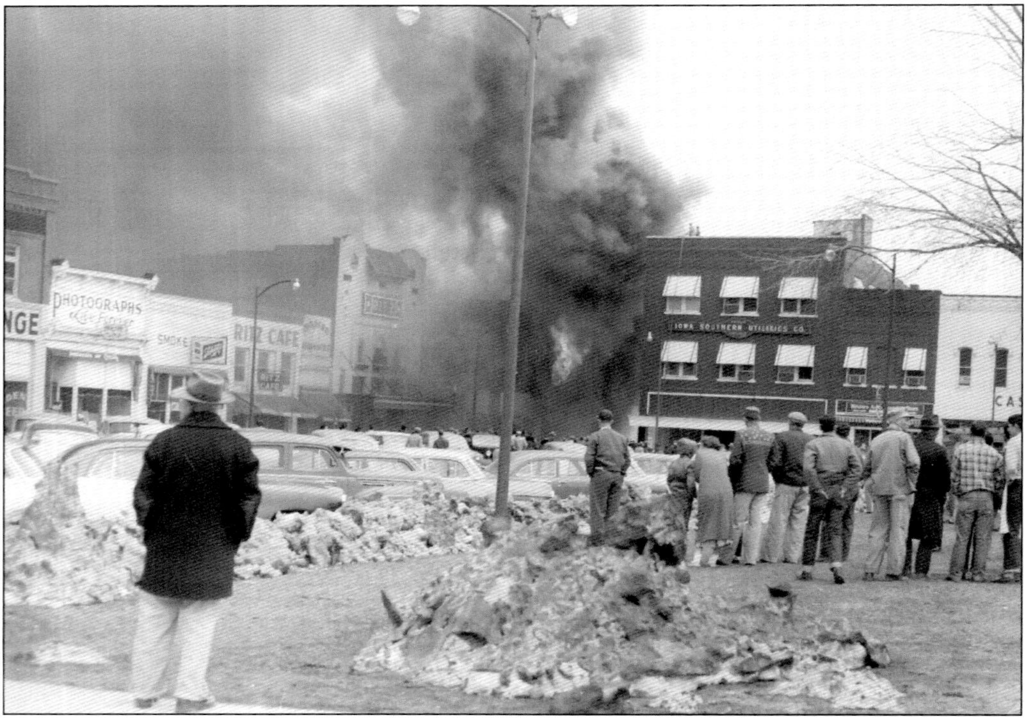

On Saturday, March 30, 1957, the Iowa Southern Utilities annex building was destroyed by fire. The annex was located across the street from the main ISU building, just off the northeast corner of the Square. Connected to the main building by an overhead walkway, the annex housed the engineering and construction departments. Many irreplaceable blueprints, maps, and years of data were lost in the fire.

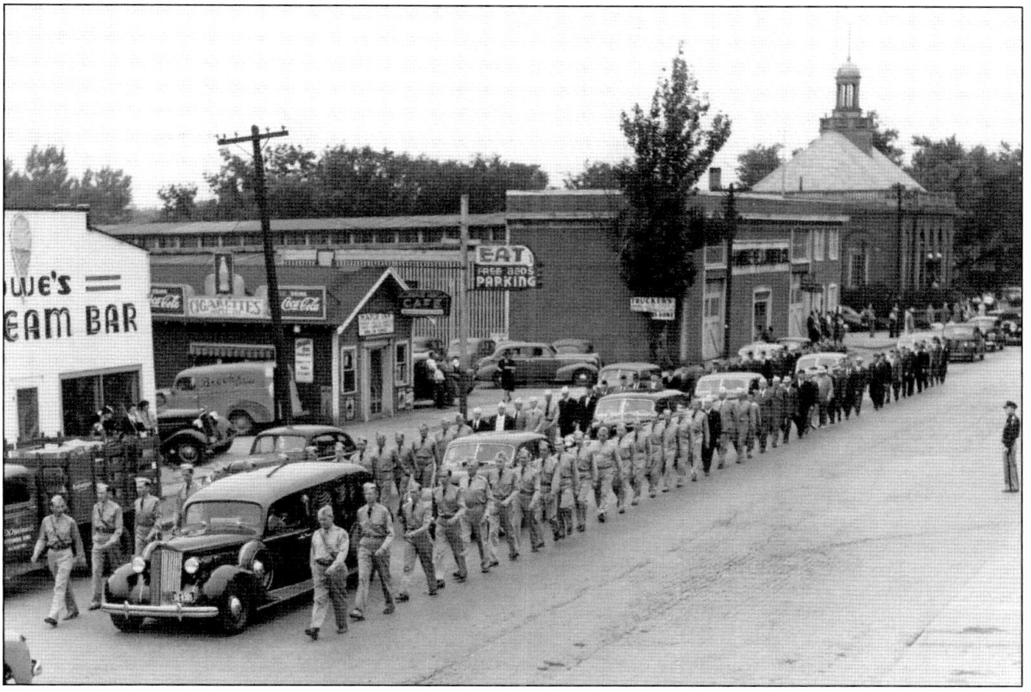

Two local members of the National Guard, Jack Packard and Robert Gilliland, were killed in an automobile accident on April 10, 1942, near Des Moines. They had been returning to Camp Dodge after an evening leave to attend the local guard ball in Centerville. The other guardsmen in the military freight truck were not seriously injured. This is a photograph of the funeral procession along Maple Street.

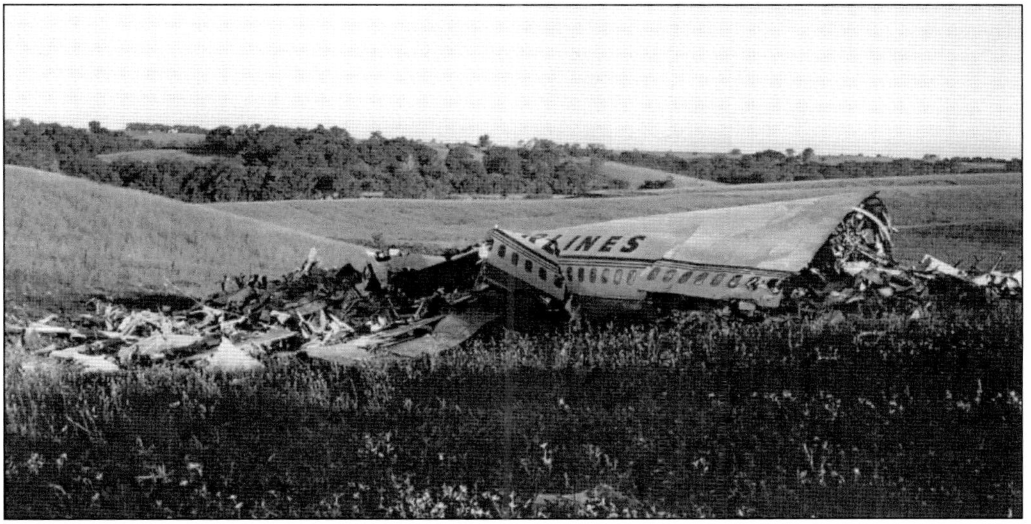

Continental Flight 11 crashed on May 22, 1962, killing 45 people Pieces of the airplane were scattered over Appanoose County. Local law enforcement and National Guard were sent to the site, just over the Missouri line. The FBI and worldwide media were headquartered in the Continental Hotel. After the FBI reconstructed the plane at the Appanoose County Fairgrounds, it was determined that a bomb had caused the crash.

Consistent with our mission to preserve history on a local level, this book was printed in South Carolina on American-made paper and manufactured entirely in the United States. Products carrying the accredited Forest Stewardship Council (FSC) label are printed on 100 percent FSC-certified paper.